Regulation
for
Revenue

The Political Economy of
Land Use Exactions

Alan A. Altshuler *and*
José A. Gómez-Ibáñez

with Arnold M. Howitt

THE BROOKINGS INSTITUTION
Washington, D.C.

THE LINCOLN INSTITUTE OF LAND POLICY
Cambridge, Massachusetts

Copyright © 1993
THE BROOKINGS INSTITUTION
1775 Massachusetts Avenue, N.W., Washington, D.C. 20036
and
THE LINCOLN INSTITUTE OF LAND POLICY
113 Brattle Street, Cambridge, Mass. 02138

Library of Congress Cataloging-in-Publication Data

Altshuler, Alan A., 1936—
    Regulation for revenue: the political economy of land de-
velopment exactions / Alan A. Altshuler and José A.
Gómez-Ibáñez, with Arnold M. Howitt.
        p. cm.
    Includes bibliographical references and index.
    ISBN 0-8157-0356-2 (alk. paper).—ISBN 0-8157-0355-4
(pbk.)
        1. Impact fees—United States. 2. Infrastructure (Eco-
nomics)—Finance. 3. Local finance—United States.
I. Gómez-Ibáñez, José A., 1948—   II. Howitt, Arnold
M., 1947—   .   III. Title.
HJ9156.A64 1992
336.1'6—dc20   92—35660
                                                          CIP

987654321

The paper used in this publication meets the minimum requirements of the
American National Standard for Information Sciences—Permanence of paper
for Printed Library Materials, ANSI Z39.48-1984

The Brookings Institution

The Brookings Institution is an independent, nonprofit organization devoted to nonpartisan research, education, and publication in economics, government, foreign policy, and the social sciences generally. Its principal purposes are to aid in the development of sound public policies and to promote public understanding of issues of national importance. The Institution was founded on December 8, 1927, to merge the activities of the Institute for Government Research, founded in 1916, the Institute of Economics, founded in 1922, and the Robert Brookings Graduate School of Economics, founded in 1924.

The Institution maintains a position of neutrality on issues of public policy to safeguard the intellectual freedom of the staff. Interpretations or conclusions in Brookings publications should be understood to be solely those of the authors.

The Lincoln Institute of Land Policy

The Lincoln Institute of Land Policy is a nonprofit and tax-exempt school organized in 1974 with a specialized mission to study and teach about land policy, including land economics and land taxation. It is supported by the Lincoln Foundation, established in 1947 by John C. Lincoln, a Cleveland industrialist. Mr. Lincoln drew inspiration from the ideas of Henry George, the nineteenth-century American political economist and philosopher.

Integrating the theory and practice of land policy—and understanding forces that influence it—is the major goal of the Lincoln Institute. The Institute brings together experts with different points of view and provides settings where they can study, reflect, exchange insights, and work toward consensus in creating more complete and systematic land policies. Through its courses and conferences, publications, and research activities, the Institute seeks to advance and disseminate knowledge of critical land policy issues. The Institute's objective is to have an impact on land policy—to make a difference today and to help policymakers plan for tomorrow.

Authors' Preface

Rarely has a government practice spread so quickly at the grass roots level as that of land development exactions. Exactions are mandated expenditures by private land developers, required as a price for their obtaining regulatory permits, in support of infrastructure and other public services. The breakneck diffusion and growth in fiscal significance of this phenomenon aroused our curiosity several years ago. What was driving it politically? Should we applaud or deplore it? Was this use of regulatory power to generate revenue for publicly defined purposes an anomaly—particularly in this era marked most visibly by deregulation initiatives and rhetoric—or did it represent a much broader, though less noticed, trend?

As our initial discussions proceeded, we discovered that we had quite different priorities in evaluating exactions, and leaned overall in different directions. Alan A. Altshuler, a political scientist by training, was intrigued by exactions as an instrument of political compromise between growth and anti-growth, service expansion and anti-tax, forces. José A. Gómez-Ibáñez, an economist, worried about the potential of exactions to accentuate inequality and their neutrality, at best, with respect to land and infrastructure use efficiency.

In joining forces initially, we hoped to clarify and refine our respective viewpoints but we did not expect to reach agreement. In the end, however, we did agree. The key to reconciling our viewpoints lay in the observation that any useful evaluation is comparative. Exactions look better or worse—in terms of equity, efficiency, or political acceptability—depending on the specific alternatives one considers most relevant analytically or most probable in reality. Our initial views had been shaped decisively by implicit assumptions that exactions should be compared with one or two of our own most favored alternatives. As we expanded the list of options systematically, however, we found that we could agree both on the significant elements of each alternative and even about which alternatives were in fact most likely. In time, we jointly came to a reluctantly favorable view of exactions—reluctant because we are deeply impressed by some of the analytic arguments against exactions, favorable because we consider the most probable alternative in many cases, growth controls, even worse.

We also concluded, as our title indicates, that in fact the pattern of revenue-raising for public purposes by regulation rather than by the imposition of overt taxes and charges is widespread and growing. While the idea that regulation is often costly to the subject parties is commonplace, the idea that public officials view regulation as a potential revenue source to be compared routinely with taxes and charges is far less well-understood. We do not seek in this book, focused as it is on just one type of regulation for revenue, to explore this phenomenon in any depth. But we do seek to highlight it as a central theme of our time, worthy of far more explicit scholarly attention than it has received to date.

Every chapter of this book reflects intensive collaboration by the two authors. Altshuler, though, assumed lead responsibility for investigating legal and political issues, and for the drafting of chapters 1, 2, 3, 4, and 9. Gómez-Ibáñez took the lead in examining issues of equity and efficiency, and in drafting chapters 5, 6, 7, and 8.

One of our colleagues, Arnold M. Howitt, was a full collaborator in the early stages of our work, until diverted by the press of other responsibilities, and he contributed significantly to what eventually became chapters 3 and 4. Our intellectual debt and warm appreciation are reflected in his listing on the title page of this volume.

Our research was supported financially by grants from the Lincoln Institute of Land Policy and the U.S. Department of Transportation (through its University Transportation Center for the New England Region). We wish particularly to thank Ron Smith, Benjamin Chinitz, and Robert Einsweiler of the Lincoln Institute, and Thomas Humphrey of University Transportation Center, for their unfailing support, encouragement, and in Chinitz's case, substantive advice.

We are likewise eager to acknowledge our institutional homes for this project, Harvard University's John F. Kennedy School of Government and Graduate School of Design, in which we both hold joint appointments. The continuing intellectual stimulus of our colleagues at both schools has assisted us tremendously. We carried out this work most directly within the Kennedy School's A. Alfred Taubman Center for State and Local Government, benefiting greatly from its excellent facilities and the efficiency of its staff. Gwen Young, in particular, who served as a graduate research assistant, provided invaluable assistance in gathering and examining materials, while Claire Brigandi and Janet Gulotta cheerfully incorporated our revisions into the manuscript again and again and again. Needless to say, all responsibility for the errors that doubtless remain is our own. And, it should be noted, our conclusion should not be attributed to the trustees, officers, or staff members of either the Lincoln Institute or the Brookings Institution.

Finally, we are indebted to our families for their constant encouragement and succor whenever we paused in our labors. Nan Wilson and José Gómez-Ibáñez were married during the course of this project, while Alan and Julie Altshuler welcomed their first two grandchildren, Jacob and Benjamin Green, into the world. In dedication of this volume, we celebrate these delightful landmarks in our lives.

Contents

Tables

1

Central Issues and Themes

SINCE ABOUT 1970, Americans have become increasingly skeptical about the local benefits of growth and increasingly resistant to new taxes. Meanwhile, citizen service demands have surged, and concern about the adequacy of the nation's infrastructure has intensified. The tensions among these trends have been particularly acute in rapidly growing localities. In this context, a widespread reappraisal has taken place of the links between real estate development, infrastructure requirements, and fiscal health at the local level.

Prior to 1970, there was little disposition among participants in local land use policy making to view real estate development as a cause of demand for new public infrastructure or to fear that growth might prove adverse to local fiscal health. The predominant view instead was that new private real estate and public infrastructure investment are both products of a common, beneficent set of root causes—population and economic growth—which tend to be associated with robust fiscal health. More people with greater purchasing power, in this view, require additional investment in both private real estate and public infrastructure. In general, fortunately, they are well able to finance both sides of the equation. Their private incomes enable them to constitute a strong market for new real estate development, which in turn generates ample local revenue, even at constant real estate tax rates, to finance the public costs of growth. Exceptions do exist, however. A pattern of new development weighted toward low-income housing or tax-exempt land uses, for

1

example, may fail to yield sufficient public revenue to cover its associated public costs. In general, though, new development tends to improve the fiscal health of the localities in which it occurs.

Over the past two decades, this viewpoint has been widely superseded. According to the new conventional wisdom, growth rarely produces sufficient revenue at constant tax rates to compensate host jurisdictions for its associated public costs. Localities generally face rising marginal costs for new infrastructure as they grow. Their existing infrastructure costs much less per unit of capacity, on average, than the current cost of expansion. Certain types of infrastructure expansion, such as new highway development, may even be impossible today in light of environmental constraints, citizen resistance, and the prohibitive cost of property that would have to be acquired. A few voters may reap windfalls from development by selling land or services to developers or by engaging in development activity themselves. Ordinary voters, however, are likely to experience tax and fee increases for the benefit of newcomers, as well as negative changes in the quality of community life.

Alternative Responses

Most politically active citizens in most growing communities today are seriously concerned about the risks of rapid development. Officials with land use responsibilities, including those most favorable to growth, nearly all want to reduce or eliminate them. Five main strategies are available.

First, a locality can reject new development, thereby diverting growth to other jurisdictions. Pressures still will exist for infrastructure expansion (because of overspill effects from adjacent communities and rising per capita demand for services) and modernization (because of federal and state mandates, the obsolescence of some older facilities, and perhaps deferred maintenance in prior years). But these pressures will be less than if development had been allowed to proceed, and the projects undertaken will mainly benefit existing residents rather than newcomers.

Second, a locality can seek assistance from higher levels of government. Progrowth views still hold sway at the state and federal levels. In practice, moreover, the taxes and fees collected by all levels of government are more likely to match public costs than those collected by localities alone. Federal grants increased only slightly during the 1970s, however they declined sharply in the first half of the 1980s, and have been static ever since.

Third, local communities can raise local tax rates, user fees, or both, to defray the public costs of growth. Insofar as old residents bear these levies, such financing can be viewed as a form of subsidy for new development. Advocates of such financing have typically argued, however, that these subsidies are generally short term and are properly viewed as investments with multiyear payback periods. In the quarter-century following World War II, local governments usually paid for the infrastructure requirements of growth from general revenues. However, increases in taxes and fees to serve new development have lost favor with voters in recent years. As a result, today few politicians are willing to advocate such financing.

Fourth, a locality can accept growth without making collateral investments in infrastructure, thereby spreading the public service costs of growth among old and new residents alike—in the form of service deterioration instead of fiscal levies. While never announced as policy, this approach in practice is commonplace. Changes in the quality of infrastructure services tend to occur gradually, so neglect can go unremarked for years. During the 1980s, however, as the capacity of infrastructure was overwhelmed in many fast-growth localities, and as the effects of deferred maintenance became apparent even in communities that were not experiencing growth, strategies of neglect became increasingly conspicuous and controversial.

Finally, localities can require that private real estate developers underwrite public investments. This strategy, of "exacting" public investment commitments from developers, has been ascendant in recent years. And it is the central concern in these pages.

What Are Exactions?

When governments mandate that real estate developers, as a condition for receiving permits, expend resources for the provision of public facilities or services, they are said to have imposed land development exactions, or, simply, exactions.

Exactions may be in-kind or financial. In-kind exactions require developers to contribute land, to construct public facilities, or to provide public services. Financial exactions, most commonly known as "impact" or "development" fees, require monetary payments into public coffers. While monetary exactions come in a variety of types and are often called by a variety of names, for the sake of simplicity we shall refer in this volume to all types of monetary exactions as impact fees.[1]

The legal theory underlying development exactions is that governments, having reasonably determined that certain public needs are "attributable" to new development, may require that their costs be "internalized" as part of the development process. From the standpoint of law, then, the costs that developers incur in fulfilling exaction conditions are user fees, not taxes. (The significance is that fees must be justified in law by a direct relationship between the payer's activities and the expenditure purpose. Taxes need not be.)

The courts consider a public expenditure attributable to new development when it is for the use of project occupants (for example, road and water system improvements to provide them with service) or to mitigate adverse project impacts on the wider community.[2] Distinguishing between these aims is not always possible in practice, but neither is it often essential for legal purposes. A widened road in the vicinity of a new office complex, for example, will both serve those who work there and protect other travelers from degradation of service (which would otherwise have occurred as a result of the additional traffic generated by the complex).

The great majority of exactions are for investment in public capital or for the mitigation of adverse physical effects (for example, air, noise, and water pollution). The rationale for exaction conditions can easily be extended, however, to include the social byproducts of new land uses. And during the 1980s, a few communities began to impose social exactions—to alleviate shortages of affordable housing, for example, that many people thought growth might aggravate.

The most obvious social exactions, those involving direct payments by the developer, have been levied almost exclusively on commercial developments. In-kind requirements for affordable housing, however, conventionally labeled "inclusionary zoning" provisions rather than exactions, have been imposed mainly on residential developments. How should these be classified? It depends, we believe, on one's analytic purpose. Economically and politically, inclusionary zoning fits squarely within the social exaction category. Legally, however, inclusionary zoning requirements rest on quite different foundations from other social exactions.

The complexity of this labeling exercise highlights a more general point: The distinction between traditional land use regulation and the imposition of exactions, while relatively clear at the extremes, often is fuzzy at the margin. Traditional regulation does not require a landowner to do anything; it simply restricts permissible uses. An exaction, by contrast, specifies that, in return for permission to develop, a landowner—over and above paying ordinary taxes—must finance certain public activities. This is clear enough. But since the 1920s traditional land use regulation has rarely been so simple.

What, for example, is a requirement that calls for an owner, in return for permission to subdivide, to set aside land for, pave, and donate to the community local access streets? It is both traditional regulation and an exaction. Which element strikes local actors as more salient is likely to hinge on historic community practices. Because consumers generally insist on the availability of paved local streets, the relevant question is simply who should pay for them. If the local norm has been public financing, the imposition of a new requirement for developer financing probably will be viewed as an exaction. If a longstanding pattern of developer financing exists, the requirement probably will be seen as a mere codification of community norms about the characteristics of responsible development. So long as exactions are synchronized with consumer expectations, developers will find it relatively easy to recoup their costs from customers, and little, if any, curtailment of development should occur because of demand elasticity in the face of exaction-induced price run-ups.[3]

What about an inclusionary zoning requirement that developers reserve 20 percent of new residential units for low- and moderate-income households? The unstated expectation is that developers will subsidize the sale or rental of these units by raising the prices of market rate units. On the one hand, this clearly is an exaction. The objective to be served has been defined by the community, not developers, and requires significant expenditures that developers never would incur for market reasons. On the other hand, traditional regulation often restricts what landowners can do with their property, constrained only by the requirements that legitimate public purposes are being served and that landowners are left with some opportunity for economic return.[4]

Legally, moreover, inclusionary zoning rests on a different basis than other exactions. Mandates for office developers to finance affordable housing have been justified on the ground that new offices attract new workers, who in turn place strains on the local housing market. By contrast, while the development of market rate housing may generate a local need for new highway lanes or school rooms, it clearly does not create a need for more subsidized housing. Stated another way, the mandate to develop subsidized housing is neither for the benefit of those who purchase the market rate units nor to mitigate adverse project impacts. The community must justify inclusionary zoning, therefore, in terms of its traditional authority to regulate the mix of uses on land within its boundaries and perhaps its responsibility, on equal protection grounds, to avoid the use of zoning for exclusionary purposes.[5]

We do consider inclusionary zoning a form, if perhaps a borderline form, of exaction. We shall have little more to say about it in this volume, however, preferring to focus sharply on the vast majority of exactions that are justified in law as serving development-generated needs.

Appraising Exactions

How exactions are viewed depends primarily on the vantage point from which they are approached and on the alternatives that are deemed most pertinent. The various participants in land use controversies all have specific orientations and values, and academic analysts bring their disciplinary perspectives to bear. Five categories of perspectives will be examined here: those rooted in the tangible interests of actors in the development process, in their value preferences, in their geographic orientations, in their functional priorities, and in their views of the relevant alternatives.

Not surprisingly, one's view of exactions is likely to reflect one's specific role in the land development process. Some categories of actors, however, typically perceive their interests more clearly than others. Local officials in a growing community, for example, view exactions as low-risk sources of revenue with which to address urgent investment needs. Developers frequently consider exactions a form of extortion, a backhanded way for communities to sell zoning permission, or a kind of double taxation (in locales where most existing public infrastructure was financed by communitywide taxes and fees). Existing property owners consider exactions an equitable means of ensuring that newcomers pay their own way. Outsiders hoping to buy in are far less prone to pay attention, but, if they do, they are likely to view exactions as a form of tariff or initiation fee. Existing renters likewise tend to be indifferent and to be among those with the most to lose in growth controversies —especially if exactions or growth controls contribute to real estate price inflation.

The impact of value, or ideological, preferences is less obvious. Many people hostile to regulation in general favor exactions in their own communities. Others, skeptical about growth and favorable to regulation, are uncomfortable with the prospect that exactions may impede the local development of affordable housing. (Most exactions are levied at a flat rate per bedroom or per dwelling unit, so they add a greater percentage to the cost of inexpensive than of luxury homes. Few communities offer reductions or waivers for affordable housing units.) Those who appraise exactions most sys-

tematically are usually academics, and they tend to be centrally concerned
with the values of fairness and efficiency. They find, however, that fairness
has numerous contending definitions and that both fairness and efficiency
often compete with the value of democratic acceptability. No consensus exists
on how to prioritize such conceptions of fairness as the following: newcomers
to a locality should not impose any fiscal burden on existing residents, communities should not discriminate between new and old residents, and public
revenue systems should redistribute wealth from those who are more affluent
to those who are less. Nor is it clear how much weight should be accorded
the goal of efficiency in designing arrangements for the financing of public
investment in comparison with the goal of political acceptability.

Geographically, nearly all participants in exaction debates assume a local
perspective. Land use permitting is predominantly local in the American system, and local governments draw approximately half their own-source revenue from levies on real property.[6] But the overspill effects of development
across local boundaries—on employment availability, on the quality of life,
and on public service demands—are anything but trivial. Any serious appraisal of exactions, therefore, must consider regional along with local effects.
As exaction requirements proliferate and become a more significant part of
the cost of real estate development, what are the effects on urban sprawl, on
regional patterns of racial and economic segregation, and on public finance
equity as viewed regionwide?

Functionally, exactions are at once instruments for shaping the physical
environment, for generating public revenue, and for resolving political conflict. Those with a land use orientation place greatest weight on the theme of
infrastructure concurrency; that is, the timely provision of public investment
in concert with economic and population growth. Those for whom the fiscal
function is paramount stress equity and efficiency criteria. Those who care
most about local politics focus on the value of exactions as a bargaining chip
in local battles between progrowth and antigrowth, prorevenue and anti-
revenue, forces. These functional perspectives are typically integrated in practice, but they are too often isolated in appraisal.

How one views exactions, finally, depends on what one considers the most
likely alternatives. We shall focus on three dimensions of comparison: with
historical practice, with other programs of regulation, and with practical options for meeting the contemporary infrastructure needs of growing communities. These themes of comparison are so central to our argument that we
devote the following three sections to introducing them.

Historical Perspective

The recent surge in local reliance on exactions may be described as either evolutionary or epochal. Exactions are evolutionary in that local governments throughout the nineteenth and early twentieth centuries commonly required property owners to finance most of the public infrastructure in their vicinity. The primary method was to levy "special" or "betterment" assessments to pay for street, sanitary, water supply, and other capital improvements. Such assessments differed from exactions in that they rarely were imposed at the time of development. Instead, they were set when the occupants of developed property petitioned for improvements, typically as ongoing levies to cover debt service on long-term bonds rather than as one-shot payments.

During the Great Depression of the 1930s, large numbers of homeowners were unable to pay their special assessment levies. As a result, special assessment bonds fell out of favor. Over the subsequent four decades, the trend was to finance local infrastructure with a mix of local tax revenues and grants-in-aid from higher level governments. Developers, particularly of large subdivisions, were also increasingly required to donate land for local streets, utility connections, parks, and other on-site public facilities. Eventually, many communities required developers to construct some of these facilities as well.

What, then, has occurred since the mid-1970s that might justify speaking of an "exaction revolution?" At least three things, in our view.

First, the number of communities relying on exactions, the range of purposes for which they are considered appropriate, and the dollar magnitudes involved have expanded exponentially. To stretch the potential of exaction financing, moreover, localities increasingly have levied cash exactions, known as impact fees, on top of traditional in-kind exactions. The impact fees collected from any project can be merged with other sources of revenue to finance investments, generally off-site, to be shared with multiple other users, while in-kind exactions are generally for the provision of on-site infrastructure.

Second, where exactions are utilized most fully, they represent an epochal shift in attitudes toward land development. Throughout American history the most consistent theme in local governance has been the pursuit of growth: more people, more jobs, and more real estate development. Local democracy has been dominated by "growth coalitions," composed of individuals and enterprises with a direct stake in real estate development. The predominant pattern of inter-local relations has been of jurisdictions competing vigorously—with subsidies, tax abatements, zoning variances, and other regulatory adjustments—for investment dollars. Localities have varied, with central cities, low-income suburbs, and rural jurisdictions typically most eager for development, high-income bedroom communities the least. But the great majority of jurisdictions has clustered near the progrowth end of the spectrum.[7]

Intense competition to attract and hold major employers still abounds.[8] But critical shifts occurred during the 1970s and 1980s. Public attitudes toward development became far more ambivalent. With the diffusion of environmental values, the number of localities determined to restrain growth for quality of life reasons increased dramatically. With rising awareness of the impact of growth on public service demand, the number of localities seeking to ensure that new development "paid its own way" likewise increased. Meanwhile, voters became increasingly hostile to tax increases at all levels of government. Localities, as a result, were required to cope at once with stagnant or declining own-source revenue and with reduced aid from higher levels of government.

The great appeal of exactions is that they generate revenue for achieving publicly defined purposes without offending any organized blocs of voters. Although developers would prefer not to be saddled with exactions, they generally are few in number, disinclined to mobilize against officials who can deny their permits, and optimistic about being able to pass exaction costs onto their customers. So long as they believe that exactions play an essential role in mitigating local skepticism about growth, that their competitors are bearing similar burdens, and that the market will support both exaction costs and healthy profit margins, they have every reason to go along.

Third and finally, the exaction revolution has had an institutional dimension. Historically, land use planning and regulation were isolated from the local government mainstream. The public agencies charged with these functions were most frequently organized as independent commissions. They generally took an abstract, long-term planning perspective, divorced from considerations of phasing, finance, and political feasibility. They concentrated in their regulatory (zoning) activities on the adjudication of private disputes among property owners. They had scarcely anything to do with public investment or fiscal decision making.[9]

Where exactions are a major source of capital financing, however, land use planning and regulation inescapably become central concerns of local government. One consequence has been greater realism in land use planning, greater interest in implementation design, and a shift in focus from ten-to twenty-five-year to one- to five-year time horizons. Another consequence, perhaps, has been heightening attention to communitywide, as opposed to neighborhood, concerns in regulatory decision making, because the effects of major developments on public infrastructure demand (road and water usage, for example) often extend far beyond their immediate vicinity.

Regulation for Revenue

Reflecting a larger trend in American government, perhaps the most striking feature of exaction policy is its reliance on regulatory power to generate revenue for public purposes. Regulation for revenue, as we label it, is a comparatively new development on the American political scene. Until the 1970s, few government regulations imposed large costs on regulated parties over and above those necessary to satisfy the immediate expectations of customers. When government bans, for example, deceptive advertising, or insider stock trading, when it mandates that utilities with franchised monopolies serve all customers impartially, or when it requires common carrier vehicles to meet high safety standards, it basically is enforcing consensual norms of market behavior. Those who violate the rules may forgo illicit gains, but collectively the regulated industries benefit from enhanced consumer confidence. Thus, even those subject to such regulations rarely view themselves as bearing large state-mandated costs.

Many regulations, furthermore, confer net benefits on regulated parties by limiting competition. The most common (for example, local tax regulations) do so by restraining entry, fixing prices, or both. Political scientists refer to programs fitting this description as "self-regulatory," noting that their main source of support, and the main source of influence upon them, tends to be the regulated parties.[10] The deregulation movement of the 1970s and early 1980s, which led to the elimination or relaxation of government control in such fields as common carrier aviation, trucking, banking, and telecommunications, was largely directed at such programs.[11]

The power to levy exactions is rooted in the power to zone, and zoning is often described as a classic example of self-regulation. The central purpose of zoning, historically, has been to enforce collective norms among the property owners of a neighborhood or locality, with the aim of enhancing property values throughout the affected area. Thus exclusionary zoning—the use of land use regulatory power to keep out racial and ethnic minorities, low-income households of all types, and needed communal facilities that might disturb immediate neighbors—has been more commonplace than unusual.[12]

Regulations that impose net economic costs on the private activities subject to them became widespread only with the rise of consumer, public health, civil rights, and environmental activism during the 1960s and 1970s. The common characteristic of such "social" regulations is that they push far beyond the norms that business leaders consider essential to maintain consumer confidence or that they desire to restrict competition.

Those who bear the costs of social regulation in the first instance and those who pay ultimately may be different. The parties directly subject to regulation often succeed in passing some or all of their regulatory costs along to customers, suppliers, or employees. The defining characteristic of social regulation, however, is that the regulated parties make expenditures for the purpose of compliance that they would not make, even if acting rationally through industrywide associations, for market reasons alone. Stated another way, some wealth is being extracted from the regulated activity for broader communal purposes.

Analogous forms of regulation are also increasingly salient within the public sector itself, where the pattern is one of mandates imposed by higher level governments on lower.[13] The only difference between such regulation in the private and public sectors is that the affected parties in the former are deflected from pursuing market interests and in the latter from pursuing public purposes of their own choice.

One way of thinking about social regulation is that it merely reflects a civilizing tendency in society, to require higher norms of responsible producer behavior than in the past. In many cases, a broad consensus supports this viewpoint. Few would quarrel, for example, with the idea that modern factories should "internalize" the cost of satisfying modern pollution control and work safety standards.

There is often considerable room for dispute, however, about the extent to which communal needs may properly be laid at the door of specific regulated parties. Social problems commonly have so many causes that attributing blame is arbitrary. As a result, tax debates typically focus on ability to pay or on the economic consequences of various revenue schemes instead of on who is responsible for the fact that revenue is needed in the first place. Consider the case of an expanding corporation that, in the course of its hiring, lures some new households to town. Their addition to the local housing marketplace may be inflationary, but overall price and rent trends will be the outcome of innumerable factors. Some of these, like growth controls and rent controls, may be directly attributable to government choices and far more significant. To what extent, then, should the employer be held responsible for averting housing price increases or for shortages of affordable housing?

The issue rarely will turn, in governmental practice, simply on an analysis of cause and effect. It is more likely to turn on custom, general attitudes toward growth, and an appraisal of possible consequences. Does the community, for example, want to encourage or discourage employers from expanding? Does it believe that a special tax or charge per new employee would significantly affect employer investment and hiring decisions?

When responsibility for a problem is widely diffused, the issue is often whether to regulate activities that contribute to it or to undertake direct government spending. The choice is often far from obvious, particularly when the activities in question are, on balance, considered valuable. Who, for example, should pay to meet emerging needs for road, school, water supply, and waste treatment investment in growing communities? Until about 1970, most debates on this topic focused exclusively on choices among conventional public revenue sources: taxes, user fees, and grants-in-aid from higher level jurisdictions. More recently, however, attention has come to focus as well on another dimension of choice: Should the payments be structured as public or private?

The need for communal action usually can be traced to private actions. Highway needs, for example, can be attributed to investor decisions to develop land in patterns that generate high motor vehicle usage. They are also attributable, however, to decisions by enterprises not engaged in land development about where to locate offices, factories, and retail outlets; decisions by auto companies to market their products aggressively; and to decisions by consumers to purchase cars, to live in low-density settings, and to eschew mass transit. With responsibility so broadly diffused, the consensus used to be that government should simply adopt broad-based taxes and get on with the job. Today, the tendency is to focus on development regulation as a lever to obtain needed revenue.

The federal Superfund program provides an extreme but informative example. The main objective of the Superfund program, enacted in 1980, is to bring about the cleanup of landfills contaminated with hazardous wastes. The program mandates that such sites should be cleaned up at the expense of those entities, public and private alike, whose waste deposits they contain—regardless of when the contamination occurred, who was responsible for it, and how many depositors can be located today. The rationale for this rule is that regulatory remedies would be frustrated unduly if enforcement were made contingent on resolving these issues, or indeed on determining that the deposits violated any regulations at the time they were made.

The legal linchpin of the Superfund program is the doctrine of "joint and several liability," which specifies that any party found to have had any involvement, however meager and nonpolluting, can be held responsible for the entire cost of cleanup. Government prosecutors are inclined in this framework to go after one or several parties with deep pockets in each case, leaving them (or their insurance companies) to sue other parties if they wish to obtain a more equitable distribution of cleanup costs. Even the legal costs of enforcement, in other words, are shifted mainly onto the private sector, and perhaps onto parties with little or no responsibility for the problem.[14]

The upshot has been far more litigation than cleanup. As of December 1990, a decade after enactment of the Superfund program, the Environmental Protection Agency had identified approximately fourteen thousand sites as serious candidates for cleanup. It had managed to commence cleanup activity (beyond study and planning) on only 287 of these and to complete work on only 63.[15] Jan Paul Acton and Lloyd S. Dixon examined the hazardous waste cleanup experience of four national insurance companies, representing 15 percent of the national market, from 1986 to 1989. Eighty-eight percent of their expenditures went for litigation and administration, only 12 percent for paying claims. They spent more on disputing coverage with their own policyholders (about whether policies were applicable) than on disputing the merits of claims with outsiders.[16] Virtually all the disputes with policyholders involved policies written before 1986; that year nearly all insurers began to exclude pollution claims from coverage in the clearest possible language.[17]

Consider, finally, New Jersey's arrangement to finance hospital care for state residents who are medically indigent but ineligible for Medicaid coverage. One might imagine that if New Jersey considered this a public need, it would appropriate general tax revenues, as both the federal and state governments do for Medicaid itself. New Jersey, however, decided to finance this objective by regulation. Its instrument was a surcharge—in effect a sales tax—on the bills of paying patients. At 19 percent in 1991–92, the surcharge generated more than $900 million a year. In May 1992, a federal judge ruled this arrangement partially invalid. New Jersey governor James J. Florio, while planning to appeal, called on the state legislature to substitute a new set of regulations, requiring commercial insurance companies to insure all applicants at the same price, regardless of age, health condition, or other actuarial factors. (Governor Mario M. Cuomo, meanwhile, was urging the New York State legislature to adopt the same idea.)[18]

In short, while a compelling case can be made in many circumstances for mandating large expenditures by regulatory means, public officials, caught between urgent service demands and antitax pressures, are often tempted to extend this approach to circumstances where, on other than political grounds, they seem inappropriate. This has become painfully obvious in recent years even to many participants in local politics who passionately support business regulation—as they have become subject to a continuing flow of expensive mandates from higher levels of government, often simultaneously with grant-in-aid cutbacks. Those who enact the rules can receive acclaim— for example, from environmental interest groups—without having to bear any of the odium associated with raising public money.[19]

To say that regulation for revenue has great political appeal is not to say that it is risk-free for public decision makers. Regulated enterprises typically are active in and adept at all aspects of politics, from financing election campaigns to public relations.[20] Particularly during periods of economic recession, and in declining urban areas, they often find a positive reception for their arguments that additional regulatory burdens will threaten large numbers of existing jobs and undermine efforts to generate new investment. During boom times nationally, however, and in growing jurisdictions, the political appeal of regulatory expansion is enormous.

Alternatives to Exactions

Whether explicitly or implicitly, all participants in local land use debates base their appraisals of exaction proposals on perceptions of what is most likely to occur if they are rejected. Local officials typically portray the realistic alternatives as growth moratoriums on the one hand, tax or fee increases on the other. Residents whose top priority is to prevent growth typically judge that, if some growth has to take place, the public costs associated with it should be financed by exactions. Those whose priority is to avoid growth controls consider exactions a price well worth paying, if necessary, to avoid them. Those whose priority is to prevent tax and fee increases vastly prefer exactions as a means of financing the costs of growth.

Scholars and other analysts without a direct stake in land use disputes often view the array of options on which key actors focus as too narrow. They ask how exactions compare on the criterion of efficiency with well-designed user charges and on the criterion of equity with progressive income taxes.[21] As might be expected, exactions come out less favorably in these comparisons. For political reasons, however, such charges and taxes are rarely given serious consideration by American local governments. Still another alternative is to shift funding responsibility to the federal and state governments, whose tax systems capture the benefits of growth more comprehensively and are more progressive than those of local governments. While attractive to local actors, they rarely consider it available to address particular growth controversies, and the overall trend from the mid-seventies to the early nineties was negative.

At the local level, in practice, the most realistic alternative to exactions in communities facing development pressure tends to be growth controls. We shall argue that exactions are strongly preferable. Growth limitations tend to be more inflationary, and to involve more perverse transfers, than exactions.[22] We shall likewise endorse well-designed user charges and greater reliance on federal and state aid, though with strong caveats about their feasibility in most circumstances. Finally, we shall offer qualified praise for two options that enjoy little support in the world of practical politics: greater reliance on property taxes and acceptance of some service degradation.

2

Sources

EXACTIONS IN their simplest forms—land dedication for and construction of basic on-site infrastructure—are among the original instruments of American land use regulation. Zoning and subdivision regulation first became widespread in the 1920s. A central objective was to mandate that developers provide essential on-site facilities, particularly streets, but often as well water supply, drainage, and sewage connections. Earlier, subdividers and developers commonly ignored such needs, leaving their customers to face large subsequent assessments, or lobbied successfully to have municipalities assume responsibility, leaving them frequently with large debt service burdens for infrastructure to serve unsold, tax-derelict lots.[1]

Little development occurred during the Great Depression and World War II. In the late forties and the fifties, however, land use regulation diffused widely, and with it on-site exaction requirements. The range of exaction objectives also broadened, with large subdividers increasingly required to donate sites for public buildings and parks in addition to providing local streets and utility connections.

During the seventies and eighties, numerous localities began further to mandate that developers share in the cost of off-site public investments. The purposes for which exactions might be imposed were extended in some jurisdictions, moreover, to include social facilities and services (for example, low-cost housing, job training, and day care) as well as infrastructure. And the total magnitude of exaction costs burgeoned.

16

Special Assessments

The practice of assessing private property owners for the cost of public works dates to at least the thirteenth century; U.S. examples extend back to the 1690s.[2] While a direct antecedent of exactions, and today often mingled with them in government revenue statistics, special assessments differ from exactions in several key respects. First, special assessments fall on all property owners in a defined benefit zone, not merely those undertaking new development. Second, they are imposed for the direct benefit of those assessed rather than of future customers or the community at large. In most cases, finally, special assessments are imposed at the explicit request of property owners in the affected benefit zone. For example, a neighborhood desiring sidewalks may petition its local government for their construction, with charges allocated among property owners by acreage or street frontage. Like exactions, though, special assessments fully embody the principle that private property owners, over and above paying normal taxes, should in some cases bear the cost of new infrastructure traceable to their activities.

During the mid-nineteenth century, special assessments became a major source of public works revenue in cities nationwide and the dominant source in some. Historian Robin L. Einhorn reports, for example, that special assessments were the main source of revenue for public works in Chicago beginning about 1850 and were viewed as an antidote to rampant corruption because the property owners paying for each project tended to monitor costs closely.[3]

Special assessments remained an important source of local revenue well into the twentieth century. In 1913, for example, cities larger than 100,000 obtained 12 percent of their total income from special assessments, a figure suggesting that special assessments may well have been the dominant source of revenue for capital improvements. Special assessment bonds proved highly vulnerable to default in the Great Depression, however, as property values and homeowner incomes fell. The investment community came to view them with extreme disfavor, and by 1940 special assessment revenues had fallen to one-tenth their 1928 level.[4]

Special assessment revenues still are tracked by the Census Bureau, but the reported figures include certain impact fee revenues. (Other impact fee revenues are classified by reporting local governments as user fees, utility revenues, and development processing fees. In-kind exactions do not show up in any government revenue tabulations.) In fiscal year 1990, special assessments were reported to account for 0.8 percent of local general own-source revenue ($2.4 billion of $322 billion).[5] True special assessments, like exactions, in recent years have come to be used for more than just capital financing. More than a thousand "business improvement" districts are in operation nationwide, for example, with their special assessment revenues commonly used to provide enhanced security, sanitation, tourist information, and other services as well as physical improvements.[6]

Pre-1970 Exactions

While active in establishing special assessment districts and providing infrastructure for developed neighborhoods, local governments until the 1920s exercised little oversight of subdivision and development activities. All they generally required was that subdividers of raw land file accurate survey maps. Streets were plotted but normally remained unimproved and in private ownership unless and until the locality chose to construct them. The typical result was a great oversupply of divided lots—often without public improvements, in bankruptcy or tax delinquency, and unattractive to those who did wish to develop. Aside from the inconvenience and financial losses experienced by those who purchased lots, or even built homes, in failed subdivisions, their presence along the path of development provided a powerful stimulus for leapfrogging. When localities did get around to providing infrastructure, moreover, their reliance on special assessment financing often meant considerable hardship for homeowners in the affected districts who were living close to the margin. Finally, special assessment bonds were extremely prone to default in periods of economic downturn, triggering widespread foreclosures against individual homeowners as well as losses for bondholders.[7]

These were highly salient concerns for the pioneers of American land use planning. Consequently, the Standard Planning Enabling Act, published (as a model for state consideration) by the Department of Commerce in 1922, authorized local governments to require that subdividers or developers provide streets, water mains, and sewer lines within the boundaries of their own sites. The Standard Planning Enabling Act language subsequently was incorporated verbatim by most states into their statutes authorizing local land use regulation, and such on-site requirements became fairly common during the 1920s.[8]

During the quarter-century following World War II, numerous localities began to mandate donations, particularly by developers of large sites in communities experiencing rapid growth, for public parks, schools, libraries, police and fire stations, and other public buildings. Developers who wished to avoid on-site land dedication frequently could substitute in-lieu payments (the direct precursors of modern impact fees).[9] Until about 1970, however, exactions for off-site improvements were rare, and exactions for social facilities and services were unknown.

Surge in Exaction Usage

Through the mid-1960s, development was, in nearly all localities, a consensual objective. Its supporters, whom scholars variously have labeled the progrowth coalition or the growth machine, included landowners, developers, and construction companies; engineering, design, law, and real estate brokerage firms; retailers, who associated growth with increased sales; banks, which envisioned new deposits and lending opportunities; media enterprises, which foresaw larger audiences and advertising revenues; and organized labor, which viewed it as a source of jobs.[10] These groups in turn virtually monopolized participation in the land use policy process. Enterprises and residents directly threatened by specific projects often sought design or siting modifications. But they rarely challenged the grand consensus head-on. Insofar as they did, they generally found themselves isolated and powerless.[11]

The consensus did not extend to every type of development. Few communities were eager to host noxious industrial plants or public housing projects. Even attractive developments were often controversial, moreover, if they entailed the exercise of eminent domain, local tax-supported expenditures, or a choice among alternative sites.[12] But the zone of consensus was broad. Local politicians did not have to be especially adept, therefore, to stake out positions on growth that would stand them in good stead on election day.

These circumstances now have been transformed—not equally in all locales, but profoundly in most of those communities with the greatest recent history of, and near-term potential for, growth. Developers today routinely spend years marketing their projects to local officials and voters before they can market to consumers.[13] From their perspective, a dramatic power shift has occurred from the owners of property to government officials. From that of local officials, by contrast, the shift has been from a relatively secure and predictable environment to one of high risk.

The progrowth coalition has by no means dissolved but is today countervailed by organized neighborhood, environmental, and taxpayer groups and by the potential votes of many residents who, while unorganized, are highly responsive to antigrowth arguments. It is hamstrung as well by numerous procedural innovations of the 1960s and 1970s, designed to ensure that the potential adverse effects of major projects are spotlighted and publicly debated, to maximize opportunities for citizen participation, and at times even to provide for decision making by referendum.[14]

What began as a pattern of neighborhood resistance to particularly unsettling projects has gradually evolved, at least in numerous communities, into one of general concern about the harmful effects of growth on the quality of life. Not surprisingly, growth critics tend to be most influential in bedroom suburbs, where the typical voter can pursue quality of life objectives undiluted by occupational concerns and where organized business and labor carry little weight. During the 1980s, antigrowth activism became a major force in the politics of some large central cities as well. The most notable examples—San Francisco, Boston, Seattle, and New York City—were all in the midst of massive, sustained downtown construction booms.

We identify seven broad developments that have contributed to the recent decline of the progrowth coalition and surge in exaction usage:
—rising citizen, and particularly neighborhood-based, activism,
—the growing influence of environmentalism,
—income stagnation for most households, intensifying their resistance to new taxes
—cutbacks in federal aid,
—growing concern about infrastructure shortfalls,
—the proliferation of new, often expensive, federal and state mandates, and
—the steady progress and diffusion of fiscal impact analysis as a guide for land use decision making.

Neighborhood Activism

The first significant crack in the progrowth consensus appeared during the sixties and early seventies, when protests erupted in numerous localities against large projects scheduled to be undertaken by government agencies. These occurred against the backdrop of a general wave of protests, including those for civil and welfare rights, against the Vietnam War, for environmental protection, for the right of public employees to organize and strike, and for greater citizen participation in governance, particularly by the poor.[15]

The urban renewal program and the interstate highway program, enacted in 1949 and 1956, respectively, were unprecedented in their vast ambition to exercise eminent domain over, and to redevelop, already settled private land. In time, they provoked an unprecedented reaction. The more densely settled the area to be cleared, the greater in general were the social costs of change. As citizen backlash developed, consequently, it emanated from some of the nation's most densely populated cities—San Francisco and New York in the early 1960s; Boston, Newark, Chicago, Los Angeles, Philadelphia, and New Orleans in the late 1960s; and finally hundreds of others during the early 1970s.[16] What seems most surprising in retrospect, given the hairtrigger readiness of most neighborhoods to mobilize that now is taken for granted, is that so many projects were carried out before the wave of protest gathered force.

The early protesters rarely sought to challenge the progrowth coalition or the basic rationales of the government programs that threatened them. Rather, they focused narrowly on the neighborhood impacts of specific projects. The urban renewal program did generate controversy of a more general nature, but few, if any, critics challenged the idea that economic growth is an overriding local priority. Conservative critics argued the impropriety of taking private land for what they viewed as essentially private purposes and the inefficiency of public land market manipulation.[17] Liberal critics spotlighted the program's perverse redistributional effects—it routinely demolished low-income neighborhoods to make way for luxury commercial and residential developments—and the social value of settled neighborhoods, including most of those viewed by renewal officials as blighted.[18]

At the beginning, the prospect of success in fighting renewal and highway plans was unthinkable to most people. When protesters in a few locations triumphed, however—often because of electoral calculations by local officials rather than any grander reason—the word quickly spread.[19] Success bred success. Residents became increasingly disposed to mobilize and increasingly adept at finding points of vulnerability in proposed projects.

Over time, protesters realized they were far less likely to carry the day if they argued exclusively on the basis of neighborhood and individual resident concerns. Insofar as they did, they left themselves wide open to the charge of placing parochial self-interest over the general community interest. So they gradually became more adept at formulating briefs with wide appeal and at forging alliances with regionwide groups organized around general conceptions of the public interest. Good government groups such as the League of Women Voters, for example, were supportive of calls for more open planning, public hearings, generous relocation benefits, and other efforts to minimize harmful project side-effects. And environmental groups, as they surged to prominence circa 1970, were eager to criticize projects that would increase traffic, noise, air pollution, groundwater contamination, wind shear, or shadows cast by tall buildings; that is, virtually all projects of any scale.

During the late sixties and early seventies, Congress added procedural and substantive requirements to be satisfied by large-scale federal aid projects. First, it mandated public hearings and humane relocation procedures. Within a couple of years, it required environmental impact statements, drastically relaxed the rules on standing to litigate against proposed projects, and prohibited the disturbance of public open spaces and historic sites when other alternatives were technically (whether or not financially and politically) feasible.[20]

By 1970 the urban renewal program had shifted almost entirely from a strategy of neighborhood clearance and redevelopment to one of neighborhood rehabilitation, and in 1973 it was effectively abolished by incorporation into the Community Development Block Grant (CDBG) program.[21] During the early and mid-1970s, the rate of new expressway development likewise fell dramatically, and the primary focus of highway expenditures ever since has been on the rehabilitation and improvement of existing roads.[22] In the wake of these early successes, the targets of local protest rapidly expanded. Soon all projects with a potential to affect neighbors adversely were fair game, whether or not they were public, were large in scale, or involved displacement of existing occupants. Routine targets included group residences for the mentally ill, drug treatment centers, electric power plants, and waste disposal facilities. And the protesters generally prevailed. The acronyms NIMBY (not in my backyard) and LULU (locally unwanted land use) came into general use as symbols of the near impossibility of locating a vast array of publicly important, but controversial, facilities and of the dramatic balance of power shift in favor of neighborhood self-defense.[23]

Environmentalism

Two key points about the rise of the environmental movement, circa 1970, from impotence to brief primacy and continuing prominence in the American political system bear emphasis here.[24] First, the heart of environmentalism was an alternative vision of the overall public interest to that represented by the historic progrowth coalition. This vision pitted modern science against the economic viewpoints that previously reigned supreme in policy debates about land development. Second, against the criteria stressed by environmentalism, virtually all development projects fared poorly.[25] As environmental consciousness spread, large numbers of Americans became accustomed to viewing not only large projects but growth itself quite skeptically. At very least they were primed to believe that the negative side-effects of development commonly outweighed intended benefits. For many it seemed only prudent to adopt the working assumption that developers are guilty of environmental recklessness until and unless they can demonstrate otherwise.

Stagnating Incomes and the Tax Revolt

From World War II until the oil embargo and price run-up of 1973, the vast majority of American households experienced rising incomes. In real terms, the average full-time worker at age fifty in 1973 enjoyed more than twice the income of his or her counterpart in 1946.[26] Moreover, the distribution of incomes remained highly stable; that is, workers in all skill categories made roughly comparable gains. Since 1973, however, earnings have increased only about one-third as rapidly as during the fifties and sixties, and the gains have been concentrated among high-income groups. Lower skilled workers, particularly men, have experienced significant real declines in income.[27] The median full-time male worker experienced a 2 percent decline in real income from 1973 to 1986, although the comparable figure for women rose 10 percent.[28] From 1977 to 1989, average household after-tax income rose 8 percent. Roughly two-thirds of this gain accrued to the top 1 percent of households; most of the remainder to the next 9 percent; and the bottom 40 percent experienced an absolute income decline. The share of total after-tax income received by the top 1 percent rose from 7 to 12 percent, while that of the bottom 40 percent declined from 18 to 14 percent.[29] In short, most households experienced very slow income growth, or actual decline, over this period. Most of the growth that did occur, moreover, was attributable to increased labor force participation by women, and households in which women work tend to have considerably higher expenses per capita (for commuting, child care, clothing, and so on) than those in which they do not.[30]

The citizen tax revolt took shape against this background of stagnating incomes. While its origin is usually traced to 1978, when California voters adopted Proposition 13, it actually was apparent at the state and local levels several years earlier. And its primary effect was to stabilize taxes as a percentage of gross national product (GNP), not to roll them back. Government receipts (taxes and charges) for all levels combined rose from 25.8 percent of GNP in 1955 to 33.4 percent in 1975. The tax revolt nearly halted this progression for a decade; government receipts totaled 34.1 percent of GNP in 1985. Growth resumed, however, if more slowly than pre-1975, during the late 1980s; government receipts totaled 35.0 percent in 1990.[31]

The post-1975 changes were particularly striking at the state and local levels. Federal receipts were relatively stable over the period 1955–75, rising from 18.0 percent of GNP to 18.5 percent. State and local receipts, by contrast, nearly doubled (7.8 to 15.0 percent).[32] During the late seventies, however, the trend of state-local revenue growth turned around, declining from 15.0 to 14.3 percent of GNP between 1975 and 1980. Federal receipts, meanwhile, rose significantly, from 18.5 percent of GNP in 1975 to 20.3 percent in 1980.[33]

As the state-local tax revolt gathered force during the middle and late 1970s, its most hated target was the property tax, which surveys consistently show to be the least popular of all taxes. Property taxes are levied on the basis of capital ownership, not current income or wealth. The tax collector does not ask whether the incomes of longtime homeowners have risen in line with property values or whether relative newcomers are carrying large mortgages. In areas where property values were rising rapidly, moreover, such as California, taxes commonly followed suit regardless of income trends.

Proposition 13 affected not only the level of property taxation—limiting it to 1 percent of assessed value—but also the manner of property assessment. It rejected the principle of current value assessment in favor of historical value assessment. The nationwide trend, enforced by state courts, had been toward requiring frequent reassessment as a way of ensuring uniform taxation of all property owners—recent purchasers as well as old-timers. California rejected this principle, however, in favor of what is often labeled the "welcome, stranger" approach. Proposition 13 prohibited localities from reassessing property except when actual sales revealed new values. Until then, local governments were permitted to raise historical (1975) assessments by only 2 percent a year or the rate of increase in the consumer price index, whichever was less. A subsequent state act provided that a California homeowner who sold one home could purchase another of equal or lesser value without losing the historically based assessment.

In the run-up of California property values that occurred in the decade following 1978, tax disparities of 5-to-1 between properties with similar current values became common—and gave rise to a constitutional challenge. To the surprise of many, Proposition 13 emerged triumphant. Critics charged that its assessment provisions blatantly violated the constitutional requirements of uniform treatment under the law and of nondiscrimination against those moving from state to state. The Supreme Court ruled in 1992, however, that a state could legitimately tax on the basis of sale prices, however disparate in time, instead of current value assessments.[34] Except as state courts rule otherwise because of state constitutional provisions, the result of this decision may well be a nationwide revival of "welcome, stranger" property taxation (which, not coincidentally, has a great deal in common with the exaction approach to financing public facilities and services).

In the years immediately after 1978, numerous other states adopted tax limitation measures, and the federal government in 1981 adopted massive income tax rate cuts. Following the New York fiscal crisis of 1975–77, moreover, a movement coalesced for reform of state-local accounting practices and for greater caution about incurring debt. By contrast with the period 1955–75, when state-local receipts and expenditures rose dramatically as a percentage of GNP, the decade 1975–85 was one of decline. Receipts declined only slightly (from 15.0 to 14.5 percent of GNP), but expenditures declined sharply (from 14.7 to 12.9 percent of GNP).

During the late 1980s, state-local expenditures rose significantly (from 12.9 percent of GNP in 1985 to 14.0 percent in 1990), even though receipts did not (declining slightly in the late eighties before rising to 14.7 percent in the recession year of 1990).[35] Meanwhile, federal claims on GNP were relatively unchanged from 1980 to 1990. Federal receipts totaled 20.3 percent of GNP in both years, while federal expenditures rose very slightly, from 22.5 to 23.3 percent.[36] The dominant theme throughout this period, however, was of unrelenting pressure to avoid tax increases and of only slightly greater flexibility on the expenditure side.

Cutbacks in Federal Aid

From 1955 through 1978, federal aid to states and localities more than quadrupled as a share of GNP (0.8 to 3.6 percent) and rose nearly eight times in real terms ($12.7 billion to $109.7 billion in 1982 dollars).[37] Federal aid contracted slightly during the final years of the Carter administration, however, and sharply at the beginning of the Reagan administration. As a percentage of GNP, moreover, federal grants-in-aid continued to shrink through fiscal 1988. The absolute volume of federal grants contracted by nearly one-fifth in real terms from 1978 to 1982 before resuming slight increases during the middle and late 1980s. As a percentage of GNP, grants-in-aid shrank by one-third from 1978 to 1989 (3.6 to 2.4 percent).[38]

Programs of direct aid to localities were particularly hard-hit by the Reagan-era cutbacks. While localities received 25 percent of federal grant-in-aid money in 1979, they received only 14 percent in 1989. Even as the national economy grew in real terms by more than one-quarter, federal grants to localities declined by 49 percent. Measured against localities' own revenue-raising efforts, the cut was two-thirds; federal grants equaled 15 percent of local own-source revenue in 1979, but only 5 percent in 1989.[39] State aid to localities rose in absolute terms during this period but failed to keep pace with local own-source revenue growth. State grants equaled 53 percent of local own-source revenue in 1979, but only 44 percent in 1989.[40] In short, localities increasingly were on their own.

Infrastructure Backlogs

Even as fiscal austerity was biting hardest in the early 1980s, Americans were learning from a panoply of study commissions and media sources that their public works facilities were in "crisis." The crisis had come about, allegedly, because long-lived capital is easy to slight in the short term. An infrastructure system in good condition, as was that of the United States during the 1960s, has considerable slack capacity and will deteriorate only gradually in the face of inadequate maintenance. The United States was severely straining this system tolerance, however. Beginning about 1965, it had turned away from physical infrastructure as a government priority—in favor of social insurance, health, and welfare programs on the domestic front and the Vietnam War and, during the early 1980s, a large defense buildup on the international front. The consequences, long invisible to the average citizen, were now manifest in such symptoms as growing highway and airport congestion, collapsing bridges, and fouled beaches. Absent major new spending commitments, such problems would proliferate and intensify in the years ahead. The costs would be borne not merely in the coins of convenience and amenity, but also of productivity, national competitiveness, and public health.[41]

A dramatic shift in national spending priorities had in fact occurred. The National Council on Public Works Improvement, a temporary federal commission, reported in 1988 that from 1960 to 1984 public sector capital spending for physical infrastructure declined from 2.3 percent of GNP to 1.1 percent.[42] Adjusted for depreciation and population growth, the figures looked even worse. Tables 2-1 and 2-2 display changes in the net stock of physical capital owned by states and localities from 1950 to 1990.[43] Table 2-1 reveals the slowdown in absolute growth beginning about 1970. Adjusted for population growth in table 2-2, the net stock of state-local capital nearly doubled from 1950 to 1970, rose just 10 percent from 1970 to 1977, and failed to increase at all from 1977 through 1984. Only in the latter half of the 1980s did capital stock growth resume, mainly as a result of increased highway taxation and spending.[44] (The per capita adjustment is conservative,

Table 2-1. *Net Stock of State and Local Fixed Capital, 1950–90*
Percent unless otherwise indicated

Year	Net stock of state and local fixed capital (billions of 1987 dollars)	Change from prior year	Average annual rate of growth per five-year period
1950	480.1	. . .	
	498.0	3.7	
	516.1	3.6	
	536.2	3.9	
	562.8	5.0	
1955	592.1	5.2	4.3
	621.7	5.0	
	653.4	5.1	
	687.5	5.2	
	722.2	5.0	
1960	756.7	4.8	5.0
	794.7	5.0	
	833.6	4.9	
	876.6	5.2	
	922.7	5.3	
1965	972.1	5.4	5.2
	1,025.7	5.5	
	1,084.7	5.8	
	1,146.1	5.7	
	1,201.4	4.8	
1970	1,249.8	4.0	5.2
	1,294.1	3.5	
	1,334.0	3.1	
	1,369.9	2.7	
	1,406.3	2.7	
1975	1,436.5	2.1	2.8
	1,462.0	1.8	
	1,481.2	1.3	
	1,498.7	1.2	
	1,517.9	1.3	
1980	1,535.9	1.2	1.4
	1,550.6	1.0	
	1,563.6	0.8	
	1,576.6	0.8	
	1,592.8	1.0	
1985	1,613.9	1.3	1.0
	1,640.3	1.6	
	1,669.8	1.8	
	1,700.3	1.8	
	1,731.8	1.9	
1990	1,771.7	2.3	1.9

Source: John C. Musgrave, "Fixed Reproducible Tangible Wealth in the United States, Revised Estimates," *Survey of Current Business* (January 1992), table 16. Percentages calculated by the authors.

Table 2-2. *Per Capita Net Stock of State and Local Fixed Capital,*
1950–90
Percent unless otherwise indicated

Year	Midyear population (millions)	Per capita net stock of state and local fixed capital (1987 dollars)	Change from prior year	Average annual rate of growth per five-year period
1950	151.7	3,165	. . .	
	154.3	3,227	2.0	
	157.0	3,287	1.9	
	159.6	3,360	2.2	
	162.4	3,466	3.2	
1955	165.3	3,582	3.4	2.5
	168.2	3,696	3.2	
	171.3	3,814	3.2	
	174.1	3,949	3.5	
	177.1	4,078	3.3	
1960	180.8	4,185	2.6	3.2
	183.7	4,326	3.4	
	186.6	4,467	3.3	
	189.3	4,631	3.7	
	191.9	4,808	3.8	
1965	194.3	5,003	4.1	3.7
	196.6	5,217	4.3	
	198.8	5,456	4.6	
	200.7	5,711	4.7	
	202.7	5,927	3.8	
1970	205.1	6,094	2.8	4.0
	207.7	6,231	2.2	
	209.9	6,355	2.0	
	211.9	6,465	1.7	
	213.9	6,575	1.7	
1975	216.0	6,650	1.1	1.7
	218.1	6,703	0.8	
	220.3	6,724	0.3	
	222.6	6,733	0.1	
	225.1	6,743	0.2	
1980	227.8	6,742	0.0	0.3
	230.2	6,736	−0.1	
	232.5	6,725	−0.2	
	234.8	6,715	−0.2	
	237.1	6,718	0.0	
1985	239.3	6,744	0.4	0.0
	241.7	6,787	0.6	

Table 2.2. *(continued)*
Percent unless otherwise indicated

Year	Midyear population (millions)	Per capita net stock of state and local fixed capital (1987 dollars)	Change from prior year	Average annual rate of growth per five-year period
	244.0	6,843	0.8	
	246.4	6,901	0.8	
	248.8	6,961	0.9	
1990	251.4	7,047	1.2	0.9

Source: Data calculated and derived from John C. Musgrave, Fixed Reproducible Tangible Wealth in the United States, Revised Estimates," *Survey of Current Business* (January 1992), table 16; and Bureau of Census population estimates as reported in Advisory Commission of Intergovernmental Relations, *Significant Features of Fiscal Federalism: 1991*, vol. 2, Report M-176-II (October 1991), table 6 (for 1970–90) and in Bureau of the Census, *Historical Statistics of the United States: Colonial Times to 1970*, part 1, series A 29–42 (for 1950–69).

because it ignores the effects on infrastructure demand of both economic growth per capita and declining household size.)

The primary responsibility for these trends has been federal. Federal grants-in-aid for physical infrastructure failed to keep pace with economic growth from 1965 to 1980 and thereafter declined absolutely. Net of depreciation—that is, over and above the new investment required just to offset official estimates of depreciation—the picture looks much worse. By this measure, federal aid for infrastructure rose a mere 9 percent from 1965 to 1980, then declined by two-thirds from 1980 to 1990.

A recent study examined expenditures—capital and operating combined—for five major infrastructure categories: highways, aviation, mass transit, water supply, and wastewater treatment.[45] After nearly quadrupling in real terms from 1956 to 1965, due mainly to start-up of the interstate highway program, federal expenditures for these purposes shrunk by two-thirds from 1965 to 1989. As a percentage of GNP, federal expenditures declined in the period 1965–89 from 2.5 percent to 0.4 percent. By contrast, state-local spending consistently rose in real terms, though it declined slightly between 1965 and 1989 as a share of GNP (from 2.5 to 2.2 percent). All of the state-local decline as a share of GNP occurred by 1976, whereas the federal trend line continued its downward course through the 1980s. From 1978 to 1989, state-local expenditures rose 47 percent in real terms, while federal expenditures fell 44 percent. In consequence, the federal share of total spending for these infrastructure purposes fell from 50 percent in 1965 to 16 percent in 1989.

According to a broader measure, the U.S. National Income and Product Accounts, the federal share of government capital outlays in 1990—excluding those for uniquely federal activities such as national defense, international relations, space research and technology, and postal service—was only 11 percent. The local share was 56 percent, while the state share was 33 percent.[46]

The favorite theme of those concerned about infrastructure backlogs at the national level is economic competitiveness.[47] At the local level, however, quality of life concerns are typically paramount. And of these the most salient, particularly in areas of rapid growth, tends to be rising traffic congestion.[48] Growth is, in fact, just one among several main generators of traffic growth. Others include rising per capita income, increases in the proportion of women in the labor force, and associated growth in per capita rates of motor vehicle ownership. Nationwide, vehicle miles of travel (VMT) rose at nearly six times the rate of population growth from 1950 to 1989: 360 percent versus 63 percent. The rate of traffic growth per capita decelerated slightly after 1970, but from 1970 to 1989 VMT still rose four times as rapidly as population (90 versus 22 percent).[49] Not surprisingly, therefore, even areas with static or declining population consistently experienced substantial traffic growth.

From the mid-1950s through the early 1970s, traffic growth was accompanied by a great surge of new highway construction. Together with improvements in traffic management, this expansion of road capacity enabled traffic conditions to improve almost everywhere. Civic protest and environmentalism brought the era of rapid highway expansion to an abrupt close in the early 1970s, however. The best available quantitative measure of this change is residential displacement by federally aided projects; from 1969 to 1975 such displacements declined 79 percent.[50] In a more recent study, including road widenings and new road development on raw land, the Texas Transportation Institute compared increases in VMT with increases in major arterial lane mileage in thirty-nine large metropolitan areas for the period 1982–88. It found that travel increased at twice the rate of lane mileage.[51]

Even in California, which once led the country in expressway development and which was among the fastest-growing states during the 1970s and 1980s, new freeway construction nearly ceased after the mid-seventies.[52] Writing specifically about Southern California, John Landis and Cynthia Kroll report that traffic growth was accommodated by slack highway capacity through the 1970s. The slack was exhausted by about 1980, but the impetus for VMT growth was not. From 1980 to 1985 VMT rose 33 percent in San

Diego County and 25 percent in adjacent Orange County (three times the rate of population growth in each case). Severe congestion became endemic, providing the main stimulus for a flood of growth control initiatives.[53]

Traffic congestion is not the only source of public anxiety about rapid growth. Others include school overcrowding, exhaustion of waste disposal sites, growing air pollution and crime rates, disappearance of privately owned open space, growing crowds at public recreation areas, aesthetic degradation, and decline of small town intimacy. Among renters and longtime residents whose adult children wish to establish households in the community, rising housing prices are a frequent concern. For growth advocates, the challenge is to demonstrate that growth can occur without such negative side-effects.

Federal and State Mandates

Even as federal aid has been contracting and voters have been revolting against new taxes, both the federal and state governments have adopted large numbers of new infrastructure objectives in recent years. Their predominant method of squaring the fiscal circle has been to assign responsibility for performance to localities.

Like the shift from taxation toward regulation for revenue in dealing with the private sector, the shift from aid toward regulation in intergovernmental relations has extended far beyond the domain of infrastructure. The federal disposition toward regulating state and local activities began to surge during the mid-1960s, but it was accompanied by a raft of new aid programs as well. The situation changed with the onset of the Nixon administration. While spending for certain programs enacted in the 1960s—most notably, Medicare and Medicaid—continued to grow rapidly, new program enactments were mainly regulatory in nature. This trend has continued. The U.S. Advisory Commission on Intergovernmental Relations estimates that 53 percent of the federal preemption (regulatory) statutes adopted from the beginning of American history through 1988 were enacted after 1969. The rate of adoptions was as rapid during the Reagan years as during the 1970s.[54]

The best-known tabulation of the mandates to which local governments are subject, by Catherine H. Lovell and associates, focused on ten local communities in five states during the late 1970s. The researchers identified 1,234 federal mandates and an average per state of 683 state mandates. Of the federal mandates, roughly one-sixth required compliance regardless of whether the federal government was providing any money; the remainder were conditions of aid. Of the state mandates, 95 percent were direct orders. Local officials estimated that 79 percent of the costs of mandate compliance were borne locally, while the federal and state aid shares were 15 and 6 percent, respectively.[55]

It bears mention that the distinction between direct order mandates and conditions of aid may be insignificant if the aid program is considered indispensable. Joseph F. Zimmerman reports a recent example from the state level. The National Governors' Association estimated in 1990 that federal mandates added to the Medicaid program over the previous three years were costing the states $2.5 billion a year.[56] Most mandates, however, are more difficult to price. For example, Florida's concurrency requirement calls for infrastructure needs to be met simultaneously with private real estate development. To estimate its cost one must not only forecast how much development will occur, but also judge how much infrastructure investment that would not otherwise have occurred will be undertaken.[57]

As local protests against unfunded federal and state mandates have escalated in recent years, fifteen states have adopted constitutional amendments prohibiting mandates without funding, while forty-two states have adopted fiscal impact assessment requirements.[58] At the federal level, Congress enacted legislation in 1981 requiring the Congressional Budget Office to prepare a fiscal impact analysis of any bill likely to cost subnational governments $200 million or more annually.[59] Observers agree, however, that these reform efforts have come to little or nothing in practice. So the pressure on localities for spending to comply with mandates seems likely to continue escalating.

Fiscal Impact Analysis

Since at least the 1940s, local officials and planners often have sought to project the net impacts of proposed real estate developments on local government budgets. What are the probable effects, for example, of permitting the construction of dwelling units for low-income renters, or of tax abatements to attract new commercial office buildings?

Most localities through the 1960s, however, took as an article of faith that in the aggregate new development generated tax revenues more than sufficient to finance the services it required. Local civic actors were not entirely undiscriminating. Virtually all recognized, for example, that housing for low- and moderate-income families constituted a net fiscal drain. In communities with substantial amounts of both commercial and residential development, however, it seemed reasonable to assume that gains and losses would even out. In pure bedroom communities, the trick was to ensure that newcomers had comparable or higher incomes and fewer children per household than existing residents.[60] Local officials who acted in accord with this rules of thumb could feel confident that they were in the mainstream of local politics—in tune with free enterprise ideology and with the broad pro-growth coalition.

The predominant view today, by contrast, is that new development rarely generates local tax payments sufficient to pay its own way. The ascendancy of this viewpoint has doubtless in part been a natural outgrowth of improvements in the state of the art of fiscal impact analysis. But three other factors have also been at play. The first is austerity; local officials have been increasingly receptive to any approach offering protection against new spending and tax pressures. The second is the rise of antigrowth sentiment, which has enhanced the political plausibility of growth control options. Finally, real changes have occurred in the fiscal effects of growth at the local level. With new mandates and rising voter service demands on the one hand, declining federal aid and stagnating local tax revenues on the other, old assumptions have seemed increasingly inadequate.

In short, even where specific types of development may once have paid their way handsomely, they are far less likely to do so today. Particularly in communities experiencing rapid growth, the amount of new investment required to maintain service quality is very high relative to current tax revenue. Growing communities that already contain large amounts of settlement are likely to suffer most severely. Retrofitting an already developed area—for example, by expanding its highway system—is much more expensive than constructing infrastructure on raw land before any development has taken place.

In most communities with great development potential, consequently, the burden of fiscal proof has shifted from the opponents to the advocates of growth. Absent developer exactions, it is generally assumed, the owners and occupants of older properties will end up subsidizing new development. Fiscal impact analyses generally confirm this view, proceeding as they typically do from the premise that new infrastructure capacity sufficient to meet existing service standards will be developed. In practice, a more common outcome is for the occupants of older properties to share in a general degradation of service quality, for example, rising traffic congestion, school crowding, and pollution. But that is scarcely attractive to existing residents either. For local politicians, the most attractive path is frequently to champion "managed" growth—that is, pursuit of only those developments able to pay their way, including exactions sufficient to finance their infrastructure requirements.

3

Evolution and Current Practice

A VIRTUAL REVOLUTION in exaction utilization took place in the 1970s
and 1980s, according to several measures: the number of localities involved,
the purposes for which exactions were considered appropriate, and the significance of exactions as an element of both local government revenue and real
estate development cost.

Unfortunately, no comprehensive data on exaction utilization exist.[1] Any
portrait, therefore, must consist of a mosaic of fragments.

From Taxes to User Charges

The exaction revolution got under way within the context of a more general shift in American local government from reliance on property taxes
toward reliance on current charges (that is, revenues from the sale of services
and products).[2] Ironically, however, the most rapid increases in exaction
charges occurred during the 1980s, after this trend had stalled.

Paul B. Downing and James E. Frank analyzed the revenues of all 943
U.S. cities for which consistent data were available from the 1966–67 and
the 1986–87 censuses of governments. Over this twenty-year period, local
revenues from current charges more than doubled in real terms while property tax revenues slightly declined. The ratio of current charge to property tax

revenue rose from 0.31 in fiscal year 1967 to 0.70 in fiscal year 1987. By 1986–87, cities in twenty-two states, as opposed to seven in 1966–67, collected more current charge than property tax revenue.[3]

More generally, current charges rose during this period from 17.5 percent of local general own-source revenue to 25.9 percent. The trend was not constant, however. The rate of increase roughly doubled in each of the first three five-year periods: 1.1 percentage point from 1967 to 1972, 2.1 percentage points from 1972 to 1977, 4.5 percentage points from 1977 to 1982. From 1982 to 1987, however, as property taxes stabilized and the local tax revolt spread to include fee as well as tax increases, the current charge share rose only seven-tenths of a percentage point (from 25.2 percent to 25.9 percent of local own-source general revenue).[4]

Why did the rate of increase in exaction charges apparently accelerate in the 1980s, even as local fee revenues more generally were stabilizing? Two likely factors stand out: the real estate boom that many sections of the country experienced during the middle and late 1980s (which offered localities great exaction opportunities), and the local fiscal pressures reviewed in chapter 2.

Incidence of Exactions

Only two nationwide surveys of exaction incidence appear to have been carried out. Each dates from the mid-1980s. The survey methods of the two studies differed in some important respects, but their findings were highly consistent. Together, they indicate that exactions other than land dedication for streets and utilities were rare prior to 1960, that the most rapid diffusion of exactions took place after 1970, that exaction usage tended first and foremost to be a function of rapid community growth, and that other key explanatory factors included local fiscal stress and state legal permissiveness.

Elizabeth D. Purdum and James E. Frank in 1985 surveyed a 10 percent stratified random sample of all U.S. cities and counties to ascertain when, if at all, they had first adopted various types of residential exactions. The response rate of 39 percent (452 localities), while less than desirable in principle, was excellent for this type of study.[5]

Prior to 1955, Purdum and Frank found, the most popular exaction types were land dedication for drainage, sewage treatment, and roads—each utilized by about 9 percent of the respondent localities.[6] The authors did not specify the degree of overlap among communities reporting adoption of each exaction category, so the percentage of communities that adopted at least one type of exaction before 1955 is unknown. Additionally, the survey responses could be only as complete as the information available to the individuals who filled out the surveys in 1985. It seems clear, nonetheless, that only a small minority of localities made significant use of exactions prior to 1955.

As of 1985, by contrast, roughly nine communities in ten made use of exactions. The survey asked about three exaction forms: in-kind land dedications, in-kind build/install requirements, and cash payments by developers. Eighty-eight percent of the respondent communities imposed some land dedication requirements; 89 percent, build/install requirements; and 58 percent, cash payments. For communities that experienced 30 percent or greater population growth from 1970 to 1980, the figures were 96 percent, 94 percent, and 77 percent, respectively. Respondents for communities that did not impose exactions most commonly explained that they were not growing or had no responsibility for development permitting.[7]

Most exactions imposed by the respondent communities were flexible, at least in part, rather than based strictly on formulas. Only 14 percent of the communities with build/install requirements, 23 percent of those requiring land dedication, and 46 percent of those requiring cash payments relied purely on formulas. The majorities that did not were more or less evenly divided between those utilizing "standards with some flexibility" and those deciding case by case.[8]

The pre-1960 exactions reported by Purdum and Frank were mainly for road and drainage work, water and sewer lines, police stations, and parks.[9] The pace of diffusion for most of these traditional exaction purposes (though not for drainage and police stations) accelerated sharply during the first half of the 1960s; and they were now commonly joined by exactions for water, sewage, and solid waste treatment facilities. After 1970, rates of adoption for all these purposes turned steeply upward, joined by exactions for fire and police stations and for drainage.[10]

The data in table 3-1, drawn from the Purdum-Frank survey, indicate broad diffusion patterns. For each exaction type examined, the "takeoff" decade (when at least 20 percent of the respondents said their jurisdiction first adopted it) and the period of most rapid adoption are noted.[11]

Gus Bauman and William H. Ethier conducted a survey in early 1985 of one thousand communities that were subscribers to the American Planning Association's Planning Advisory Service.[12] Only 220 communities (22 percent) responded, but they were distributed across forty-six states. Two-thirds (66 percent) reported levying on-site exactions; 58 percent, off-site exactions; and 45 percent, impact fees. (As employed in this study, the term "exaction"

Table 3-1. *The Diffusion of Exactions*

Takeoff decade	Exaction purpose	Period of most rapid adoption	Exaction types used by 40 percent or more of localities by 1984
1955–64	Police stations	1970–84	Build,[a] land
1955–64	Parks	1970–84	Build, land
1960–69	Roads	1970–84	Build, cash, land
1960–69	Schools	1970–79	Build, land
1960–69	Water lines	1960–64, 1970–74	Build, cash, land
1960–69	Water treatment facilities	1960–74	Build, cash, land
1960–69	Sewage treatment facilities	1960–74	Build,[b] land
1960–69	Solid waste	1960–64, 1970–74, 1980–84	Build,[a] land
1965–74	Affordable housing	1965–74, 1980–84	Build, cash, land
1970–79	Sewer lines	1970–79	Build, cash, land
1970–79	Open space	1970–84	Cash, land
1970–79	Fire stations	1970–84	Build, land[a]

Source: Data drawn from Elizabeth D. Purdum and James E. Frank, "Community Use of Exactions: Results of a National Survey," in James E. Frank and Robert M. Rhodes, ed., *Development Exactions* (Chicago and Washington: Planners Press, 1987), table 6-9.
[a]Also, cash by just under 40 percent of localities.
[b]Data on cash not available.

included in-kind requirements and fees in lieu of performance. The term "impact fee" included payments toward the cost of off-site facilities with no option of in-kind performance.)

Of those communities that imposed impact fees as of 1985, 10 percent reported that they had first done so prior to 1960. Nineteen percent began levying impact fees in the 1960s, 36 percent in the 1970s, and 35 percent during the first half of the 1980s. (No data were reported on the diffusion of other types of exactions.) Bauman and Ethier did not carry out a sophisticated analysis of the causes of variation in exaction usage. Their simple cross-tabulations, however, suggested that rates of in-kind exaction usage differed only slightly by region, but that rates of impact fee usage varied much more widely. For example, 82 percent of the California respondents reported levying impact fees, none of the New England respondents, and only 13 percent of those in the Middle Atlantic states.[13] Nationwide, 46 percent of the communities that experienced more than fifty housing starts in 1984 imposed impact fees, as compared with 33 percent of those with fewer starts.[14]

Two other surveys conducted in the mid-1980s provided stronger evidence of the prevalence of exactions in growing communities. Edward J. Kaiser, Raymond J. Burby, and David H. Moreau surveyed water and sewer fee usage as of 1986 by 148 localities in nine southeastern states. Finding state averages ranging from 13 to 71 percent, they conducted a multiple regression analysis to determine the sources of variation. Differences in state institutional arrangements became insignificant as explanatory variables in the context of this analysis. The factors that proved statistically significant were all locality-specific. In descending order of significance, these were: rate of increase in water and sewage volume, coordination of local utility planning with comprehensive land use planning, presence of water and sewer system stress, and staff attitudes toward new ideas. Of respondents that had actually invested in system expansion over the past several years, 93 percent said that they had relied wholly or in part on developer financing for extensions within the boundaries of their jurisdictions, while 100 percent said that they had done so for extensions beyond their jurisdictional limits.[15]

James E. Frank, Elizabeth R. Lines, and Paul B. Downing surveyed a random sample of localities that made sewage capital investments in 1985 (as indicated by their expenditure reports to the Census Bureau). In distinguishing those that levied sewage impact fees from those that did not, Frank, Lines, and Downing found only three variables statistically significant: magnitude of population growth, own-source revenue level as a percentage of personal income (a measure of fiscal stress), and judicial permissiveness toward development regulation.[16]

We are aware of only one data series that traces the diffusion of exactions into the 1990s. Although confined to one state (Florida) and one exaction type (impact fees), it provides striking evidence of the continuing rapid pace of exaction diffusion beyond the mid-1980s, when all the studies cited above were carried out. The surveys of Florida cities and counties in question indicate that the number of jurisdictions levying impact fees rose from about 5 in 1972 to at least 125 in 1991. As of 1991, 53 percent of the cities responding and 49 percent of the counties levied impact fees. The number of specific fees reported rose from 5 in 1972 to more than 400 in 1991. Nearly all of this growth occurred after 1977, when the number of fees in effect still was only about 20. Nearly all of the pre-1978 impact fees were for water and sewage improvements. The range of purposes became highly diverse thereafter, but transportation (almost all road), sewage, and water fees accounted for 78 percent of total impact fee revenue in fiscal year 1991. Park, police, and fire protection fees accounted for another 16 percent.[17]

Dollar Magnitudes

Determining whether exactions are imposed in a given jurisdiction is much easier than figuring out what they cost developers. Most exactions are negotiated (at least in part) rather than set by formula, moreover, so exaction costs may vary widely within the same jurisdiction.[18] Finally, many exactions are still in-kind, so they do not show up on local government books as revenue, nor are developers required to report what they cost to fulfill. Not surprisingly, therefore, the available data on exaction costs are particularly fragmentary and focus almost exclusively on impact fees.

James C. Nicholas and colleagues surveyed 100 local governments during the first half of 1991 to ascertain their impact fee levels. The sample was drawn from high-growth states where impact fees were known to be especially prevalent. It consisted of seventy-eight California localities, fourteen from the upper northwest (Oregon and Washington), seven from Florida, and eleven from seven other states.

The survey requested impact fee magnitudes for a three-bedroom, single-family, detached home of two thousand square feet, and for three standard, hundred thousand square foot, nonresidential structures (general industrial, general office, and general retail). Numerous localities were unable to provide comprehensive data because some or all of their fees were variable. The survey obtained overall data on impact fee magnitudes, therefore, only from those localities that imposed all of their fees by formula.

Bearing these caveats in mind, impact fees averaged more than $12,000 per dwelling unit in early 1991 while nonresidential impact fees averaged $5 to $7 per square foot, depending on use category (see table 3-2). While development costs varied widely from project to project, these fee totals were probably in the range of 5 percent of average development costs.

Comprehensive national data are lacking, but four recent studies indicate that impact fee growth rates during the 1980s were prodigious. Likely reasons include the scarcity of alternative resources for local infrastructure investment, the great real estate boom that many areas experienced during the 1980s, and the growing familiarity of local officials with impact fee financing. During the early years of impact fee usage in each state, local officials have typically been uncertain about what the courts would permit, as well as about

Table 3-2. *Impact Fee Totals, California and Other Localities, 1991 Dollars*

	Impact fee total		
Type of building	Average	Low	High
Industrial building (per 1,000 sq. ft.)	4,998	1,035	24,659
Office building (per 1,000 sq. ft.)	6,052	790	33,888
Retail building (per 1,000 sq. ft.)	7,061	841	52,219
Single-family home	12,368	605	55,070

Source: Growth Management Studies Program, School of Law, University of Florida, "Levels of Impact Fees," memorandum with data attachments, June 12, 1991.

what developers might be induced to pay. Thus impact fees have generally been set very low to start, so as to minimize the likelihood of litigation by developers and to be easily defensible in court if necessary. Over time, as confidence about the legality of impact fees has grown, most early adopters have become far bolder, and new adopters have felt free to set higher rates from the outset.

Thomas P. Snyder and Michael A. Stegman studied changes in the development fees levied from 1975 to 1983 by twenty-three Southern California localities on new single-family homes. They found that such fees (mainly for road, school, park, water, sewer, and flood control purposes) rose 511 percent in real terms over the eight-year period, from an average of $1,087 per house to $6,647 (1983 dollars). Road and school fees, which were not levied at all in 1975, accounted for 38 percent of the total in 1983.[19]

The San Francisco Bay Area Council surveyed thirty-four Bay Area communities in both 1981 and 1987. They all levied development fees, and the median for a "starter" house (defined as 1,434 square feet on a lot of 5,500 square feet) rose 87 percent in real terms over the six-year period. "Growth" fees (for example, for the construction of streets, schools, and parks), as opposed to those for permit processing and utility hookups, rose 250 percent in real terms. The most rapid growth was in school impact fees. Only 24 percent of the respondent communities levied such fees in 1981; 93 percent did so in 1987. Furthermore, the median school impact fee had increased from $650 to $2,151 (current dollars). The overall median fee per house in 1987 was $9,110.[20] By comparison with this surge in development fees, the respondent communities reported per capita declines in local tax and intergovernmental aid revenues of 50 percent or more from 1978 (the year of Proposition 13) to 1985.[21]

According to the Florida surveys cited previously, impact fees in that state more than tripled from 1985 to 1991. By far the greatest reported increase was in the category of road impact fees, which accounted for just 8 percent of total revenue in 1985 but grew to 55 percent in 1991. (The other main categories as of 1991 were water and sewer, 24 percent; parks and recreation, 8 percent; and police and corrections, 6 percent.)[22]

Finally, the Growth Management Studies Program of the University of Florida surveyed thirty-two large jurisdictions (mainly counties) that experienced rapid growth in 1988, 1990, and 1991. Of these, twenty-two were in Florida, six in California, two in Maryland, and one each in Colorado and New Jersey. During this brief period, the real estate economy went from the crest of a boom to deep recession. Impact fees rose sharply nonetheless. The average impact fee total for a two thousand square foot single-family home, exclusive of water and sewer fees (for which 1988 data were unavailable), rose 85 percent in real terms. The total per thousand square feet of industrial space rose 184 percent; per thousand square feet of office space, 96 percent. Retail fees went up the least (23 percent) but were considerably higher than office and industrial fees throughout this period.[23] Surprisingly, the rate of increase was much more rapid during the recession years of 1990–91 than in the two prior years. The average impact fee per single-family home rose only 26 percent in real terms from 1988 to 1990, but 47 percent from 1990 to 1991. The same trend was observable in each of the three nonresidential categories.[24]

Impact Fees and Urban Sprawl

A frequent query about exaction financing is whether it tends to stimulate urban sprawl. The question is highly pertinent because many other public policies have done so, from the federal highway and mortgage insurance programs of the early postwar decades to suburban growth controls in recent years.

If exaction levies were higher in central cities and close-in suburbs than in far suburban locations, they reasonably could be seen as encouraging sprawl. The one study we have located that bears directly on this topic, however, indicates the reverse. The San Francisco Bay Area Council, in its 1981 survey, distinguished localities in three concentric zones: the urban core, the inner suburbs, and the outer suburbs. Basic fees at the time for permit processing and building inspections were virtually identical in all three zones, roughly $700. Utility hookup fees were nearly four times as high in the outer suburban zone as in the core, however, and growth (impact) fees were twenty-four times as high. Overall, hookup and growth fees averaged $920 per dwelling unit in the core, $2,809 in the inner suburban zone, and $5,519 in the exurban zone.[25]

Social Exactions

Broad surveys of the incidence of exactions typically spotlight residential development, because it is ubiquitous, whereas many jurisdictions have little or no commercial development. It is where pressures for commercial development are particularly intense, however, that social exaction requirements are prone to become most expansive.[26] The main reasons, presumably, are that large commercial developments are popularly perceived to yield great profits and to have large side-effects (for example, on peak period travel volumes). Additionally, given that the intended customers of commercial developers are other businesses, the tendency is to worry far less about potential exaction impacts on affordability than when dealing with residential development.

Numerous jurisdictions still offer generous inducements to commercial developers in such forms as tax abatements, land cost write-downs, and public works improvements. In the hottest markets, though, particularly where the booms are extended in duration, local officials typically see little need to court development and may be emboldened to extend the reach of their exaction objectives. Furthermore, some of these markets, particularly in California and the Northeast, experienced dramatic run-ups in housing prices during the 1980s, while dramatic cutbacks were taking place in federal housing aid. From fiscal years 1981 to 1987, federal housing grants declined from $30 billion to less than $8 billion, and the number of households receiving assistance declined by 74 percent.[27]

Between 1979 and 1988, at least ten jurisdictions adopted mandatory "linkage" (social exaction) programs in connection with new commercial development. These programs invariably required developers to finance new housing units for low- and moderate-income households. Some required developers as well to provide free space in their projects for community services, to finance social services on a continuing basis, or both. At least another half-dozen cities adopted "voluntary" linkage programs—focused more exclusively on housing and, in most cases, offering density bonuses to developers as an inducement.

Of the ten jurisdictions with mandatory programs, six were in California, two in Massachusetts, and two in New Jersey. By far the largest programs were those of Boston and San Francisco, where developer commitments were estimated as of 1990 to exceed $46 million and $28 million, respectively. Of the six voluntary programs, three were in Florida and one each in Connecticut, New Jersey, and Washington State.[28]

Whereas most exactions are justified by the anticipated service demands of project occupants (for example, for potable water) or by community standards for environmental impact mitigation (for example, sewage treatment), the typical rationale for social exactions is socioeconomic "linkage." The argument is that new office space generates employment growth, which in turn stimulates demand for new housing and for such services as day care. Unless developers arrange to serve these demands, all community residents will experience shortages and price increases. Those affected most adversely will be those with low and moderate incomes. (Low income is most often defined as less than 80 percent of the local median, adjusted for household size, moderate income as 80–120 percent of the median.)

The proposition that housing and social service shortages are attributable to office development is far from universally accepted. Community activists generally consider it so obvious, however, that they view documentation as superfluous; and their views have at times prevailed in local politics. The Boston program, for example, has never rested on any technical analysis. Linkage first emerged in the late 1970s, during an intense public controversy over a large mixed-use development (Copley Place) in Boston's Back Bay, which involved both the use of public land and a $19 million federal Urban Development Action Grant. To secure the needed political approvals, the developer agreed to set aside one-quarter of the one hundred residential units to be developed for low- and moderate-income households and to set aside a fixed percentage of construction employment for city residents, minorities, and women. Linkage subsequently became a major issue in the 1983 Boston mayoral campaign, championed by, among others, the eventual victor, Ray Flynn. The city council formally authorized it even before Flynn's inauguration. Linkage payment revenues were to be expended by the city in support of affordable housing, job training, park restoration and maintenance, and athletics.[29]

The city never conducted a study to justify its linkage policy; and a developer brought suit in 1985. Ten months later, a state superior court ruled against the city, finding that linkage as practiced in Boston "more closely resembles a tax than a fee" and that "its primary purpose is to raise revenues . . . to be expended for the common good" [rather than to accommodate demands generated by specific new developments].[30] Leading developers, convinced that linkage had become an essential underpinning of local political support for new development, rushed to announce that they would continue making linkage payments regardless of the program's legal status. Subsequently, the Supreme Judicial Court of Massachusetts overturned the Superior Court ruling on a technicality. Realizing that the program's legal status was in doubt, however, the city sought and obtained explicit state legislative authority for its program in 1987.[31] Since then, in effect, developer linkage payments have been taxes, not impact fees; that is, despite the label, Boston has been under no legal obligation to demonstrate actual linkage.

San Francisco has been more punctilious. Critics maintain, however, that its housing shortages are far more attributable to the city's own policies than to developer actions. San Francisco first adopted its linkage policy in 1980. Only three years previously, in 1977, it massively downzoned its residential neighborhoods in response to pressures from existing residents, and it continued to downzone on a spot basis thereafter. The city also discouraged for-profit housing development by requiring that developers of market-rate housing provide subsidized housing as well. The city's Southeast Waterfront Plan, for example, stipulated that 50 percent of all new housing be for low- and moderate-income households.[32]

The San Francisco linkage program was based on a detailed study of the employment and housing correlates of office development. This study estimated that, for each one million square feet of new office space, 386 new dwelling units would be required within the city limits of San Francisco. (As is typical of local impact studies, no attention was paid to spillover effects on other jurisdictions.) Because of the high cost of San Francisco housing, the study assumed, all new residents earning less than 150 percent of the local median would require some housing subsidy. The total subsidy required, in the form of an initial capital cost write-down, would be $9.47 per square foot of office development if the linked housing was for sale, $10.47 if it was for rent. As a matter of policy, the city chose to levy a housing linkage fee of $5.34 per square foot on new office development, which also could be satisfied in-kind.[33] This figure has been updated periodically since 1988 to reflect housing price inflation; it stood at $8.10 per square foot in 1992.[34] In practice, linkage contributions are negotiated case by case in San Francisco and have varied considerably.[35]

For all of its surface rigor, the San Francisco linkage study notably ignored a key feature of the city's recent history that had been spotlighted by critics of growth for other purposes. From 1965 to 1980, even as the city's booming economy had generated 166,000 new jobs, the number of employed San Francisco residents had declined by almost 18,000.[36] In short, while job growth had doubtless stimulated housing demand in the city, this effect had been more than offset by the ongoing trend toward central city jobs, new and old alike, being filled by suburban residents.

The jurisdiction that seems to have been most aggressive in levying social exactions is Berkeley, California. Berkeley's current menu of exactions includes housing, child care, public art, preferences and placement services for local residents seeking project-related jobs, and commitments to make payments in lieu of taxes should space within the project ever become tax-exempt because it is leased for public use. City officials, who exercise discretionary authority over all development proposals, examine each project at the planning stage to determine what the developer can afford. Their calculations take into consideration the anticipated needs of "indirect" employees—those working elsewhere who provide services to businesses located within the project—as well as on-site employees. Neil S. Mayer and Bill Lambert analyzed Berkeley exactions as applied to two recent office development proposals. One project was approved with an exaction package totaling about $12.50 per square foot plus potential in-lieu tax payments should any space become tax-exempt. The prospective developer in the other case agreed to an even larger package ($12.50 per square foot plus $0.35 per square foot a year in perpetuity) but met rejection anyhow in the face of neighborhood opposition.[37]

All localities that have initiated social exaction programs to date were in the midst of prolonged, intense real estate booms. Few jurisdictions experience such booms in any decade, however, and the turnover rate among them tends to be high from one decade to the next. The number of jurisdictions that experienced commercial real estate booms in the 1980s, moreover, was highly unusual. Commercial real estate values have since fallen by half or more in the strongest markets of the 1980s, vacancy rates have soared, and development activity is at a standstill. Over the longer term, whereas the national rate of office development in the mid-eighties was roughly twice the level of normal demand growth, vitually all analysts forecast rates well below normal through the 1990s.[38]

Had the boom conditions of the eighties persisted, a wide diffusion of social exactions, along with expansion of their scope and magnitude, could have been expected during the nineties. Now, however, the question has become whether localities that adopted social exaction policies will scale them back to achieve economic revival. (For reasons of local political symbolism, outright repeal does not seem likely.)

4

Political Wellsprings, Legal Constraints

WHILE LOCALITIES VARY over the full spectrum in their attitudes toward growth, the most common shift of recent decades has been from consensus about the desirability of growth to fierce controversy. In striving to navigate the shoals of development conflict successfully, local officials typically claim to favor "desirable" growth while opposing "harmful" growth. The obvious question is how to distinguish one from the other—or, stated another way, how to craft viable compromises between progrowth and antigrowth forces. The challenge is vastly complicated by contemporary requirements for environmental, fiscal, traffic, and other types of impact reviews. While such studies are useful in determining whether plans merit approval, they also clarify points of group conflict, expanding the range of issues to be resolved.

In searching for positions that can attract broad support, local officials invariably feel pressured to demonstrate that all of the projected infrastructure needs associated with growth will be met without placing new fiscal burdens on, or reducing any of the amenities and services enjoyed by, existing local residents. It is here that exactions come in. By obtaining developer commitments to finance public facilities and services, local officials can maintain that they have protected the interest of current residents and, more generally, that they are "managing" growth rather than caving in to either developers or antigrowth extremists.

With growing local tax resistance and declining federal aid, moreover, both taxpayer and antidevelopment groups have honed their analytic skills in recent years: the former to ensure that fiscal benefits promised by developers actually materialize, the latter in search of ammunition to shoot down development proposals. As a result, in most communities with great development potential, the burden of fiscal proof has shifted from the opponents to the advocates of growth. It is now widely assumed that, in the absence of exactions, development will result in local tax increases or service cutbacks.

The growing determination to ensure that development both "pays its own way" and is accompanied by adequate investment in public facilities is manifest today even in communities highly favorable to growth.[1] For these communities, exactions are simply the local revenue source least likely to generate voter backlash. Their exactions are usually based on solid technical studies, are embodied in clear formulas, and are allocated entirely for conventional infrastructure purposes (for example, roads, sewers, schools, and park sites). Progrowth communities tend further to be conservative in setting exaction levels, keeping developer costs well below the levels that their studies have shown to be justifiable. And they are frequently willing to accommodate developers on matters of procedure—deferring the collection of impact fees, for example, until projects are ready for occupancy.

Localities ambivalent about growth often have more complicated exaction agendas, involving conflict resolution as well as the search for revenue. Elected officials in such communities, for example, often consider it vital to balance their pro- and antidevelopment actions. Exactions are valuable symbolically as well as fiscally in this respect, because their apparent effect is to "make developers pay." Communities of this type are likely to take fewer pains in developing technical justifications for their exaction levies, to rely significantly on negotiated exactions, to utilize them for social as well as conventional infrastructure purposes, and to insist on collecting at least some impact fees before construction begins.

Finally, a few communities—such as San Francisco and Petaluma, California, and Boulder, Colorado—have adopted explicit policies of growth limitation, forcing developers into competition for a limited number of development unit slots. The result, when markets are hot, is to encourage a bidding war of "voluntary" exaction commitments by developers, calibrated to win community support rather than merely to finance investments clearly attributable to their projects.

From the standpoint of local politicians, the greatest appeal of exactions is that they seem free to voters. Except for those who engage in land development, no one gets a tax bill or pays an explicit fee. Nearly all citizens view exactions as a straightforward method of requiring developers to "pay their own way" and, perhaps, of enabling the community to share in their windfall profits. Even those who buy or rent newly developed property know only what they pay; they never see a breakdown of the exaction portion. Indeed even professional economists have difficulty determining how costs have been allocated in any particular case.[2]

Sophisticated owners of existing property, finally, increasingly realize that they stand to reap windfall benefits when exactions are imposed on new development. If, on the one hand, exactions deter some developers from proceeding, the supply of property on the market will be less than it would have been otherwise, enhancing the value of existing property. If, on the other hand, developers go forward but raise prices to cover their exaction costs, the value of existing property is likely to rise in tandem (because new and old properties compete in the same marketplace).

In short, exactions provide something for just about everyone in local politics. Even developers benefit insofar as they receive permissions that would otherwise have been blocked by community opposition.[3] Future voters may be disadvantaged, but they will never know how much. Nor will they receive any cues to arouse their curiosity. No account exists of a politician suffering at the ballot box because newcomers to a community became angry in retrospect about the exactions imposed on the developer of their property.

Judicial Oversight

American law provides that government may take private property only upon payment of just (market value) compensation. Exactions, however, and particularly land dedication requirements, constitute partial takings of property without compensation. The law provides further that private owners have a right to use and develop real property as they see fit, except as regulated for specific, valid public purposes. That is, local governments do not have unlimited discretion in attaching conditions to development permits. Finally, localities exercise land use authority only by explicit delegation from states. With rare exceptions, states have not conferred broad authority on localities to tax development. Thus, the great majority of exactions are rooted in regulatory authority; when challenged in court, they must be defended as instruments for the achievement of valid regulatory objectives.[4]

In short, while the motive forces of land use regulation may be political and fiscal, localities must act within a web of legal constraints. Most local officials assign high priority to avoiding litigation, moreover, and thus do not press the limits of their authority. They stress that litigation is risky, expensive, time-consuming, and unproductive. The risk is in part personal; officials who invite lawsuits and lose may be widely perceived as incompetent. But it is also communal. A locality defeated in court, whether by developers or critics of development, may be forced to accommodate unwanted development or fail to secure intensely desired projects.

Some localities, nonetheless, choose to push the limits of their land use authority, counting on the time and financial costs of litigation to deter most private parties, or simply preferring the risks of aggressiveness to those of (as they see it) timidity. When such localities prevail in court, or manage for sustained periods to escape challenge, they expand the range of options available to more cautious officials elsewhere.

Developers likewise are averse to litigation, probably more so than any other private actors who regularly participate in land use affairs. While better financed on the whole than most opponents of development, they are also more driven by economic calculation. Time is money for them more than for anyone else in the land use process. They also appear as petitioners before the same regulators again and again. The last thing they want is to antagonize those on whose goodwill they so profoundly depend. Even when a developer prevails in a lawsuit, the typical outcome is a court order for the local regulatory body to reconsider. The explicit rules may have become more favorable to the developer, but the regulators almost invariably have other grounds available for saying "No" or for prolonged delay.[5]

During each major phase in the evolution of exactions, nonetheless, some developers have litigated, and some developer associations have lobbied for state legislation to constrain local initiative. The consequence, over time, has been the adoption in most states of a clear set of rules. The courts have led the way in framing these rules, with high convergence from state to state. Where state legislatures have acted, they have generally sought to codify prevailing judicial guidelines and give them statutory force, thereby reducing uncertainty (particularly in states that have not had many lawsuits in this area) and the potential for litigation.

The core legal standards that exaction ordinances must satisfy in most states revolve around interpretations of the police power and cost accounting issues. During the early days of land use regulation, prior to the enactment of specific state enabling statutes, local land use regulatory authority rested on the common law of nuisance. Even at that time, landowners desiring permission to subdivide their land were commonly required to dedicate some portion of it for public roads and utility lines. Since purchasers expected these amenities, most subdividers were pleased to provide them. Disputes did occur, however, and when they led to litigation the central issue was whether governments, in effect, could take private land without paying for it. State courts, by and large, said they could. Their core argument was that land subdivision is a privilege, not a right, and that consequently governments may require land donations for valid, related public purposes as a condition of subdivision.[6] This is still good legal doctrine and has been extended far beyond the issue of land donation to cover a broad range of exaction circumstances, but it has become just one way of expressing a much broader doctrine.

As the states have authorized local governments to regulate land use, they have relied on their police power. The police power, reserved to the states under the Constitution, provides general authority to regulate in furtherance of public health, safety, and welfare. Where localities have ventured beyond the land use regulatory powers explicitly conferred by state acts, moreover, they have normally relied on general grants of police power under state acts establishing local home rule.[7] (The doctrine of privilege, in consequence, today generally is viewed as just a particular expression of the principle that land use is subject to the police power.)[8]

Governments may regulate and impose fees on the basis of their police power, but they may not impose taxes. A tax can be used for any purpose; no connection, in principle, need exist between the source of revenue and the purposes for which it is used. Fees, on the other hand, must be justified with reference to the cost of providing services to the payers or of mitigating harm to others that would otherwise be caused by the payers' activities.[9] The explicit purposes of exactions, in particular, must be to finance service capacity for future occupants or to alleviate negative project impacts on the wider community.[10]

It has fallen mainly to state courts to elaborate these general rules as cost accounting standards.[11] How tightly and conclusively, for example, must the connection be established between a development project and the public actions that a government wishes to finance by exaction? Where project occupants are to share services financed in part by exactions, how compelling must be the analyses underlying cost allocation? How much time should localities be allowed before having to refund unexpended impact fee revenues?

Through the mid-1970s, judicial answers to these questions varied widely from state to state. Since then, however, the courts of most states have adopted a middle path, known as "rational nexus," first suggested in a 1965

Wisconsin case but most fully developed by the Florida courts beginning in 1976.[12] As most commonly applied, the rational nexus standard includes the following elements:

—Each exaction must be well-designed to meet service needs directly attributable to the project bearing its cost.

—Where facilities are to serve more than a single development, costs must be allocated in proportion to services rendered.

—Such facilities must be elements of a comprehensive local plan for service improvements.

—Where facilities are to be financed by a combination of tax and impact fee revenues, special care must be taken to ensure that project occupants, who pay taxes like everyone else, are not double-billed. The impact fee calculation, in other words, must be net of anticipated tax contributions.[13]

—Impact fee revenues must be segregated until used and must be expended in timely fashion (generally, within five or six years) for the purposes originally designated.

A local system may, of course, appear to satisfy all these requirements at the time of development permitting but then fail in practice to carry out its commitments. When that happens, the developer generally is entitled to a refund.[14]

Other standards that have been adopted by a few state courts include, most notably, the "specifically and uniquely attributable" test and the "reasonably related" test. The former was adopted by the Illinois Supreme Court in the early 1960s and was taken up by the judiciaries of several other states. At its most stringent, this standard requires a conclusive, precise showing that the public need to be served is 100 percent attributable to the development in question. Facilities to be shared among the occupants of several developments cannot, in jurisdictions subject to this standard, be financed by exaction contributions. The Illinois Supreme Court is generally thought to have adopted a more lenient interpretation of the "specifically and uniquely attributable" standard without rejecting it explicitly in 1978, though controversy remains about its current position. Few, if any, other states today give even lip service to this standard.[15]

By contrast, the California courts until recently utilized a far more permissive standard than rational nexus. Beginning in 1949, they required simply that localities demonstrate a "reasonable relationship" between development impacts and exaction levies. As applied over most of the next forty years, this standard provided localities with such broad discretion that it came to be known as the "anything goes" rule.[16] California has arguably moved

toward a rational nexus standard in recent years, because of statutory provisions adopted at the state level and because of the U.S. Supreme Court's
decision in the case of *Nollan* v. *California Coastal Commission* (1987).
Whatever change has occurred has been subtle, however.[17]

The *Nollan* case, one of the very few on the subject of land use regulation
ever considered by the Supreme Court, turned on the lack of any direct relationship between the condition imposed by the Coastal Commission and
the proposed development. The Nollans wished to construct a 2,500-square-
foot house on a site currently occupied by a 500-square-foot bungalow. The
Coastal Commission ruled that they could do so, but only if they granted a
lateral public easement along the beach in front of their house. Forty-three
of their neighbors had already granted such easements, without litigating,
under similar pressures from the Coastal Commission.[18] The Nollans, however, viewed this as an unconstitutional taking of part of their property without compensation. The Court decided in their favor, finding no significant
relationship between the issue of public easement and that of whether to
permit the house. The public had no right of passage with the bungalow in
place, so it would be no worse off with a larger structure on the site. The
Court did not explicitly adopt any of the exaction standards discussed above.
Rather, it specified that a "close nexus" must be shown between the regulatory
condition imposed and the development impacts of concern, and that the
regulatory action must "substantially advance legitimate state interests."[19]
Some legal scholars have read this decision as a restatement of the rational
nexus doctrine, others read it variously as a more permissive or tighter standard. What seems clear, however, is that the Court wished to slap down the
California policy of virtual carte blanche for exactions. Five years after *Nollan*, the Court has given no further indication of its views, and the rational
nexus standard continues to dominate at the state level.[20]

The body of rational nexus case law has evolved nationally to the point
where substantial support exists for statutory codification. The advantages of
codification are, first, that it can shortcut the need for a particular state to
replicate, at vast litigation cost, the full national experience, and second, that
it may provide a more unambiguous set of guidelines than a cluster of state
court opinions. Because judicial opinions do vary at the margin, however,
there is often considerable room for controversy about precisely what to
codify.

In general, it is developers who have taken the lead in pursuing legislation—primarily to secure state protection against new local practices that they
find threatening. Where they have succeeded, it has been by forging alliances

with significant groups of local officials. Officials joining in such alliances have typically been motivated by prodevelopment sentiment, a desire for legal clarity to reduce litigation risks, and hope that such clarity would provide a buffer against political criticisms that they did not demand enough from developers.

Nine states adopted impact fee enabling statutes in the decade through 1990, mostly codifying the rational nexus standard and in some cases specifying additional constraints.[21] Illustratively, Georgia's statute, enacted in 1990, codifies the rational nexus standard with two additional restrictions. It precludes the use of impact fees to finance capital facilities with useful lives of less than ten years and solid waste facilities of any type. Additionally, it authorizes (but does not require) localities to grant impact fee waivers for projects likely to "create extraordinary economic development and employment growth or affordable housing."[22] In California, where state law authorizes impact taxes as well as fees, developers played a key role in securing adoption of a 1986 state ballot initiative (Proposition 62) requiring two-thirds voter approval of all local tax increases.[23] They also secured the enactment of new statutory provisions in 1981, 1986, and 1987 tightening impact fee standards.[24] Maine's legislation, enacted in 1988, not only codifies the rational nexus standard but also restricts the use of impact fees to localities with state-certified comprehensive growth management plans.[25]

Escape from Oversight: Negotiated Exactions

A reader of judicial opinions and law journals might conclude that virtually all exactions are imposed by formula or on the basis of detailed impact studies. However, most exactions are negotiated, and judicial oversight is rare.

Development permitting, especially for large projects, is increasingly discretionary.[26] Wherever real estate markets are strong, developers generally can be induced to proffer "voluntary" contributions, often at multiple stages in the approval process. It is virtually impossible for courts to oversee such subtle interactions between local regulators and developers. Developers maintain that such contributions are rarely voluntary. Most local officials, however, perceive developers as reaping windfall profits from booms they did nothing to create and have few compunctions about asking, on behalf of their constituents, for all they can get.

The courts press for consistency and fairness. Their preference, consequently, is for rules that are precise and strictly enforced. Local officials, meanwhile, view each case as unique. They are preoccupied with the difficulty of evaluating development proposals until they are fully fleshed out and until all community interests have been heard. They believe as well that ingenious developers are likely to run rings around any system of fixed rules. Their preference, consequently, is for flexibility—to exercise judgment case by case and to exact the largest possible contributions from each development.

Until the 1960s, nearly all state courts insisted on rigid, precise zoning regulations, with property owners free to develop "as of right" if they conformed. The courts also enforced a vision of regulatory purpose—the protection of property values—that seems unduly narrow by current standards. Over the past several decades, however, a major shift has occurred. The courts have become increasingly permissive with respect both to zoning discretion and purposes. While still seeking fairness in the treatment of like cases, they have accepted the regulator viewpoint, by and large, that, because of the variety of development proposals and the many valid purposes to consider, the requirements of fairness cannot be reduced to formula.[27]

Numerous localities, as a result, have adopted land use regulatory systems in which all permission to develop is discretionary. This is particularly common for large projects. The most common label for a system in which negotiated agreements can override the formal rules is planned unit development (PUD) regulation.[28] Almost everywhere, moreover, projects of substantial scale are subject to environmental reviews, which conclude with discretionary judgments about the balance of advantages and drawbacks and about suitable mitigation requirements.

Even where traditional zoning still exists in form, opportunities for negotiation abound. The density rules for downtown Boston, for example, were traditionally clear on paper. Until the recent collapse (circa 1989) of commercial property values, however, land values reflected density expectations considerably in excess of those specified in the zoning ordinance. The result was that developers could not buy land in the Boston core and develop it profitably within existing zoning constraints. They understood that the norm was to negotiate for variances, typically pledging "voluntary" exactions in return—outside any framework of law.[29] Justice Antonin Scalia, writing for the Supreme Court majority in the *Nollan* case, took specific note of the possibility that local governments would tighten their regulations merely to establish a favorable negotiating position, and he called for strict judicial scrutiny to preclude this. He wrote,

One would expect that a regime in which this kind of leveraging of the police power is allowed would produce stringent land-use regulation which the State then waives to accomplish other purposes, leading to lesser realization of the land-use goals purportedly sought to be served than would result from more lenient (but nontradeable) development restrictions. [30]

In calling for precise exaction rules, however, the courts are swimming against a powerful tide of regulatory flexibility in which they have acquiesced. Not surprisingly, many jurisdictions have perceived the contradiction and sought means to exploit it. Lawrence Susskind and Gerard McMahon, who applaud this trend, observe that it requires "the city and the developer [to] bargain over the scope and character of each project and agree on the value, timing, and format of compensatory payments or actions for which the developer will be held responsible." [31]

Localities, when negotiating exactions, must avoid the appearance of "selling" development permissions, because that is illegal. Many local officials believe, however, that selling the privilege of developing in their community is entirely legitimate, if "to sell" means to seek the best possible financial outcome for one's clients (or, in this case, constituents). How to square the circle? The answer is to induce developers to "volunteer" exaction commitments. Having done so in the context of complex negotiations, developers can scarcely turn around and seek judicial relief. Nor are they disposed to. Their strategy, with rare exceptions, is simply to walk away when they consider local exaction demands excessive.

Developers find the whole system of negotiated regulation a source of enormous frustration and uncertainty. Because their business is characterized by very high risk, they seek, as Douglas R. Porter has observed, as many "points of certainty" as possible. [32] The fact that public policy has been evolving so as to greatly increase uncertainty is a source of intense grievance. In good times, however, most accept the system stoically, professing confidence that they can manage any new wrinkle in the development game as well as any competitor.

In some circumstances, developers may actually benefit from a system of negotiated, as opposed to formula, exactions. Formulas are rigid and their revision typically requires legislative action, which is often politically difficult. Thus downward adjustments may lag considerably behind the weakening of markets. Where fees are negotiated project by project local officials can adjust in relative obscurity. Developers take little comfort from this, however, because much more of their activity occurs during booms than recessions and because they cannot raise financing for projects on the basis of possible, but highly uncertain, local negotiating concessions.

While systems of negotiated exactions typically function with few if any rules, they are increasingly gaining explicit legal recognition as legitimate. The Virginia courts, for example, have actually rejected formula impact fees while indicating that "voluntary proffers" by developers are acceptable.[33] And California has, since 1979, by statute authorized localities to negotiate project development agreements that supersede all other local regulations. These agreements have been characterized as "legal vehicles for engaging in open-ended bargaining on virtually all aspects of a community's land use controls."[34] By 1985–86, more than 30 percent of California local governments had concluded at least one project development agreement or were in the process of doing so. Similar statutes, though less widely used, were in books in Florida, Hawaii, and Nevada.[35]

The extreme case of a negotiated exaction system is that of San Francisco. Since 1986, new commercial projects there have been required to secure permission competitively under a tight development cap or from the voters directly by referendum. Either procedure is well designed to maximize the pressure on developers to "volunteer" exactions.[36] Seattle voters adopted a similar though less stringent set of controls in 1989.[37]

Some observers believe that the courts will eventually seek to pierce the veil of "voluntarism" that now surrounds negotiated exactions, subjecting them to the same constraints as formula exactions. This will be extremely difficult, however, and developers willing to litigate will be scarce, so long as land use permitting itself remains an arena of discretion and negotiation.

Bargaining Dynamics

All exaction systems, whether formula-based or negotiated, rest on market estimates. Where development pressures are strong, a community will find potential developers eager to satisfy all but the most extreme permit conditions, and sometimes even these. Where development pressures are weak, communities are more likely to be offering inducements than imposing exactions.

Localities enter negotiations with prospective developers armed with the legal power to regulate. Developers are not at their mercy, however; they can lobby and litigate at the state level, and they can withhold their investments. This may not count for much in a hot market environment, when other developers are lined up for the chance to invest. But such circumstances are not the norm, as even those communities that enjoyed the greatest booms during the 1980s have discovered in the early 1990s. Developers, finally, are often more adept negotiators than local officials, particularly the officials of small and medium-sized jurisdictions.

Communities in the vanguard of exaction utilization tend to be among those least concerned about attracting investment. Even some that are eager for growth, however, are today often vigorous employers of exaction financing. Consider the case of Aurora, Colorado, as reported by Peggy L. Cuciti. Aurora, a suburban city to the east of Denver, has actively sought to annex unincorporated land on its periphery with strong development potential. Its strategy has been to make itself optimally attractive to developers but then negotiate hard as they appear. Specifically, Aurora has assured itself of ample water rights (a critical factor in this arid region), so that developers can hook up whenever they are ready. The city facilitates long-term, tax-exempt financing of exaction commitments by establishing each development as a special assessment district. It allocates a quarter of the sales tax receipts from each assessment district to help finance the district's infrastructure. Finally, Aurora is eager to accommodate developers who wish to construct high-density, nonresidential properties. Aurora bargains with great skill and adaptability. Depending on how eager it is to attract a particular development and its sense of what the developer is prepared to pay, it drives a more or less hard bargain. The city negotiated thirty-six annexation agreements covering 40 square miles in the brief period from April 1985 to February 1987.[38]

Few localities have negotiating strategies as well-developed as Aurora's. A more frequent pattern, especially in small jurisdictions and in localities just beginning to experience development pressure, is for local officials to negotiate in ad hoc fashion. They tend to be inexperienced, particularly in comparison with large developers, and to have far less access to analytic talent. They can and do seek advice from consultants, but they generally are unwilling to incur the costs of independent studies. Thus, while striving to be available to local interest associations, to sort out local priorities, and to organize a cohesive local bargaining team, they often find themselves dependent on the developer for cost, pricing, and environmental impact estimates. The developer may in such cases be able to deflect attention from the most critical issues of substance to peripheral or symbolic issues that can be addressed at relatively low cost.[39] Differentials in experience and expertise can also cut the other way, of course. Small, particularly neophyte, developers may be at a serious disadvantage in dealing with governments that, over time, have assembled strong and experienced staffs.[40]

Potential for Corruption

Scandals have been common in land use regulation. One might expect greater discretion to render them even more so. Bernard J. Frieden and Lynne B. Sagalyn, however, who have studied numerous recent developments in large city downtowns, observe that scandal has been rare. They speculate that it has been discouraged by two factors working in combination: first, media and community group vigilance, and second, the wide diffusion of real estate analytic skills. While the negotiations leading up to public-private agreements often are secret, Frieden and Sagalyn note, they are today invariably followed by public hearings and frequently as well by litigation, referenda, or both.[41] In many cities, finally, the negotiations themselves are subject to open meeting requirements.[42] Thus, whatever agreements local officials may be tempted to conclude in private, they know that their decisions will be subject to close and perhaps highly probing scrutiny.[43]

While persuasive as far as it goes, the Frieden-Sagalyn analysis is scarcely conclusive. First, the authors were not looking for evidence of corruption. Second, they focused on large, high-profile downtown projects. The negotiations surrounding smaller and more routine projects are considerably less likely to attract sophisticated scrutiny. Whether recent trends toward greater openness and citizen participation can adequately offset the potential for corruption opened up by greater flexibility, therefore, remains to be seen. Given the prevalence of public cynicism about government, one would expect more than cursory attention by scholars to this topic. It has to date, however, virtually been ignored, perhaps because evidence is so hard to obtain.

Why Don't States Impose Exactions?

The factors that have inspired greater reliance on exactions at the local level—voter resistance to new taxes, pressures for environmental protection, severe cutbacks in federal aid, and so on—have profoundly affected the states as well. The states, moreover, have vast infrastructure responsibilities, they are the basic repositories of land use authority under the Constitution, and they rely significantly on fee revenues (even if less heavily than do local governments).[44] Yet no state has ventured substantially into the exaction arena.[45] Why not?

Each level of American government has a different angle on land use policy. Local governments deal mainly with site-specific controversies. The residents and enterprises most affected by each development proposal generally dominate public debate about it. They are able to estimate their interests with relative precision and—whether seeking to bring about or prevent development—typically pursue them with righteous intensity. Even broad legislative initiatives, such as a new zoning ordinance, are typically debated in terms of their parcel-by-parcel impacts. The central features of land use policy making at the local level, in short, are particularity and passion.

At the national level, by contrast, urban land use issues appear in abstract terms. Legislatively, for example, how much money should be allocated for highways, and what levels of air pollution should be deemed permissible? Judicially, how should the threshold be defined at which land use regulation becomes so burdensome as to constitute a taking (requiring compensation) under the Constitution? As the nation's largest landowner, the federal government does confront a vast array of site-specific management and leasing issues relating to its own properties. It is not significantly involved in the regulation of private land, however, and little of its own land is in urban areas.

State governments have traditionally viewed their role as one of local oversight. Thus, like the federal government, they have focused mainly on broad principles of policy and law rather than on site-specific considerations. Legislatively, the usual question has been "What should localities be authorized to do?" rather than "Should this particular real estate project be allowed to proceed?" Judicially, it has most typically been "What are the rules?" rather than "How desirable is the project?"

The states also engage, far more commonly than the federal government, in siting and constructing specific public works (for example, new highways). These activities might have been expected to stimulate their interest in development exactions. This has not occurred, however. We suspect that the reasons are as follows.

First, states are much less prone to ambivalence about development than localities. Voters everywhere are preoccupied with earning their livelihoods. The residents of a bedroom suburb can segregate their interests, counting on other jurisdictions to provide sites for industry, commerce, and low-cost housing while maximizing amenities where they vote. Most voters, however, work and live in the same state. As a result, even those who concentrate in local politics on the preservation of amenities generally accept the need for development at the state and regional scale.

Second, states are far less likely than localities to perceive new development as overwhelming. Even the fastest-growing states contain a mix of developing and fully developed localities. So no state ever faces growth pressures nearly as great as its most rapidly developing localities; and every state contains numerous localities eager to attract development.

Third, states are much less likely than localities to view growth as involving an invasion of newcomers. Fast-growth localities, with rare exceptions, draw most of their new residents from other places in the same state. From the state perspective, therefore, most of the new residents of any locality are not new at all.[46] States might be inclined to levy special taxes on in-migrants or to impose waiting periods for entitlements, but the U.S. Supreme Court generally has barred such measures as infringements on the constitutional right to travel.[47]

Fourth, state governments are much less accustomed to raising revenue from real property. In 1989–90, for example, states raised less than one property tax dollar for every twenty-five raised by localities, and property taxes generated only 1.5 percent of states' own-source general revenue.[48]

Finally, with a richer mix of potential revenue sources than localities, and a greater capacity to capture revenue from interlocal transactions, states are not disposed to focus on whether specific parcels or categories of real property pay their own way. Instead, state revenue debates focus on issues of equity and incentives for broad classes of taxpayers—individuals versus corporations, rich versus middle-class households, capital-intensive versus labor-intensive enterprises, and so on.

In sum, states are far less prone than localities to get caught up in the passions of site-specific disputes and far better able to internalize both the benefits and costs of development. Politically, ordinary citizens as well as business interests are more likely to look to state officials to promote their economic welfare. And business interests carry far more weight in state capitals than in those localities that have pioneered in restraining, and levying exactions upon, new development.

5

Local Infrastructure Demands and Costs

A KEY PREMISE of the argument for exactions is that land development is a major cause of escalating local infrastructure demands and costs. For example, most state courts regard an exaction as a tax, and not a fee, unless the local community can demonstrate that infrastructure costs are the result of development. Even without legal requirements, local communities might be wary of charging developers for infrastructure costs that were unrelated to their developments. The practice not only would be difficult to defend politically but also could make the local community fiscally dependent on continued land development.

Since the early 1980s, policy makers and analysts have debated whether a national "infrastructure crisis" exists and, if so, how severe it is.[1] The focus here, however, is on a narrower and less-studied question: How often is land development an important cause of infrastructure expansion requirements.

Development generally is a less important cause of increasing infrastructure demand than other forces, such as rising standards for infrastructure services and rising incomes. Contrary to popular belief, moreover, low-density sprawl and other often-criticized types of development probably do not add greatly to the costs of servicing infrastructure demands. Development can be a major cause of infrastructure demands or costs in at least two circumstances, however: when communities are experiencing extraordinarily rapid growth and when development takes place in already built-up areas (and thus requires costly rebuilding and expansion of existing infrastructure facilities).

Other Causes of Rising Infrastructure Demand

Land development often is blamed for the rising demand for local infrastructure services. When local roads become congested and the local water supply is overdrawn, newly built subdivisions and office parks are the most visible and obvious cause. Moreover, a direct and immediate link exists between development and the types of infrastructure commonly provided by city or county government. Developing a parcel of land would be impossible without access roads, water and sewer lines, and other locally provided infrastructure, and the parcel needs infrastructure only if it is to be developed.

Land development is not the only cause of rising demand for infrastructure, however. Several other factors contribute significantly, some of which clearly can be distinguished from land development and some cannot.

The former category includes higher standards for the quality of infrastructure services. Federal regulations adopted during the 1970s and 1980s, for example, raised standards for air quality, drinking water, sewage treatment, and solid waste disposal, and most communities still are struggling to achieve full compliance.[2] The 1970 Clean Air Act Amendments, for example, forced many communities to install expensive emissions controls on solid waste incinerators or to close them. The Resource Conservation and Recovery Act (RCRA) of 1976 established strict controls over the design and operation of landfills and required separate hazardous waste treatment facilities. As a result, according to the Environmental Protection Agency, more than 70 percent of the fourteen thousand landfills operating in 1978 were closed by 1988 and about 40 percent of the remainder would be closed by the mid-1990s. Their replacements—safer (and often more distant) landfills and waste recovery plants—tended to be far more expensive.

Two factors that are difficult to distinguish from land development are economic growth and demographic change. Economic and population growth often lead to land development. As incomes grow, for example, households usually move to larger and higher quality housing, which may require more infrastructure services. And population growth or demographic shifts usually lead to the construction of new houses and workplaces.

Nevertheless, economic growth can contribute to the demand for infrastructure without leading to land development. As real per capita incomes increase, for example, households buy more cars, drive more miles, consume more water, and produce more sewage and solid waste, even if they continue to live in the same houses. Thus, not surprisingly, regions or cities with relatively stable populations (and fairly limited new land development) and growing per capita incomes still experience rising traffic congestion, water consumption, solid waste generation, and so on.

Similarly, population growth and demographic changes also can affect the demand for infrastructure services independently of land development. The growth in automobile travel since the 1950s is the result not just of the rising population but also of the increasing labor force participation of women and the aging of the baby boom generation. As an increasing percentage of women joined the workforce, the percentage of adults commuting to work grew. In addition, the baby boom of 1946 to 1964 meant a surge in the proportion of the population that reached driving age between the 1960s and the 1980s, which contributed to the fact that auto ownership and travel grew at faster rates than the population.[3]

Economic growth and population changes collectively appear to have had a powerful independent effect on national infrastructure demands in the past several decades. If land development was the primary cause of infrastructure demands, then infrastructure use would be expected to increase at about the same rate as the population or the formation of new households (which presumably would trigger a need for new dwelling units and places to work). Highway travel, the only infrastructure demand for which historical national statistics are readily available, grew two to four times faster than population or households in the 1950s, 1960s, and 1980s, however (see table 5-1). Even in the 1970s, the decade of two oil price shocks and slower income growth, motor vehicle travel increased more rapidly than the rate of household formation. Based on these figures, land development nationally might have accounted for as little as one-fourth to one-half of the increase in driving demand in the postwar period, although the conclusion is speculative.

Some analysts argue that economic growth and demographic changes will exercise a smaller independent effect on per capita infrastructure demands in the future. Additional income growth may not stimulate increased driving per capita, for example, because almost a majority of households already own at least one car for each licensed driver.[4] Similarly, demographic changes may not be quite as powerful because the baby boom generation now is licensed to drive and the female labor force participation rate cannot increase as rapidly as it has.[5]

Table 5-1. *Average Annual Increases in Population, Households, and Vehicle Miles of Highway Traffic*
Percent

Decade	Population	Population old enough to drive	Households	Vehicle miles of travel
1950s	1.7	0.7	1.0	4.6
1960s	1.3	1.6	1.8	4.4
1970s	1.1	1.9	2.5	3.2
1980s[a]	1.0	1.2	1.6	3.6

Sources: Household and population data calculated from *Statistical Abstract of the United States, 1991* (1991), tables 2, 13, and 56. Vehicle miles from Department of Transportation, Federal Highway Administration, *Highway Statistics, Summary to 1985* (n.d.), pp. 225–28; and Department of Transportation, Federal Highway Administration, *Highway Statistics, 1989* (n.d.), p. 181.
[a] To 1989.

Economic growth and demographic changes are likely to continue to influence infrastructure demand significantly, however. Even if income growth has less effect on per capita driving, for example, it probably still will be a powerful stimulus to demand for water, solid waste, parks, and other infrastructure services. Similarly, demographic shifts will affect infrastructure demands as the children of the baby boom generation reach driving age during the 1990s.

National or Regional versus Local Perspectives

Isolating the effects of land development from other factors is much harder when the problem is viewed from the national or regional instead of the local perspective. The simple analysis of national trends derived from the data in table 5-1 may understate the role of land development, for example, if the suburban housing built after World War II typically required more infrastructure services per dwelling unit than older and more densely built housing. However, even if modern or suburban housing does require more infrastructure per unit, the changing characteristics of new housing stock arguably were caused by the rising incomes of the population, not land development per se. In principle, this controversy could be resolved by comparing actual trends in infrastructure demand with those that might have prevailed had stringent and widespread development controls forced population and income growth to be accommodated in the existing building stock (or new houses built to traditional densities or designs). We have no experience to draw on for such comparisons, however, because there has never been a national will or policy to impose such development constraints.[6]

Isolating the effects of land development is simpler if the perspective of a single local community is taken. Land development usually is the villain at the local level because it is the physical manifestation of economic and population growth and it locates that growth at a particular point on the map. Additionally, local officials often have the option of trying to capture many of the benefits of economic growth for their residents without suffering the costs of land development. A local government can try to push the traffic-generating regional shopping center into a neighboring jurisdiction, for example, knowing that the jobs and services it provides still will be reasonably available to its residents. By contrast, the possibilities for enjoying the benefits of economic and population growth without accepting land development are far more limited from the regional and national perspective.

Calculating the local effects of land development on infrastructure thus seems fairly straightforward. Local officials usually deem a new residential or commercial development responsible for the demands on infrastructure services made by the new local residents, customers, or employees that the development attracts. Presumably, if local development permission is denied, the development and population or workforce growth, along with their associated infrastructure needs, will be displaced to some other community.

Growing communities, as a result, blame local land development for most of the increase in local infrastructure demands. Growth may have to reach high levels, however, before land development accounts for more than half of the increase in infrastructure demand. If higher standards for infrastructure services, real income growth, and demographic shifts increase per capita demands for infrastructure services by 2 percent per year, for example, then development would account for more than half the growth in infrastructure demand in communities that were growing faster than 2 percent per year.[7]

From the regional perspective, local calculations often ignore important infrastructure demands that spill over jurisdictional boundaries. This is particularly true if some local communities are attempting to shift infrastructure burdens of new development on their neighbors. The spillover problems can be particularly acute for transportation, for example, because motorists driving from residences in one town to shopping or employment centers or jobs in other towns often use roads that pass through communities that had no say in the siting of those facilities. Similarly, development may impose costs across local boundaries by straining regional watersheds, reservoir systems, or waste treatment facilities.

Such displacement options are much less available on the regional and national scale. Stated another way, the infrastructure demands of land development are practically indistinguishable from those of economic and population growth at the regional or national level.

Suburban Sprawl and Jobs-Housing Imbalance

Some planners argue that new development contributes disproportionately to the demand for infrastructure services, or the costs of meeting those demands, because it is so poorly planned or designed that unnecessary burdens are placed on the infrastructure system. The local problems created by rapid development often are compounded, according to this view, because growth is planned without adequate attention to infrastructure requirements.

In this regard, suburban "sprawl" has been viewed in some quarters as a serious problem since the 1940s. The term "sprawl" has been used to refer to at least three different forms of development: continuous low-density residential development on the metropolitan fringe, "ribbon" low-density development along major suburban highways, and development that "leapfrogs" past undeveloped land to leave a patchwork of developed and undeveloped tracts. Each often is alleged to require more infrastructure than more compact or better planned development. Continuous low-density or leapfrog development, for example, would require more miles of road or pipe to connect residences with major employment centers, sewage treatment plants, or reservoirs than more compact and contiguous development.

In the 1980s, a new concern emerged among planners about the "job-housing imbalance" in urban development. While the previous preoccupation with sprawl focused largely on patterns of residential development, the new critics stressed the problems created by mismatches in the locations of new jobs and new housing, particularly for transportation infrastructure. For example, according to California environmental officials, the coastal strip of Los Angeles and Orange counties has been the location of approximately 80 percent of the new jobs created in the Los Angeles area since 1970, but only 40 percent of the new housing. Most of the new housing has been built inland, which, the planners hypothesize, adds to the average commuting trip length and to the air pollution problems of the region. The Air Quality Man-

agement Plan adopted in 1989 by the Southern California Association of
Governments recommended that a larger portion of new jobs be required to
locate inland to reduce commuting demand and help meet ambient air quality standards.[8]

The fundamental cause of the jobs-housing imbalance is alleged to be
fiscal and exclusionary zoning.[9] Communities in the most advantageous locations tend to zone for high-income housing or commercial development
and to exclude low- and moderate-income housing. Low- and moderate-
income household members end up having to commute long distances from
remote suburbs.

The concerns about sprawl and jobs-housing imbalance appear inconsistent with one another at first glance. The usual remedy for sprawl is a more
compact urban form, for example, while the most feasible remedy for a jobs-
housing imbalance, given residential sprawl, is greater job dispersal. The
jobs-housing imbalance argument does not imply that development ought to
be high or low density, however, only that it ought to be heterogeneous in
jobs and housing types. While the old concern about sprawl attacked low-
density residential development on the fringes, the new concern about jobs-
housing imbalance strikes at traditional patterns of job concentration (for
example, the downtown) and of segregation between high- and low-income
residential areas.

Research has not fully borne out the fears about either sprawl or jobs-
housing imbalance.[10] Four separate issues should be distinguished. Three
relate primarily to sprawl: the effects on infrastructure costs of residential density, of leapfrogging, and of distance between residential neighborhoods and
central infrastructure facilities. The fourth, which relates to job-housing balance, is the effect of employment dispersal.

Residential Density

Most research on sprawl focused on how the density of residential neighborhoods affected the costs of providing infrastructure within them. This research typically considered the costs of local streets, sewage collection lines,
water distribution pipes, storm drainage systems, and neighborhood schools.
Regional links, such as arterial roads connecting the residential community
with employment centers, usually were not considered. In the 1950s, this
research focused primarily on the costs of serving single-family homes on
different sized lots. In the 1970s, the focus turned to comparisons among
conventional single-family homes on grid lots, clustered single-family hous-

ing surrounded by larger open space, townhouses, walk-up and high-rise apartment buildings.[11]

Cost comparisons are complicated by whether the standards for infrastructure improvement can or should be allowed to vary with the density of the residential neighborhood. The issue is most relevant in comparisons of neighborhood infrastructure costs for single-family residential communities with varying lot sizes. Increasing the size of the lot (or more precisely, the lot frontage) increases the length of the streets, sidewalks, sewer and water lines, and storm drainage systems. But as lot sizes increase to one-half acre or more, the added length can be offset at least partly by economies in design. In low-density residential communities, for example, swale drainage can replace curbs and storm drains, sidewalks can be eliminated on one or both sides of the street, and narrower local streets can be built because of reduced vehicular traffic. Where soil conditions permit, large lot developments also can substitute septic systems for more expensive sewage lines to central treatment facilities. Several studies done in the 1950s concluded that, where such substitutions were permitted, the costs of neighborhood infrastructure per dwelling unit were relatively constant for single-family lots ranging from one-quarter acre to two acres or more.[12]

As densities increase beyond three or four dwelling units per acre, neighborhood infrastructure costs decline, although the magnitude of the saving is open to dispute. Many of the analytic problems are illustrated by the widely publicized *The Costs of Sprawl* study done in the 1970s for the Environmental Protection Agency by the Real Estate Research Corporation (RERC).[13] RERC analyzed infrastructure and other costs for five prototype neighborhoods, each consisting of one thousand units of either conventional single-family homes on one-third acre grid lots, clustered single-family homes on smaller lots surrounded by open space, townhouses, walk-up apartments, or high-rises. Estimates showed that road and street systems cost 33 percent less to build and 51 percent less to maintain in a neighborhood of townhouses than a neighborhood of single-family conventional houses, for example (see table 5-2). Utilities (water, sewer, storm drainage, gas, electricity, and telephone underground cables) cost 58 percent less to build and 30 percent less to maintain for townhouses than conventional single-family houses. Costs for other infrastructure, such as parks, public buildings and schools, varied relatively little across the neighborhoods and are not reported in table 5-2.[14]

The principal problem with the RERC study is that finding meaning in the cost differences is difficult because the quality of the housing units in the different communities is not comparable.[15] In particular, the single-family

Table 5-2. *Profile of Five Prototype Neighborhoods of 1,000 Dwelling Units*

Profile category	Single-family conventional	Single-family clustered	Townhouses	Walk-up apartments	High-rise apartments
Uses of land (acres)					
Public facilities, open space, and transportation	154	184	166	134	67
Residential	330	200	100	66	33
Vacant	16	16	34	0	0
Total	500	400	300	200	100
Residential density					
Units per gross acre	2	2.5	3.3	5	10
Units per net acre	3	5	10	15	30
Capital cost per unit (1973 dollars)					
Roads	3,080	2,661	2,111	1,464	801
Utilities	5,483	3,649	2,369	1,579	958
Total	8,563	6,310	4,480	3,043	1,759
Annual operating cost per unit (1973 dollars)					
Roads	37	28	18	11	6
Utilities	484	483	340	278	243
Total	521	511	358	289	249

Source: Real Estate Research Corporation, *The Costs of Sprawl: Detailed Cost Analysis* (1974), p. 3, tables 2, 6, and 7.

houses include private backyards, while the apartments do not, yet the acreage of public parks is the same in the different communities.[16] Many households probably would be willing to pay the modest increases in road and utility costs to gain the larger private backyards and more open space of the low-density neighborhoods. Indeed, many of the neighborhood infrastructure costs estimated in the RERC study often are paid for by developers as part of the requirements for on-site infrastructure in large subdivisions and therefore already are reflected in the prices for housing of different densities. Where this is true, households effectively face the full costs of neighborhood infrastructure and have the option of economizing on infrastructure costs by opting for smaller and less private units in high-density neighborhoods.

Leapfrogging

Infrastructure costs also might increase if new residential development leapfrogs over undeveloped land so that additional roads and water and sewer

Table 5-3. *Profile of Six Prototype Communities of 10,000 Dwelling Units*

Profile category	Low density		Mixed density			High density
	Planned	Sprawl	Planned	Partly planned	Sprawl	Planned
Dwelling types (percent)						
High-rise apartments			20	20	20	40
Low-rise apartments			20	20	20	30
Single-family clustered	75	25	20	20	20	10
Single-family conventional	25	75	20	20	20	
Townhouses			20	20	20	20
Uses of land (acres)						
Public facilities and transportation	1,780	1,590	1,590	1,460	1,330	1,440
Residential	2,333	3,000	1,450	1,450	1,450	733
Vacant	1,064	0	2,352	1,955	1,552	3,392
Vacant improved or semi-improved	823	1,410	608	1,135	1,668	435
Capital cost per unit (1973 dollars)						
Roads	3,377	3,796	2,707	2,977	3,235	2,286
Utilities	4,744	6,197	3,323	3,604	3,868	2,243
Total	8,121	9,993	6,030	6,581	7,103	4,529
Annual maintenance cost per unit (1973 dollars)						
Roads	35	40	26	26	26	21
Utilities	513	514	399	399	399	333
Total	548	554	425	425	425	354

Source: Real Estate Research Corporation, *The Costs of Sprawl: Detailed Cost Analysis* (1974), pp. 3, 90, 92, 97, and 98; tables 43, 44, and 45.
ªIncludes land used for road or utility right-of-way.

lines are required to connect the development with its older neighbors. The Real Estate Research Corporation study addressed these concerns by estimating costs for six prototype communities of ten thousand dwelling units consisting of ten neighborhoods each. The six communities include low-density communities composed entirely of conventional and clustered single-family neighborhoods, mixed-density communities with equal numbers of the five neighborhood types, and a high-density community predominantly of townhouses and apartments (see table 5-3). Moreover, three of the communities are "planned," so that development is compact or contiguous, while three are characterized by some degree of sprawl, in which the neighborhoods are not contiguous. Each community consists of six thousand acres, so that some land is left vacant. In the planned communities, the vacant land is largely on the periphery, but in the sprawl communities it is scattered among the neighborhoods and crisscrossed by roads and utility lines. The three different mixed-density communities (the third, fourth, and fifth columns of table 5-3) provide the most direct estimates of the added costs of leapfrogging.[17] Compared with the planned mixed-density community, roads and utilities cost 18 percent more to build in the sprawl community and 9 percent more to build in the partly sprawl, partly planned community.

These estimates probably overstate the added costs of leapfrog development, however, in communities that expect continued growth and eventual infill development on the vacant land. Compared with the planned communities, the sprawl communities contain substantially more vacant land that is improved or semi-improved by some road and utility access. Developing improved vacant land in the future presumably would cost less than developing unimproved land. If infill development is expected, then a portion of the added costs of leapfrogging eventually will be recouped—the cost of sprawl would be the cost of supplying some infrastructure in advance of its eventual need and would be lower the more rapidly infill was expected.

The possibility that the costs of leapfrog development are reduced by eventual infill is supported in part by a study by Richard B. Peiser, which compared the hypothetical costs of planned and unplanned development of a 7,500 acre tract in Houston.[18] The housing types in both developments were similar. In the unplanned development, small housing subdivisions were built in a piecemeal and uncoordinated fashion, leaving vacant land to be filled in later with commercial and other uses. In the planned development, however, housing was developed according to a master plan for the entire area, and commercial and other users were sited to minimize transportation costs and other conflicts.

Peiser estimated that capital costs for infrastructure (roads, sewers, water, and drainage) would be only 5 percent lower in the planned community than the unplanned community.[19] Water, sewer, and drainage capital costs were estimated to be higher in the unplanned community because it failed to exploit economies of scale in service areas, pipe dimensions, or treatment facilities. Road capital costs were slightly lower in the unplanned community, however, because developers built only roads connecting their subdivisions with major highways and not roads that connected their subdivisions with others. The residents of the unplanned community had to drive farther to compensate for the lack of direct connections among subdivisions, but total transportation costs (including travel time as well as road costs) were only 3 percent lower in the planned than the unplanned community.[20]

Distance to Central Facilities

A few analysts have estimated the cost impacts of increasing distance from central infrastructure facilities, such as sewage treatment plants, waste disposal facilities, and drinking water supplies. These are costs above and beyond those associated with neighborhood density, compact versus leapfrog development, and so on. Paul B. Downing, for example, extended the Real Estate Research Corporation's analysis by estimating the added public service costs per mile of distance from centrally located facilities. For water, sewage, and storm drainage, Downing calculated that the capital cost of more piping would add approximately $500 per household (in 1973 dollars) for every mile of distance from the central plants, a substantial addition to the RERC's community utility capital costs of $958 to $5,483 per household (see table 5-2).[21] Downing also estimated the operating cost increases for police, fire, schools, and garbage collection per mile of distance from relevant central facilities.

Downing's estimates overstated the effects of distance because they ignored potential scale economies in both pipe sizes and central treatment plants. Significant economies of scale exist in central sewage plants and water supplies, for example; otherwise linking many neighborhoods or communities to a single source of treatment or supply would not be economical.[22] Trunk transmission line capacities also increase more than proportionately with the radius and cost of the pipe, so that a community can economize in serving more distant neighborhoods if it has the foresight to install larger trunk lines when the close-in neighborhoods are developed. Costs, in short, may be less strongly related to distance if the area can exploit these economies of scale in trunk line capacities or central plants.

Employment Dispersal

Relatively little research has been done on the jobs-housing imbalance. Much of the existing literature points with alarm to statistics indicating that some communities in major metropolitan areas have three to five times as many jobs as residents, that only a small fraction of employees typically work and live in the same town, and that low-income workers often have longer commutes than more affluent employees because of the high price of housing around suburban workplaces.[23] Theoretical simulations, not surprisingly, have shown that transportation infrastructure costs can be reduced significantly if employment is dispersed among residences in a metropolitan area instead of concentrated in a central location surrounded by residences.[24] To-ronto's planners reported that their policy of encouraging housing downtown reduced the amount of commuting into the city's central area.[25]

Severe jobs-housing imbalances probably are temporary and self-correcting phenomena, however. Residences tend to decentralize faster than employment, as young or moderate-income households search for housing they can afford. Initially, then, the residents of a newly developing suburb may have to commute long distances to find work. But employers eventually recognize the advantages of locating closer to the workforce. In time (and presumably with the approval of local planning and zoning officials), jobs follow residences. Genevieve Guiliano showed that the outlying communities in Los Angeles had low jobs-housing ratios when they were first developed, for example, but that they later increased.[26] Similarly, Peter Gordon and others demonstrated that the decentralization of jobs in U.S. metropolitan areas appears, on balance, to have reduced the distance of commuting trips.[27]

Where jobs-housing imbalance persists, moreover, it may reflect the preferences of businesses and households as much as zoning or other impediments. Many factors in addition to poor regional land use planning contribute to the jobs-housing imbalance and long commutes.[28] Many businesses prefer to locate near other businesses, so, even if unconstrained by zoning, they probably would not spread themselves uniformly over a metropolitan area. A household may find selecting a residential location close to the workplaces of its members difficult because of occasional job changes or because the household has two or more employed people. Households consider a wide variety of other factors besides proximity to job sites in selecting residential location, such as distance to family and friends and preferences for certain types of neighborhoods, building types, churches, or schools. Perhaps for these reasons, residents in communities planned for greater jobs-housing balance appear to commute about as far as residents of unplanned communities.[29] Given the complex considerations that affect residential and workplace location, the notion that better land use planning might allow many households to live close to where they work may be more of a romantic dream than a practical reality.

In sum, sprawl and low density appear to increase the burden new development imposes on infrastructure, but only slightly. The studies of residential sprawl suggested that if housing quality and amenities were held constant, good planning could reduce infrastructure costs in residential neighborhoods by perhaps 5 to 10 percent. Similarly, the jobs-housing imbalance research suggested that severe imbalances were a self-correcting phenomenon and that limits existed to the willingness or abilities of households and businesses to locate close to one another.

Redevelopment and Infill Development

The sprawl and jobs-housing imbalance literature focused primarily on the costs of building on large tracts of vacant land. A great deal of development involves building on isolated vacant lots in already built-up areas, however, or the redevelopment of existing parcels or districts to higher densities. A low-density, outlying community may be engulfed by an expanding metropolitan area, for example, and the old, large lots subdivided to make way for more units. The older buildings in a metropolitan area's central business district may be demolished to create taller structures. A shopping center or office park built only a decade or two earlier may be significantly expanded.

Accommodating such redevelopment often requires rebuilding or retrofitting existing infrastructure facilities. For example, septic systems may have to be replaced by a municipal sewage system, old water and sewer lines rebuilt with larger pipes, existing roads widened, and existing sewage and water treatment plants expanded.

Virtually no research compared the costs of rebuilding or retrofitting facilities with those of building on vacant land. Studies of leapfrog development, for example, typically focused on the added costs of building trunk lines or streets through vacant land that could be developed, but not of rebuilding facilities in already developed areas.

Retrofitting infrastructure facilities to accommodate the demands of added density is, in general, expensive. The cost of adding two new lanes to an existing two-lane road, for example, probably would far exceed the original cost of its development, especially if the area has developed in the meantime, new right-of-way is required, and existing bridges, sidewalks, and drainage systems must be rebuilt. Similarly, the cost of creating an additional unit of sewage or water carrying capacity may be much higher than the unit cost of existing capacity if the old sewage or water lines must be dug up and replaced with larger ones.

The costs of rebuilding may be reduced if the need for eventual expansion was anticipated when the initial facilities were built or if rebuilding allows the community to exploit the economies of scale present in some types of facilities. Purchasing excess right-of-way or installing oversized pipes that will not be needed for many years is costly, however, and the anticipated future demand for capacity may never develop (or it may develop much later than forecasted). As expensive as rebuilding may be, it may be less costly than building or reserving excess capacity that is not needed for a long time.

Redevelopment and development on vacant land, then, have strikingly different implications about increasing development densities. Each increment of density and infrastructure capacity usually will be more expensive than the last if development involves the rebuilding or infilling of existing communities to higher densities. While higher density may provide modest infrastructure savings over low density when development occurs on vacant land, higher density also may cause disproportionate increases in infrastructure costs if the development occurs within existing built-up areas.

In sum, viewed nationally, regionally, and even from most local communities, land development tends to be a less important cause of rising infrastructure demand than other forces, such as rising incomes or stricter standards for infrastructure services. Variations in urban form (such as sprawl or jobs-housing imbalance), moreover, appear to have modest effects on infrastructure costs. Development often is a major cause of local infrastructure demand in two important circumstances, however: in communities experiencing rapid growth and in built-up communities where new development requires a retrofitting of existing infrastructure facilities at great cost.

6

Does Development Pay Its Own Way?

EVEN WHERE NEW development accounts for only a modest portion of infrastructure demand, local officials will be concerned whether the tax and other revenues the development generates are greater than the costs of providing the infrastructure and other services it requires. If revenues are less than costs, new development will either add to the backlog of unfinanced and unprovided infrastructure (or other public) services or require politically unpopular increases in local tax rates.

The available evidence shows that development does not cover new public costs; that is, it brings in less revenue for local governments than the price of servicing it. Development typically pays its way less often than was thought in the 1950s and 1960s, partly because of changes in fiscal conditions and partly because past studies understated the capital costs of growth. Many types of development probably do not meet rising infrastructure demands, particularly in rapidly growing communities, at difficult-to-service sites, and where costly retrofitting of existing infrastructure is required. Such generalizations must be heavily qualified, however, because cost and revenue allocation involve difficult methodological problems and costs greatly depend on specific local circumstances.

Conventional Wisdom and New Doubts

Planners and other local officials have long analyzed the financial impacts of new development on local governments. In the 1940s and 1950s, these studies were called "cost/revenue analyses" and focused on the financial implications of either new, large residential subdivisions or annexation of fringe rural areas by local governments.[1] In the 1970s, the term "fiscal impact analysis" came into popular use, and planners broadened their focus to include commercial, industrial, and smaller infill projects as well as residential subdivisions and annexation proposals.[2] In the 1980s, the spread of exactions generated a new genre of fiscal impact analysis focused on development's effects on the specific public services for which exactions were being levied.[3]

The conventional wisdom that emerged from the fiscal impact analyses of the 1940s through the 1970s was that housing for low- and moderate-income families often did not pay its way but most other forms of development did. Low-income housing was thought to impose fairly heavy burdens, particularly for schooling, while contributing little revenue to local coffers. Commercial or industrial development and high-income housing, by contrast, required relatively fewer local public services and generated more revenues. Many localities, therefore, sought to capture such development while preventing the construction of low-cost housing.

Recently, some local planners and budget analysts concluded that "profitable" development is far more rare than previously believed. Their skepticism stems in part from the changing circumstances of public finance in the late 1970s and 1980s. A variety of forces both increased the burden of infrastructure costs on local government and reduced local tax revenues from development. Federal cutbacks in infrastructure spending increased local responsibilities for the public costs associated with development, for example, while popular tax resistance reduced the local property tax revenues generated by new development in many communities. At the same time, local governments came under pressure to improve and expand their services in a variety of ways. Federal standards for drinking water supply, sewage, and solid waste disposal and other local infrastructure services were tightened, while demands for social and educational services also increased dramatically.

Capital and Marginal Costs

Concern about infrastructure and development also directed local planners' attention to two longstanding analytic problems in conventional fiscal impact analyses. First, most fiscal impact analyses prior to 1980 focused on operating expenses, to the virtual exclusion of capital costs, probably because operating costs were more easily estimated. Even when included, capital costs generally were estimated on the basis of historical costs or book values, which invariably are far lower than current expansion or replacement costs. In many cases, additionally, the only capital costs included were payments on bonds that still were outstanding.

Common financing practices may prevent even the most sophisticated or best-intentioned local governments from allocating capital costs fairly between current and future budgets, and thus between current and future residents. Thomas P. Snyder and Michael A. Stegman argued, for example, that current and future residents will face the true economic costs of the facilities they use if the local government finances all capital facilities through bonds and if the terms of the bonds are identical to the useful lives of the facilities. State laws, however, often limit the terms of local government bonds to twenty years or less and limit the amount of debt that a local government can issue. As a consequence, local governments may be forced to finance many facilities out of current revenue or with bonds that have terms shorter than the useful lives of the facilities. If the terms of the bonds are shorter than the lives of the facilities, capital costs will be allocated fairly between current and future users only in the unlikely event that the community's population growth rate is equal to the annual real interest rate on the bonds. Where the growth rate is lower, current budgets will understate the true current economic costs of facilities; where it is higher, current budgets will overstate current capital costs.[4]

Snyder and Stegman's results suggested that current residents are at substantial risk of subsidizing future residents only in communities growing faster than 3 or 4 percent per year (approximately the real interest rate). Few communities grow so rapidly for an extended period. This analysis assumed that bond term limitations were the only barrier to assessing cost appropriately. However, other problems exist as well.

A second problem with the early fiscal impact analyses was that they focused on the average instead of the marginal, or incremental, costs associated with new development. Economists have long argued, though, that marginal costs are the most relevant measure of the costs development places on a community and that average costs may differ widely from marginal costs for several reasons.[5]

One commonly cited possibility is that new development allows the community to exploit economies of scale in some public services, so that the marginal costs of new development are less than average costs. The mayor's staff and the central branch of the municipal library, for example, may not have to expand proportionately as the city's population increases. With respect to infrastructure, moreover, growth may allow small or low-density communities to take advantage of the economies of scale (in sewage treatment plants, solid waste disposal, or similar facilities). In practice, however, economies of scale tend to be insignificant in all but the smallest communities. And even in these, cooperative arrangements with other localities often are an option.[6]

Excess capacity and "lumpiness" of capital investments are other reasons sometimes given for differences in marginal and average costs. If growth is anticipated, building facilities larger than necessary to accommodate immediate needs may be more economical than expanding facilities incrementally as the community develops. Under such a strategy, the marginal costs of growth would appear to fluctuate, being extraordinarily low (relative to the long-term average costs) during the periods of excess capacity and then extraordinarily high once the capacity was absorbed and another round of investment was required.

The problems created by lumpiness probably also are exaggerated. Many facilities can be expanded incrementally with few cost penalties (especially when the expense of building capacity that is underutilized for many years is considered), so the cycles of investment are not so long or extreme. Lumpy investments only make sense when future growth is considered a high probability, moreover, and the apparent fluctuations of marginal costs may be reduced if capital costs are financed through bonds. Such capital cost allocations raise difficult conceptual and practical problems (notably those cited by Snyder and Stegman), but they are common to all long-lived investments.[7]

Finally, marginal costs may exceed average costs if accommodating growth requires the rebuilding or retrofitting of existing facilities. Where retrofitting infrastructure facilities is required, marginal costs often far exceed average costs. This problem may be more common than economies of scale or lumpiness, particularly in communities that already are built up.

Montgomery County, Maryland, Studies

The potential effects of including better estimates of the marginal capital costs of infrastructure are illustrated by two studies carried out twenty years apart in Montgomery County, Maryland. Montgomery County provides all local public services to residents outside the cities of Bethesda and Silver Spring and also has many responsibilities within those cities. The 1969 Boise-Cascade Center for Community Development study reflected the state of the

Table 6-1. *Montgomery County, Maryland, Revenue/Expense Ratios for Various Types of Businesses and the Residences of Their Employees*

	Business and residences separately			Business and residences combined	
Enterprise Activity	Business activity alone	Employee residences alone	Percentage of employees living in Montgomery County	Business plus employees living in Montgomery County	Business plus all employees
Commercial recreation[a]	3.72	0.61	50	1.51	1.13
Construction	7.27	0.58	58	1.03	0.85
Federal government office	0.54	0.73	51	0.69	0.71
For-profit medical	2.67	0.67	62	1.09	0.95
Hotel or motel	4.13	0.56	76	1.59	1.40
Large white collar installation	9.81	0.65	33	2.34	1.29
Major shopping center	2.14	0.61	82	1.06	1.00
Manufacturing plant	3.70	0.56	65	0.79	0.71
Research and development installation	6.13	0.72	66	0.96	0.88
Service distribution center	3.59	0.61	46	0.89	0.74
Smaller rental office buildings	3.95	0.71	74	0.99	0.92
Tax-exempt, large white collar installation	0.12	0.65	33	0.55	0.61
Tax-exempt medical center	0.15	0.67	62	0.56	0.59

Source: Adapted from Boise-Cascade Center for Community Development, *The Relative Importance to Montgomery County of Selected Economic Activities: A Benefit/Cost Study*, report prepared for the Economic Development Commission, Montgomery County, Maryland, 1970, tables III-1, V-1, B-46.
[a]For example, golf courses.

art in fiscal impact analysis.[8] The 1989 study was conducted by Henry Bain, the county's chief legislative analyst.[9]

The 1969 study first examined the fiscal impacts of business and residential activities separately, and then considered their combined effects. The estimated fiscal impacts of thirteen different types of business activities alone can be determined from the data in the first column of table 6-1. (The assump-

Table 6-2. *Assumptions for Allocating Montgomery County, Maryland, Expenses and Revenues among County Businesses and Residents*

	Method of allocation	
Category of expenses or revenues	*To businesses*	*To residents*
Expenses[a]		
Education and recreation		
Education K-12	None	Per student
Libraries and recreation	None	Per household (survey of use)
Montgomery County College	None	Per student
Protection and justice		
Crimes against persons[c]	None	Per person
Protection of property[b]	By assessed value	By assessed value
Shoplifting	By retail sales	None
Development, transportation, environmental quality		
Environmental protection	None	Per person
Highway construction, maintenance, and police and safety	Per vehicle trip generated[d]	Per vehicle trip generated[d]
Zoning and building inspection	Per dollar of new construction	Per dollar of new construction

Source: Extracted from Boise-Cascade Center for Community Development, *The Relative Importance to Montgomery County of Selected Economic Activities: A Benefit/Cost Study*, report prepared for the Economic Development Commission, Montgomery County, Maryland, 1970, tables III-1, V-1, and B-46.

[a]Education and recreation $72 million; protection and justice, $10 million; development, transportation, environmental quality, $9 million; health and welfare, $5 million; county overhead functions, $5 million; and general county government, $1 million.

[b]For example, robbery.

[c]For example, assault, murder.

[d]Unclear is whether work trips made by Montgomery County residents to Montgomery County businesses were charged to the residents or to businesses. See Boise-Cascade Center for Community Development, *The Relative Importance to Montgomery County of Selected Economic Activities*, pp. B-11, B-44.

tions used to allocate county expenses between business and residential activities are summarized in table 6-2.) The study indicated that large white collar office installations, such as corporate headquarters, had the most favorable fiscal impact, generating $9.81 in county tax revenues for every dollar in county expenditures required to serve them. The nonresidential activities with the least favorable impacts were tax-exempt institutions. A federal government office building, for example, generated only 54 cents in revenue for every dollar it cost the county. A nonprofit hospital brought in 15 cents; a foundation office, 12 cents. Excluding the tax-exempt institutions, however,

Table 6-2. (continued)

Category of expenses or revenues	Method of allocation	
	To businesses	To residents
Health and welfare		
Inspectional	Per medical care licensee	None
Public health	None	Per person
Welfare	None	Per low-income household
County overhead functions and general county government	e	e
Revenues		
Personal income tax	None	By income
Property tax		
Business	By assesssed value	None
Residential	None	By assessed rate
County taxes stimulated by purchases[f]	$.01404 per dollar spent in county	$.01404 per dollar spent in county

eCounty overhead functions (such as the county manager and finance department) were allocated in proportion to other expenses; general county functions were allocated among residents and businesses according to assessed value and then among residential households on a per capita basis and among businesses according to assessed value. See Boise-Cascade Center for Community Development, *The Relative Importance to Montgomery County of Selected Economic Activities*, pp. B-3–B-5, B-11–B-13.

fThe source of this estimate was not given, and its inclusion may be criticized because county expenses stimulated by purchases were not included. This element counted for more than half of the revenue credited to "construction and allied services" and one-quarter of the revenue credited to "research and development," but a much smaller proportion of the revenues of other business activities. See Boise-Cascade Center for Community Development, *The Relative Importance to Montgomery County of Selected Economic Activities*, p. B-38 and B-43.

all enterprises paid at least twice as much in revenues as they cost to serve, the best being those with relatively large amounts of taxable property per employee, such as corporate headquarters or golf courses.

The figures in the second column reflect the costs and revenues of the residences of typical workers in the thirteen enterprise activities. The ratio of county revenues to county costs varied because the average income, house value, and number of children of the typical worker varied by category. All categories generated less revenue than costs, however. The residences of workers in offices and research and development installations generated 65 to 70 cents in tax revenue per dollar of expenditure, for example; the residences of manufacturing and hotel workers, 56 cents.

One difficulty, which the consultants recognized, was uncertainty about the extent to which business activities would attract particular kinds of workers to reside within the county (and vice versa). Two alternative estimates of the combined fiscal impacts, using different assumptions about the relationship between business and residential locations, are provided in the fourth and fifth columns of table 6-1. The fourth column adopts the definition used by the county's consultants: Combined fiscal impact is the direct impact of the business plus the impact of the residences of its workers who reside in the county. The fifth column includes the fiscal impacts of the residences of all county workers, whether they reside in Montgomery County or not. The consultants' definition assumed that, if the businesses relocated to another county, their workers would move, too (and that workers employed in other counties would not have occupied their housing sites or residences). The alternative definition assumed that local residences would be provided for all locally employed workers, which is more realistic at the metropolitan or regional level than for an individual county.

Business appears significantly less attractive when its effects on residential location are considered, regardless of which definition is used. If the residences of all workers are included (regardless of where in the region they are located), even office parks and hotels appear only marginally profitable. The figures support the conventional wisdom of fiscal impact analysis: The most profitable local strategy is to attract regional office complexes and similar business activities but to avoid housing their employees, particularly those with low or moderate incomes and school-age children.

Bain's 1989 study came to strikingly different conclusions, largely because of the way he estimated the cost of public infrastructure required to serve development. The earlier study included two components of capital cost: debt service for county bonds that were outstanding in 1969 plus the amortized cost of the county's current five-year capital plan (that is, the cost of investments planned for the next five years, amortized over their expected lifetimes). These two components greatly understated infrastructure costs, as the county did not include depreciation in its 1969 budget and many of its existing facilities had been financed on a pay-as-you-go basis or by bonds paid off long ago. Furthermore, the 1969 consultants made no effort to calculate the marginal, as opposed to the average, capital costs of development.

Bain's study was narrower in certain respects than the previous study, to devote more attention to capital costs. Bain considered the fiscal impacts of office buildings only, one of the best performers in the earlier study, and did not make estimates for residences. Bain counted all forms of county revenue generated by office buildings, and he estimated only the expenses that the county would incur for highways used by commuters to the office buildings.

The prototype office building was in an office park outside downtown Silver Spring or Bethesda, so that virtually all workers would drive to work instead of taking the Washington, D.C., Metrorail (which stops in Silver Spring and Bethesda) or bus. Highway capital costs were estimated by calculating how many lane feet (one foot of one lane) the county would have to build to accommodate one more commuting office worker, given the average distance office workers commute on county roads, the average capacity of those roads, and the cost to the county (over and above state aid) of building new lane feet of road. To these capital expenses, Bain added highway maintenance and operating expenses.

Bain's calculations, summarized in table 6-3, suggested that a new office building would generate $409.81 in tax revenue per office worker per year for the county but would cost the county $346.68 per office worker per year to build and maintain the roads needed to get the worker to the office building. With such a slim margin, little tax revenue was left over to fund other county services that the office building might require (such as sewer, water, solid waste, police protection, or fire protection), let alone those required by the households of employees. If this result held for office parks, the most profitable form of development under the 1969 analysis, it doubtlessly was even more true of other types of businesses or residential developments.

Both the 1989 and the 1969 studies can be faulted on a number of grounds. Both studies required Solomonic judgments about whether costs of commuting should be assigned to the residence or the workplace of a worker, for example. By assigning all the commuting costs to the workplace, Bain assumed that all new office workers would live outside the county (or that residences did not yield any fiscal surpluses for highway capital investment).[10] Both studies also used fairly simplistic methods for allocating operating costs to different types of development. Despite these limitations, Bain's cost estimates, which amounted to only 5 cents per vehicle mile traveled, seemed fairly consistent with other careful attempts to estimate the costs of peak hour auto travel.[11] Refinements in the calculations probably would not affect the central result of Bain's study: Development often fails to generate sufficient local tax revenue to cover the costs of the infrastructure it requires.

The contrast between the two Montgomery County studies raises interesting questions. Would Bain's methodology yield similar results in other communities? Had Bain's methodology been applied to Montgomery County in 1969, would it have generated the same results as it did in 1989? Bain's methodology probably would have brought conclusions considerably more favorable to development in 1969 because Montgomery County had become far more built-up over the intervening twenty years. However, development

Table 6-3. *Comparison of Montgomery County, Maryland, Revenues and Transportation Costs for an Office Building Worker*

Category of revenues or expenditures	Amount	Measurement
		County Revenues
Interest on early property tax payments	10.24	In dollars, per worker year
Personal property tax on office building	69.42	In dollars, per worker year
Property tax on office building	250.61	In dollars, per worker year
Transfer tax and other new development fees (amortized over 20 years)	71.77	In dollars, per worker year
Utility taxes paid by office building	7.77	In dollars, per worker year
Total county revenues	409.81	In dollars, per worker year
		Transportation Expenditures
Peak hour travel induced by office worker	8.0	Vehicle miles per worker day (one way)
Divide: Effective peak capacity of road	2638.3	Vehicle miles per lane-mile
Multiply: Length of mile	5280	Feet per mile
Total road required by one worker	16.0	Lane feet per worker
Multiply: Capital cost to county of roadway capacity (half of $2.4 million per lane mile cost amortized over 20 years at 4 percent)	16.72	In dollars, per lane foot year
Total highway capital costs	267.52	In dollars, per worker year
Add: Other highway costs[a]	79.16	In dollars, per worker year
Total transportation expenditures	346.68	In dollars, per worker year

Source: Adapted from Henry Bain, "Highway Costs and Revenues of an Additional Worker in Montgomery County, Maryland," report prepared for the Transportation and Environment Committee, Montgomery County, Maryland, especially pp. 2–6, by excluding all noncounty revenues and expenses and by using a lower real discount rate (4 percent per year instead of 7 percent).

[a]For example, maintenance, planning, police.

likely would have never paid as much of its way in Montgomery County as the 1969 study suggested.

Fiscal Impact Analyses

No systematic canvasses are available of the results of fiscal impact studies; they rarely are published or widely distributed. Clearly, however, results vary widely. Many recent studies support the conventional wisdom (that most types of development, except low-income housing, pay their way), while others, such as Bain's, do not.

Fiscal impact analysts confront several formidable methodological problems whose solutions are far from obvious and may depend on local circumstances. As a consequence, judging the believability of a fiscal impact analysis is difficult without examining the analysis in great detail. Absent such scrutiny, analysts often have a great deal of discretion in their methods and results.

Three Methodological Problems

To estimate the effect of a new development on local services and revenues, a baseline must be established of what the alternative might be.[12] What might happen to the pattern of local land uses and public service demands in the absence of some contemplated or proposed new development?

One difficulty in determining the baseline is that changes in income, demography, and service standards may alter community demands for public services even in the absence of new development. Another complication is the potential for spillovers. If local development permission is denied, the development may be displaced to neighboring communities, and the local community still may bear the burden of some of its traffic or other costs.

If a new development would displace existing land uses or attract new ones, these effects also should be included in the baseline and the alternative. Will new commercial development, for example, intensify pressure for local residential development? To the extent that the two are related, any analysis of the fiscal impacts of new commercial development must consider the fiscal impacts of the residential development it attracts, and vice versa.

A second major problem is calculating the marginal costs and revenues of development (even when the distinction between the new development and the baseline alternative is clear). Calculation of the marginal costs requires that public service standards be held roughly constant between alternatives, for example. More important, marginal costs typically vary by location within a community. Service expansion may be unusually costly in areas that already are built-up, that are remote, or that have difficult topography. It may be less expensive than average in areas that have excess service capacity or favorable topography. The difficulties of calculating marginal costs are especially complex in the case of infrastructure, because the facilities are long-lived and investments tend to be made in large increments, which raises difficult questions about how to allocate costs between current and future residents when the facilities are to be used by both groups.

A third problem is how to allocate responsibility for overhead or social service costs that society cannot, or will not, finance on a fee-for-service basis. Some types of development have to generate revenues beyond their marginal costs if communitywide overhead costs and subsidies to needy groups are to be financed. The question of which types of development should bear these burdens is less a technical issue than one of politics and equity.

Of the two types of costs, overhead is the less important. Overhead means those functions that are subject to large economies of scale and thus are not greatly influenced by new development. If the mayor's office does not increase with the size of the community, for example, then its costs do not enter into marginal cost analyses. Strictly speaking, such overhead costs would be assigned entirely to existing development. This implies that new development might generate a profit even when existing development was failing to cover its full cost. As a practical matter, however, few costs are so invariant.

More troubling are social and regulatory services that localities choose to provide without considering the ability of users to pay. Educational expenditures will increase with the number of children enrolled, for example, but problems may arise from assigning special responsibility for paying educational costs to families with children (or to the developments that house these families) because of society's commitment to provide a basic education for all regardless of ability to pay. Similarly, the poor or near-poor cannot bear a proportionate share of local health, welfare, or criminal justice costs. The issue of who should finance such services is of enormous significance given that they routinely make up half or more of the budgets of state and local governments.[13]

Two conventions for allocating such costs have emerged, but neither is completely satisfactory. The first, typically adopted in the analyses dominant until the 1980s, focuses on whether development pays its way for the entire range of public services, not just infrastructure. The manuals or handbooks for such analyses usually allocate the costs of social services (such as education or public welfare) entirely to residential development.[14] This convention is inconsistent with the popular principle that education, welfare, and many other services should not be rationed on the basis of household ability to pay.

The second convention emerged during the 1980s in analyses that focused on whether new development contributed its fair share of infrastructure costs. These studies typically assumed that new development should pay the same proportion of its tax revenues toward general public services as existing development.[15] If, on average, 20 percent of local tax revenues are used to finance infrastructure and the balance for other public services, for example, then new development should do likewise. This convention perpetuates the historical pattern of cost sharing, but it does not determine the fairness of that pattern.

Office Development in San Francisco

Two competing studies of office development prepared during San Francisco's growth control debate of the early 1980s illustrate the problems of fiscal impact analysis (see table 6-4.). The first analysis, prepared by the accounting firm of Arthur Andersen for the San Francisco Chamber of Commerce, reported that, in fiscal year 1979, the downtown high-rise district generated 50 percent more in local tax revenue ($53 million) than it cost the city to serve it ($36 million).[16] The tax revenues Arthur Andersen credited to the downtown consisted primarily of the city property, payroll, and sales taxes paid by downtown businesses, although a share of state grants to the city and various miscellaneous revenues (such as fines for downtown traffic violations) also were included. The expenses consisted mainly of transit deficits (net of fares) incurred by the city's Municipal Railway (MUNI) in transporting downtown office workers to and from their jobs and the costs of police and fire units assigned to cover the downtown district.

David Jones of San Franciscans for Reasonable Growth prepared an alternative analysis showing that city revenues from the downtown district ($42 million) were only half as great as city costs ($94 million) in the same year.[17] Jones did not dispute many of Arthur Andersen's tax revenue estimates, but he chose not to credit state grants and other miscellaneous revenues to downtown because they were not clearly attributable to downtown activities (compare the first and second columns of table 6-4). His main criticism of the Arthur Andersen figures was on the expenditure side. Jones argued that the downtown should contribute the same proportion of its revenues to support such social overhead services as schools, parks, hospitals, and jails as other neighborhoods. If public health absorbed 15 percent of all city revenue, for example, then 15 percent of downtown revenue should be dedicated to public health. Once Jones added these expenses, downtown appeared to cover less than half its properly attributable costs.[18]

Both studies illustrate how misleading taking a purely local point of view may be. Each ignored the income, sales, and other tax revenues that downtown generated for the state of California, regional authorities, and neighboring cities. They also excluded the costs imposed on other governments by the downtown, which were large in the case of infrastructure services. Only about 30 percent of downtown workers used the San Francisco Municipal Railway for their entire commuting trip, for example, while 11 percent used MUNI in combination with another mode of transportation and 59 percent either drove or patronized other transit systems (such as Bay Area Rapid

Table 6-4. *Alternative Estimates of Revenues and Expenditures to the City of San Francisco, Generated by the Downtown High-Rise District*
Millions of dollars

	Downtown district in fiscal year 1978–79		
Category of revenues or expenses	Arthur Andersen study	David Jones study	City of San Francisco
Tax Revenues			
Business inventory tax	0.82	0.82	5.00
Cigarette taxes	0.23	0	3.00
Hetch-Hetchy project revenues	0.67	0	6.07
Hotel tax	2.77	2.77	17.60
Interest revenue	1.25	0	14.71
Other taxes less than $1 million	2.39	0	28.07
Parking meter revenues	0.52	0	3.00
Parking tax	2.22	2.22	4.50
Payroll tax and gross receipts	11.98	11.98	40.40
Property taxes	13.54	13.54	121.98
Property tax transfers	0.28	0.28	7.70
Sales tax	6.60	6.60	40.00
San Francisco Airport revenues	0.22	0	2.00
State/federal grants and aid	0	0	193.02
State surplus funds	6.13	0	55.18
Traffic fines (city)	1.11	0	9.93
Traffic fines (state)	0.13	0	4.40

Source: Arthur Andersen, Inc., *Downtown Highrise District Cost-Revenue Study Update*, report prepared for the San Francisco Chamber of Commerce, April 1981, as cited in Brad Paul, "San Francisco Growth Management," case C16-90-948.0 (John F. Kennedy School of Government and Graduate School of Design, Harvard University, 1988), exhibits 3 and 4; David Jones, *Downtown Highrise District Cost/*

Transit's rail system or the buses of the Alameda Contra-Costa Transit Authority and the Golden Gate Bridge Authority). Downtown commuters almost surely cost the California Department of Transportation and regional transit authorities more than they did the San Francisco Municipal Railway. While such a parochial analysis may have been appropriate for the city of San Francisco, it was misleading for the region as a whole.

Even from a purely local perspective, both studies can be faulted for failing to distinguish what would have happened if recent downtown growth had not taken place. Did the older buildings demolished during the 1970s benefit (or cost) the city more, for example, than the high-rises that replaced them? To the extent that development of the downtown influenced residential and

Table 6-4. (*continued*)

| Category of revenues or expenses | Downtown district in fiscal year 1978–79 | | City of San Francisco |
	Arthur Andersen study	David Jones study	
Utility users tax	2.24	2.24	16.60
Miscellaneous revenues	0.19	1.59	26.15
Total[a]	53.29	42.04	599.31
City Expenses			
Bay Area Rapid Transit (BART)	0	25.60	30.10
Bond interest	1.14	0.58	8.57
Fire	2.09	4.44	65.61
General government	3.33	4.26	63.05
General government-related	0.28	0.36	5.28
Library	0.36	0.42	5.94
Mental health	0.23	2.02	29.73
Parks and recreation	0.19	2.28	33.84
Planned unit development (PUD) administration	0.80	0.16	2.31
Police	3.05	5.58	82.61
Police-related	1.31	2.40	35.50
Public health	0.40	6.26	91.82
Public works	0.92	2.15	31.88
San Francisco Municipal Railway (MUNI)	21.27	29.50	45.24
Social services	0.02	8.29	122.63
Other	0.62	0.17	2.49
Total[a]	36.01	94.47	656.60

Revenue Study, report distributed by San Franciscans for Reasonable Growth, February 1981, as cited in Paul, "San Francisco Growth Management," exhibits 5 and 6.

[a]All items in columns except the totals are from the original source; the totals in the original were incorrect because of minor errors of addition and have been corrected.

commercial development in other parts of the city, how were city costs and revenues affected?

Nor did either study calculate the marginal capital costs of downtown development. Both examined current city expenditures only and failed to make an estimate of the depreciation of existing public capital that might be charged against the downtown. If downtown growth required some costly expansions of transit, highway, and water and sewer capacity, its marginal costs likely were to be far above average.

Finally, neither analysis offered a compelling rationale for deciding how much revenue the downtown should contribute toward citywide social service and overhead expenses. David Jones's proposal (that each type of activity should contribute the same proportion of its general revenue) is no more defensible than many others. If a development does not cover its directly attributable expenses through user charges and tax revenues, as Bain alleged was true of Montgomery County office buildings in 1989, then it clearly does not pay its way. But if development does cover its directly attributable costs, as both studies of San Francisco's downtown suggested, how much it should contribute toward the cost of nonattributable services is less a matter of economics than politics.

Evaluating Impact Studies

The solution to these methodological problems often depends on the specific circumstances that the local community faces. The relevant alternatives to development will vary from one community to the next, for example, as will the specific problems in estimating capital costs. As a consequence, fiscal impact analysts must exercise a fair amount of judgment and discretion in tailoring their approach to the specific situations before them.

An analyst may easily influence the outcome of a fiscal impact analysis by judicious choice of assumptions and approaches. Strikingly, the results of most fiscal impact analyses conform with the policy inclinations of the governments or organizations that sponsored them.

Most fiscal impact analysts are not unscrupulous, and fiscal impact analyses are not impossible to evaluate. However, taking the results of a fiscal impact study at face value is risky. A simple inventory of the results of local fiscal impact analyses might provide little information on the circumstances under which development does or does not pay its way. Without a detailed evaluation of each study, determining how much of the variation in results was caused by differences in local circumstances and how much by questionable differences in the assumptions or approaches used is difficult.

Spending and Revenue Trends

Another approach to estimating whether development covers public costs is statistical analysis of government spending and revenue trends in slow- versus fast-growing communities. A study by Helen F. Ladd illustrates the limitations of such analyses.

Ladd's study, by far the most comprehensive of its type, examined the effects of changes in residential population on local spending and revenue in the 248 largest U.S. counties or county equivalents between 1978 and 1985.[19] The data included spending and revenue for all local governments within each county, including cities, towns, and special districts as well as the county itself. Approximately one-quarter of the counties in the sample experienced population growth in excess of 15 percent over the seven-year period (or more than 1.3 percent, compounded, per year). Ladd attempted to estimate the independent effects of population growth on real (net of inflation) spending and revenue per capita by controlling for the influence of several other factors, including changes in real per capita incomes and in the proportion of the population that was school age or elderly.

Ladd found that population growth was associated with modest but statistically significant increases in total real local government spending per capita. Once the effects of income growth and demographic changes (other than population growth) were eliminated, per capita spending grew 1.6 to 2.4 percent faster in areas with 10 percent population growth over the seven-year period than in areas with no population growth.[20] Transportation, capital, and interest expenses per capita all were strongly and positively associated with higher population growth, which supported the popular impression that growth places particular burdens on infrastructure.[21] Education spending per capita, meanwhile, exhibited a U-shaped pattern, growing more rapidly than average only in the fastest- and slowest-growing counties.

Ladd found that rapid population growth also was associated with above-average real revenue growth per capita. Local own-source revenue per capita grew 6.1 percent faster in counties that experienced population growth of 10 percent or more than in those that did not grow. Local revenue as a percentage of local resident incomes grew 4.3 percent faster in counties with 10 percent population growth than in no-growth counties.

The increases in local revenue per capita probably were driven by a combination of spending pressures and cutbacks in intergovernmental aid. Per capita intergovernmental aid declined between 1978 and 1985 in the 248 counties, as modest increases in state aid failed to fully offset federal aid cutbacks (see table 6-5). Local own-source revenues per capita increased by more than enough to offset the lost intergovernmental aid, with most of the added revenues being collected in the categories of miscellaneous revenue (which included exactions) and user charges instead of taxes.

At first glance, Ladd's results seemed to contradict the conventional wisdom that most development pays its way: Higher population growth rates appeared to require higher per capita spending, particularly for infrastructure,

Table 6-5. *Average Local Government Revenue Per Capita in 248 Large Counties, 1978 and 1985*
1982 dollars

Category of revenue	1978	1985
Intergovernmental aid		
From federal		
governments	128	78
From state		
governments	374	403
Subtotal aid	502	481
Local source revenue		
General sales taxes	36	51
Property taxes	422	409
Other taxes	57	67
Subtotal taxes	515	527
User charges	123	164
Miscellaneous	57	133
Subtotal local source	695	824
Total revenue	1,197	1,305

Source: Bureau of the Census data as reported by Helen F. Ladd, "Effects of Population Growth on Local Spending and Taxes" (Cambridge, Mass.: Lincoln Institute of Land Policy, April 1990), table 8.

and higher spending required increases in local revenue collections (both per capita and as a percentage of income). The results, however, offered less of a challenge to the conventional wisdom than originally thought and should be regarded as inconclusive.

A major problem, which Ladd recognized, is that spending does not measure the quality of services provided. The spending data could not be adjusted for service quality because no broad-gauge measures of the quality of local public services are available. The fastest-growing counties may have been improving service quality (in response to the demands of new residents, for example), which would mean that the spending trends overstated the financial burdens of growth. However, the fastest-growing counties also could have failed to hold service levels constant, which would mean the spending data understated the financial burdens of growth.

The published statistics on government spending, on which researchers such as Ladd necessarily rely, also include poor estimates of current capital costs. The statistics on current spending included the total gross investment in any new capital facility built during a particular year (even if it was financed with bonds) but omit current depreciation and opportunity cost of older facilities. This practice overstated the true economic costs of new facilities but understated the costs of existing ones. If fast-growing communities were investing heavily in new capital facilities with long, useful lives, the spending data would exaggerate the financial burdens of growth, particularly for capital intensive services such as infrastructure. [22]

Conclusions

A few tentative conclusions about when development pays its way can be drawn, even if much of the evidence is inconclusive or flawed. First, if development now pays less than the conventional wisdom once suggested, the shift probably was caused by both real fiscal changes and a growth in awareness of longstanding problems with fiscal impact analysis. The revenues generated by development almost certainly have declined somewhat in the last decade or two, because of a combination of taxpayer revolts and declines in intergovernmental assistance. An equally serious challenge to the conventional wisdom, however, has arisen from a more careful accounting of marginal and capital costs. To the extent that this new accounting now makes particular types of development appear unprofitable, some of those types of development may have never paid their way.

Second, the focus on capital costs probably will reduce (but not eliminate) the fiscal advantages of commercial over residential development. The conventional wisdom that commercial development generally was more profitable than residential development depended largely on the practice of allocating educational expenditures entirely to residences and understating capital costs. Commercial developments place few immediate demands on local educational services (although they may eventually lure new residents). Commercial developments ask more of capital facilities, such as roads and water or sewage systems. A more careful accounting of capital costs therefore is likely to narrow the gap in profitability between commercial and residential development.

Third, the new emphasis on capital costs suggests several local circumstances and conditions that probably will strongly influence whether a development covers public costs. Development (without exactions) is less likely to pay its way when a community is growing very rapidly, for example, if only because state laws limiting the terms of local bonds and the amount of local debt are expected to force current residents to pay an excessive share of future capital costs. Chances are great that developments on sites that are unusually costly to service also will have weak revenue-cost profiles. Developments in communities that already are heavily built-up also are among those least likely to pay their way, because they typically require costly rebuilding of existing infrastructure. Development thus may be profitable for a community in the early stages of development but eventually become unprofitable as rebuilding infrastructure, instead of building from scratch, becomes the norm.

Finally, calculations of whether development pays its own way are inevitably political as well as technical. The political dimension is inescapable if one believes that local government should not require users to finance their own social, protective, and educational services. If a development does not cover expenses that can be comfortably allocated, then it clearly does not pay its way. But how much more beyond that it should pay is a political question.

7

Equity Considerations

IF DEVELOPMENT DOES not always pay its way for infrastructure or other local government costs, are exactions an equitable solution? Some proponents of exactions argue that requiring developers to pay for needed infrastructure is only fair, because they are the parties who profit from development. Other proponents contend that exactions are equitable even though developers can pass fees back to landowners or forward to customers because exactions ensure that existing taxpayers do not subsidize the infrastructure needs of newcomers. Critics of exactions argue that they allocate costs and benefits perversely, tending particularly to benefit the affluent over low-income households and older over younger households.

Neither the proponents nor the skeptics, however, are entirely correct. The equity of exactions depends largely on how they are structured, on the specific circumstances of their application, and on the alternatives to which they are compared. Exactions may include exceptions for affordable housing, for example. They may be applied only during periods when the local real estate market is overheated or consistently, regardless of market conditions. The realistic alternative to exactions may be to collect revenue by other means, such as raising taxes or user charges; to curtail new development; or to allow new development but tolerate some deterioration in the quality of public services.

The longer exactions are in place and the more widespread they become, the more likely they are to cause equity problems for younger generations and the poor. In the short term, this is not always the case, however, and long-term exactions still may be preferred if the only realistic alternative is to stop development altogether.

Who Pays Exactions?

All the arguments about exactions depend on who pays for them. While limited, the empirical evidence available suggests that developers and land-owners are unlikely to bear the exaction cost in many situations. The evidence is consistent, moreover, with economic theory.

Exactions nominally are paid by the developer in most communities, but the developer may pass all or part of the cost back to the original landowner (in the form of a lower price for the land than the developer would have paid otherwise) or forward to the purchaser or renter of the developed property (in the form of higher purchase prices or rents). The ultimate burden or incidence of exactions, like that of other taxes or fees, falls on the parties that are least able to evade them—for example, by moving to another locale or shifting to another line of business. The incidence of exactions thus is greatly affected by their design and by the specific market conditions and circumstances in which they are applied.

Long-Term and Widespread Exactions

Most economists agree that developers will pass on most of the cost of exactions to buyers and renters if exactions are applied over a long period of time and the level of exactions does not vary much within the relevant property market.[1] Residential consumers have the fewest opportunities to hold their exaction costs down because, unlike land or property taxes, exactions usually do not change significantly with the dwelling size or value.[2] Those determined to minimize their exaction costs may move to another community or metropolitan area where exactions are lower or may be able to defer forming a new household (for example, by remaining with their parents). Generally, however, they have few other options.[3] As exactions remain in place for a long time, moreover, and diffuse regionwide, the avoidance options tend to evaporate.

By contrast, developers virtually are forced to pass on most or all of the cost of exactions to either consumers or landowners in the long run, because development is a competitive business. Local developers will remain in business only if they earn returns comparable to those available in other communities or other lines of business. If the returns to capital and entrepreneurship in development temporarily are driven below normal levels because a community imposes exactions, the local development industry gradually will contract until returns (after exactions are paid) once again are at normal levels.

Owners of undeveloped land also can avoid most of the burden of long-standing and widespread exactions by holding the land in agricultural or other undeveloped uses longer. Developed property on the periphery of a metropolitan area sells or rents for less than developed property closer in because commuting to centrally located workplaces is not as convenient from peripheral sites. The price for developed property at any given location is rising constantly in a growing metropolitan area, because the periphery (where land conversion takes place) is moving out and the commuting advantage of a developed site over the periphery is increasing. The owner of an undeveloped site will wait until the interest saved by postponing the development investment by one period equals the increase in rents for developed property expected from waiting one period.[4] The imposition of exactions increases the development investment required, thereby delaying development (because a larger increase in expected developed property rent now is needed to trigger conversion).[5] By slowing the rate of land conversion, exactions will reduce the amount of developed property available in any given year and therefore (all else being equal) drive up prices for developed property throughout the metropolitan area.

Owners of undeveloped land on the periphery of the metropolitan area likely are to suffer losses immediately after exactions are imposed. Property on the periphery typically is valued at more than agricultural land farther out in anticipation of the commuting premium it will eventually command when the metropolitan area expands around it. By slowing the rate of growth, exactions delay the date that commuting premium is realized and thus reduce the value of undeveloped land that already has appreciated in anticipation of development. This effect may be partially offset, however, because the conversion slowdown also will increase developed property prices, and thus the price the landowner eventually expects to realize on conversion.[6]

Farther out and in the long run, however, landowners should be only minimally affected. Competitive markets would require that the rate of return on all types of investment be roughly equal over time. Thus owners of undeveloped property on the periphery (or elsewhere) would earn, on average, the same returns on their investments as others do. In such a situation, the exaction could not be absorbed in the long run by reducing the returns to land speculation but would have to be passed on to buyers.[7]

Neither how the proceeds of the exaction are spent nor the alternatives to exactions have been considered yet. The exaction may finance public improvements for which consumers are pleased to pay (for example, local access streets), so that, on the whole, they feel better off even though the exactions are passed on to them. At this stage of the analysis, however, assuming that all other government services and taxes are held constant and focusing only on the effects of collecting an exaction will be less confusing. Subsequently, the effects of taxes, service cuts, and other alternatives to exactions will be discussed.

Four Exceptions

Four important exceptions exist to the generalization that buyers and renters of developed property usually bear most exaction costs: In the short run, in communities with unusually high exactions, in hot real estate markets, and in communities committed to growth control.

The short run is the period soon after a community decides to impose exactions and before local developers and landowners have adjusted their activities and investments to the new situation. How long it takes developers and landowners to pass exactions on to buyers depends upon the extent of their sunk investments in the local community. A developer who owns options on undeveloped land at the time exactions are imposed, for example, may have little choice but to develop and absorb the exactions or to write off the options as a loss. Developers' ties to the community may take other forms, such as an understanding of the local real estate market or of the land permitting process. Similarly, landowners may suffer a loss immediately after exactions are imposed if, as noted earlier, they own property so close to the urban periphery that its value already has appreciated (above agricultural values) in the expectation of imminent development. Once exactions have been in place for a while, however, developers and land speculators will leave the market unless they can earn competitive returns.

The second exception is where the level of exactions varies significantly among local communities that potential buyers and renters of developed property view as close substitutes. In this case, the owners of undeveloped land probably will bear most of the exaction burden in communities with exceptionally high exactions. If a suburban community imposes high exactions, for example, while nearby comparable communities impose only modest exactions or none at all, developers (and their prospective buyers or tenants) easily can avoid the high exactions by shifting their operations to the close substitute communities. Development will proceed in the community imposing high exactions only if owners of undeveloped land are willing to write down their prices sufficiently to offset the exaction differential, enabling the developers to keep their prices competitive while earning competitive returns. Landowners may choose not to write down their land, particularly if the returns from holding undeveloped land in agricultural, recreational, or other uses are competitive with those from development. But if exactions are collected in the community imposing high exactions, they will be paid mainly by the owners of undeveloped land.

This situation—where one community imposes significantly higher exactions than its close competitors—may be common when exactions first are adopted or during subsequent run-ups in exaction charges (as in the 1980s), but it is unlikely to persist for long. Public officials understand that unusually high exactions can deter development. Meanwhile, communities that buyers and renters regard as comparable typically have similar attitudes toward growth. As a result, exactions over time tend to become uniform in comparable localities within a given metropolitan area. Where variation persists, the basic or common exaction cost (that is, the exaction charged by most communities in the relevant housing or office market) eventually will be passed on to the buyers or renters of developed property.

A third exception, of greater practical significance, is common in hot real estate markets. In a hot market, developers have a hard time keeping up with the demand for newly developed property. Markets do not stay hot indefinitely; the situation typically is relieved by some combination of a cooling off of demand and the expansion of developer capacity and production. While the market is hot, however, prices can surge above the levels dictated by long-term supply and demand because of the temporary shortage in the supply of developed properties. The imposition of exactions cannot force prices any higher in a hot market because prices are being determined by the temporary shortage of supply, not the long-term developer costs. Thus, in this situation, exactions probably will tap into some of the windfall profits (over and above those typical in the long run) that developers and landowners are earning in the hot market.

A final exception frequently occurs when local government chooses to limit the number of building permits below the level that the market would otherwise demand. Here, too, the developers or landowners will bear the primary burden of exactions instead of consumers. The scarcity of building permits creates artificial hot markets, driving up prices for newly developed property above those dictated by the normal forces of supply and demand. Developers and landowners with permits reap windfall profits from the government-imposed scarcity, which the government may be able to recapture, wholly or in part, by levying exactions. Buyers and renters of developed property experience artificially high prices. The permit constraints, not the exactions, however, are to blame.

At first glance, this situation may seem fairly common. Exactions typically are imposed by communities concerned about the effects of growth, which often leads them to limit building permits as well. However, except for the most affluent bedroom suburbs, communities rarely constrain building permits over an extended period of time. Limits on permits may hold back development when the local market is very hot, but not when the market cools off and vacancy rates are high. If the limit on permits is not binding over the extended cycles of expansion and slowdown, then buyers and renters still are likely to bear the primary burden of exactions.

Empirical Evidence

Few empirical studies are available on exactions payments. Those that are, however, tend to support the view that exactions are passed on to property buyers or renters in most cases. Consider, for example, two studies—one of Loveland, Colorado, and the other of Dunedin, Florida—of the effects of exactions on new housing prices. The Loveland study analyzed housing prices eighteen months before and eighteen months after impact fees first were introduced (in July 1984).[8] The researchers estimated that the average price of a new home increased by $3,800 after fees of $1,182 per unit were imposed, while building permits declined by 11 percent. Prices may have increased more than exactions because the fees were imposed when the Loveland market was hot or because the developers responded by building higher-quality housing.[9] However, the investigators attempted to control carefully for both possibilities in their statistical analysis.[10] Another possible explanation is that the developers marked up the fees to recover interest and administrative costs and to earn a normal profit.[11]

The Dunedin study examined new housing prices three years before and nine years after an impact fee of $1,150 per single-family housing unit was imposed (in June 1974).[12] Unlike Loveland, a relatively isolated community, Dunedin is one of four communities on a peninsula, and home buyers view them as reasonably close substitutes. Dunedin's three neighbors imposed no fees or much smaller fees during the period studied. The researchers estimated that new housing prices in Dunedin increased relative to those of its neighbors once Dunedin's intention to impose impact fees became known, although the size of the differential declined after six years.[13] As in Loveland, prices increased by two to three times the amount of the fee.[14] That Dunedin's developers and landowners were able to pass on the fee to buyers for at least six years is surprising, if, as the researchers claimed, houses in neighboring communities were regarded as reasonable substitutes. The Dunedin study incorporated less elaborate controls for housing quality than the Loveland study, however. Some of the Dunedin price differential likely were attributable to upgrades in the development mix (perhaps in response to the new fees).

Studies in three cities concluded that exactions were associated with increases in the prices paid for developable building lots.[15] The land price increases were too large to be explained by chance alone in two of the cities (Toronto, Canada, and Sarasota, Florida), although not in the third (Loveland, Colorado). In Toronto, where fees were paid at the time of the land sale, land prices increased by 20 to 80 percent more than the amount of the fee.[16] In the other two cities, where fees were paid at the time of actual development (instead of at the land sale), land prices increased by slightly less than the fee.[17]

Nonresidential Exactions

Exactions on office, industrial, and other commercial developments are subject to many of the same forces that affect exactions on housing. The one important difference is that nonresidential buyers and tenants have customers and employees and can try to pass on any price premiums to them.[18] The ability to do so will depend on the competitive situations faced. Commercial tenants will pass space cost premiums along to customers if demand is not price sensitive, for example, a situation more likely if the firms have little competition from companies in other metropolitan areas providing the same products or services. Commercial tenants also may pass on costs to their workers (in the form of lower wages) if local labor demand is weak and workers are unwilling to move from one metropolitan area to another in search of higher wages. In short, the costs of nonresidential exactions may be more widely distributed than those of residential exactions. To the extent that this is true, there may be less reason for concern, at least on equity grounds, about the effects of business space costs than residential space costs on low- and moderate-income households.

When Developers and Land Speculators Lose

The suggestion, then, is that the developers and landowners bear exaction costs only in four exceptional circumstances. Considered together, they appear to add up to many situations, but the four typically occur in combination and not randomly. Communities mostly likely are concerned about the costs of growth in a hot market, for example, which may lead them not only to impose new exactions but also to impose new limits on building permits. Once exactions have been in place for a while, moreover, the exceptional circumstances become much rarer.

By the same token, the chances for keeping the burden on developers and landowners, and off buyers and tenants, can be enhanced when local governments adjust their exactions to prevailing market conditions—raising them, for example, when the market is hot, reducing them as it cools off. In this respect, negotiated exactions may be superior to formula impact fees if local officials find adjusting them in response to changing market conditions more feasible. Decisions on formula exactions, by contrast, may be more politically visible, symbolically charged, and difficult to adjust.

Would the alternatives to exactions—growth limitations, increases in taxes (property or sales) or user fees, and toleration of deteriorated service levels for lack of funding—impose more of a burden on developers and owners of undeveloped land? A stringent limitation on growth is the only clearly inferior alternative from the standpoint of developers and landowners. A long-term limitation would force most local developers to move elsewhere or enter another line of business. It also would significantly reduce the value of undeveloped land by lessening the possibility that a commuting premium could be commanded once it was developed. The few developers and landowners who were allowed permits would earn windfall profits, but the rest would be shut out.

All the other alternatives have burdens that are spread widely within the community and not focused on the development and landowning community. Take the property tax, for example, which at first glance appears the most likely of the remaining alternatives to impose significant burdens on developers or landowners. Most economists believe that the property tax is borne partly by owners of capital (including landowners) and partly by consumers of capital (such as renters and owner-occupants of developed property). Capital owners bear the portion of the property tax rate that is the common or minimum rate charged in most jurisdictions; consumers bear the increment beyond the common or minimum rate in jurisdictions with high rates.[19] This implies that increases in property taxes would be borne primarily by consumers and not owners in jurisdictions with average or above average rates. Even in jurisdictions with below average rates, where capital owners might bear the brunt, undeveloped land is only one form of property, so the burden still would be widely shared.[20]

In sum, developers and owners of undeveloped land always will prefer exactions to growth moratoriums. Exactions will not hurt them much except during the adjustment period immediately after enactment or in hot markets. And they have little to fear from the alternatives of tax increases and service cuts, which will be borne largely by other members of the community.

Newcomers, Existing Residents, and Intergenerational Equity

Some proponents argue that exactions are fair, even if the buyers and renters of developed property ultimately pay, because existing residents and businesses are saved from having to pay costs attributable to new development. This argument assumes that newcomers will bear most of the burden of exactions. In fact, however, many existing residents and businesses will share in the burden.

When the price of newly developed property rises (because exactions are passed on), the price of already developed property, which is a close substitute for new property, also will increase. Thus owners (but not renters) of developed property at the time an exaction is imposed reap a one-time windfall, while future buyers, and both existing and future renters, lose. The Loveland, Colorado, study, the only empirical analysis to consider exaction impacts on existing as well as new home prices, bears this out. Prices for existing homes increased more than prices for new homes after Loveland imposed exactions.[21]

Exactions, therefore, may not shift costs between new and existing residents as much as they do between younger and older generations. Older residents are more likely to be property owners at the time the exactions are imposed. Younger people tend to be renters or to enter the market for ownership after the imposition of exactions.

The distinction between newcomers and existing residents is more helpful when a community is imposing higher exactions than the communities from which the newcomers migrate. As exactions become more uniform across jurisdictions, however, this situation becomes less important. Even in high-exaction communities, many of the newcomers are often children of existing residents, while many of the existing residents may be renters.[22]

Whether the shift in wealth from younger to older residents is fair or not depends on the assumptions made about how equitable infrastructure finance was in the past and how it recently has changed. Those who believe that exactions promote intergenerational equity assume that the system of infrastructure finance was equitable in the past, that something happened to shift the burden from new to existing property owners, and that exactions are necessary to restore the balance. In particular, they argue that development used to pay its way, that it began not to do so recently (perhaps because infrastructure costs increased faster than taxes or because of federal aid cutbacks), and that exactions compensate for the changes.

These assumptions are debatable. Putting aside the conceptual and practical obstacles of determining whether development covers public costs in any particular set of circumstances, new development probably was subsidized by existing development for quite a while, although perhaps not always to the degree that it is now. If new development never fully paid its way, then the imposition of exactions removes a subsidy that new homebuyers and renters traditionally enjoyed in the past. The older generation experienced the benefits of this arrangement when it was young. Now it escapes having to pass on the subsidy to the next generation, and it also reaps a new windfall in the form of property value inflation.[23]

The only alternative to exactions that could be worse for newcomers or renters is stringent limitations on development. Local tax increases or service deterioration presumably would be shared by both groups. Like exactions, however, growth limits would run up developed property prices, which would leave younger generations and newcomers worse off. Whether growth limits would cause larger price increases than exactions depends on the stringency of the growth limits and the amount of exaction levied. An absolute moratorium on growth would cause greater price increases than all but the highest exactions, for example, because a greater shortage of developed property would result.[24]

The Progressivity of Exactions

Another equity consideration is whether exactions or alternative policies place a disproportionate burden on poor households. The standard yardstick is the degree of progressivity or regressivity. A progressive revenue source requires poor households to pay a smaller share of their income than rich households, while a regressive revenue source asks the poor to pay a larger portion of their income than the rich.

Other Local Revenue Sources

Property taxes accounted for 25.6 percent of all 1988 local government revenue (see table 7-1), while sales taxes accounted for 5.3 percent and user charges for 12.1 percent. Most of the balance was from intergovernmental aid (32.8 percent) or other sources not easily increased by local officials.

Most economists believe that the progressivity of property tax increases depends upon whether the community starts from a rate that is above or below the common rate charged in most jurisdictions. Increases in low-rate communities usually are regarded as progressive, because capital owners assume property tax costs up to the common rate. Increases in high-rate communities generally are regarded as regressive, however, because consumers of capital bear the increment beyond the common rate.[25]

Both sales taxes and user charges are mildly regressive in most communities. The burden of sales taxes falls mainly on consumers. Sales taxes therefore are considered regressive because consumption is a higher proportion of current income for low- than high-income families. Some jurisdictions moderate the regressivity of their sales taxes by excluding food, clothing, and other goods that account for a large share of the purchases of low-income households, however, and sales taxes appear less regressive if the consumption of taxable items is compared with long-term or lifetime instead of current household incomes.[26] The regressivity or progressivity of user charges depends on the types of services involved. Infrastructure user charges typically are mildly regressive, because water, sewage, road, and other infrastructure usage increases less than proportionately with household income.[27]

Determining whether exactions on nonresidential development are progressive or not is difficult. Assuming that developers and owners of undeveloped land avoid them in the long run, exactions probably are borne in part by the owners of the businesses that buy or rent nonresidential developed property, in part by their consumers, and in part by their workers. To the extent that their owners pay, the burden is probably progressive.[28] To the extent that consumers or workers pay, the burden is similar to that of a sales or consumption tax (mildly regressive). One advantage from a strictly local perspective, however, would be that some consumers and workers live in other jurisdictions.

Table 7-1. *Sources of Local Government Revenue, 1988*

Source of revenue	Amount (billions of dollars)	Percentage
Insurance trust revenue	14.3	2.9
Intergovernmental aid	162.7	32.8
Local taxes		
Income	10.3	2.1
Corporate	2.1	
Individual	8.2	
Property	127.2	25.6
Sales	26.1	5.3
General	18.2	
Special[a]	7.9	
Publicly owned utilities and liquor stores	46.7	9.4
User and current charges[b]	60.1	12.1
Airports	3.7	
Education[c]	7.7	
Hospitals	18.7	
Housing and community development	2.3	
Sewage and sanitation	13.5	
Miscellaneous general revenue[b]	39.6	8.0
Interest	24.3	
Sale of property	0.9	
Special assessments	2.4	
Total	496.3	100

Source: Bureau of the Census, *Statistical Abstract of the United States* (1991), table 466.
[a]For example, alcohol.
[b]Includes other items not shown separately.
[c]For example, school lunch and higher education.

Exactions on residential development have a greater chance of being far more regressive than most alternative local taxes or user charges for four reasons.[29] First, housing costs absorb a greater proportion of income in poor households, so, if exactions increased the price of all types of housing by the same percentage, poor households would suffer more than rich.

Second, exactions generally impose a greater percentage cost increase on low-value than high-value houses. Impact fees usually vary only slightly with the value of the housing unit. They typically do differ according to the number of bedrooms in a house, for example, because bedrooms often are used to predict household size (and thus the number of miles driven, gallons of sewage produced, or water per housing unit consumed). Detached single-family and multifamily units also often are charged slightly different fees, given that they tend to be occupied by different types of families that place different demands on infrastructure services. The resulting fees almost certainly increase less than proportionately with the value of the unit, however, particularly in communities where multifamily housing is permitted. The percentage price increase will be far greater on a $50,000 than a $150,000 single-family home if both are subject to a similar fee. The impact fee programs described in published journals only rarely include provisions to waive fees for low- or moderate-income housing, although it is possible that such waivers are granted on a case-by-case basis.

Third, the trend toward using exactions to fund social services as well as infrastructure may make exactions more regressive. While roads and sewers are the services most commonly funded by impact fees, for example, fees for schools, police, and fire protection are increasingly popular. Fortunately school, police, and fire fees usually are less than a quarter of overall fee charges, because fees generally are utilized to defray only capital costs (for example, for classroom construction) as opposed to operating costs (for example, for teachers' salaries, which on an annualized basis are much larger). Nevertheless, given that a large portion of the poor are families with children, the burden of exactions for schools, police, or other social services likely is to fall disproportionately on poor households (compared with property tax, sales tax, or other alternatives).

Finally, residential exactions may impose a much higher absolute burden on poor households than tax increases because of their narrow revenue base and their ripple effects on housing prices. Exactions generate revenue only from newly built houses, while causing price increases throughout the housing market. In contrast, property tax increases generate revenue from the entire housing stock and either reduce or leave unaffected housing prices.[30] In a community with housing stock increasing at 2 percent per year, for example, an exaction of $1,000 per new housing unit will raise only as much revenue as a property tax increase averaging $20 per unit. If borne fully by buyers and renters, the exaction will generate an annual (amortized) price increase of around $40 per unit at a 4 percent real interest rate, twice the absolute burden of the property tax increase. In this simple calculation, the exaction-induced price increase will be smaller than the property tax increase only in the unlikely event that the community's growth rate is higher than the real interest rate.[31]

The windfall to property owners from the run-up in housing prices makes the burden of exactions even more regressive. In the example above, owners of developed property when exactions are imposed will avoid a $20 per year property tax increase and will capture a windfall increase in their property values worth $40 per year. For those who rent or have not bought yet, however, the situation is reversed: Instead of a $20 per year property tax increase (passed on in higher rents), they will pay a $40 per year rent increase (caused by the inflation in property values). The poor probably are underrepresented among the owners of developed property when exactions are imposed and overrepresented among the renters or would-be property buyers.

Growth Limits or Deteriorated Services

A fairly strong case can be made that stringent growth limitations impose greater burdens on the poor than exactions because the increases in housing prices and rents will be greater. Allowing services to deteriorate is more difficult to evaluate on equity grounds. The major factor to consider is which public services are permitted to deteriorate. On the one hand, if road investments are curtailed and traffic congestion increases, the poor might experience a less adverse impact than from exactions. Members of poor households generally drive fewer miles each year than more affluent people and place a lower monetary value on time wasted in traffic. On the other hand, if the deterioration occurs in public education, the poor may experience a more adverse impact than from exactions.

Conclusions

The equity arguments for exactions are not compelling. Exactions can serve as a form of windfall profits tax on developers or landowners if they are applied selectively and temporarily when markets are hot or when the local government is restricting building permits. If exactions are in place for a long time and do not vary with market conditions, however, they generally are borne by property buyers and renters. Exactions tend to redistribute wealth from younger to older and from poorer to more affluent households. They have these effects more than most of the relevant alternatives, although less than stringent growth limitations. This is particularly true of exactions on residential development and of exactions charged for social services, such as education or public safety. The key problem with residential exactions is that they reduce housing affordability for low- and moderate-income families by raising prices for both new and existing homes. The widespread use of waivers for low- and moderate-value housing could bring significant relief, but such waivers still are relatively rare.

8

Exactions and Efficiency

ADVOCATES OF EXACTIONS frequently argue that they not only are equitable, but also can be a useful tool to encourage efficient land and infrastructure use.[1] Such a scenario is easily imagined. A central authority in each metropolitan area would calculate the infrastructure costs of serving different types of developments on every available site. Developers would be offered a schedule of impact fees, based on these costs, so that they would consider the infrastructure costs of their development decisions.

In the real world, however, exaction practice falls so far short of this ideal that the question arises whether exactions will ever make significant contributions to efficiency. If a case can be made for exactions on efficiency grounds, the reason is that most realistic alternatives may be worse. Growth controls, for example, often are less efficient than exactions. While infrastructure user charges have great efficiency potential in theory, they rarely are structured to enhance efficiency in practice.

Infrastructure versus Social Services

The basic thrust of the efficiency argument is based on the idea that consumers of public services should be required to pay for them. If that were the case, consumers would have an incentive to use services only when and where they are valued at least as much as they cost. Making the responsible parties pay, in essence, assures that the benefit received is as great as the cost of providing it.

Society, however, has decided that numerous public services should be provided regardless of willingness or ability to pay. Such services include those thought important to ensure equality of opportunity for all citizens and to provide a safety net for the less fortunate.[2] The minimum level of service that society is obligated to provide is controversial. Primary and secondary education are offered without tuition, for example, to ensure equality of opportunity and a well-educated citizenry necessary for a democracy. Some argue, however, that the quality of free public education is too low or that the principle should be extended to the university level. Similarly, assistance is provided to the poor in the form of welfare, but some believe society should expand its obligations to include universal access to health care, affordable housing, affordable day care, and other services.

Water, sewage, solid waste disposal, and transportation services are likewise important to poor households. The arguments for free provision are less compelling, however, than those for education, health, or other services that seem more central to ensuring equal opportunity. Charging users for these services is unlikely to cut off access entirely for any household and would encourage households to consider carefully the amount of service demanded.

Although exactions are assessed most commonly for core public infrastructure, they also are assessed for public services for which equity considerations are thought more important, such as schools, police stations, or day care. Charging exactions for such social services or facilities is inconsistent with the principle that they should be available regardless of ability to pay. An exaction for school buildings or police stations, for example, effectively amounts to a charge on the users of school or police services (insofar as home buyers and tenants bear exaction costs).[3]

These social services must be financed somehow, and the question becomes whether alternative financing sources would be less like an indirect user charge than exactions. Low-income families and other recipients pay a share when social services are financed out of general property, sales, or income taxes. But general taxes are spread more widely over the community than exactions and more likely are to be designed with concern for ability to pay.

Incentives for Low Exactions

The present system establishes incentives for local governments to under-charge developers even for services or facilities for which a broad consensus exists that users should pay. In the first place, local governments are not encouraged to consider the infrastructure costs that their developments impose on neighboring communities or higher levels of government. Courts generally have prohibited local communities from including these spillover costs, even if they were inclined to do so. As a consequence, under present incentives and constraints, exactions can be utilized only to promote efficiency in the use of locally provided infrastructure, which may be a small portion of the total infrastructure system.

Local communities also tend to be conservative in calculating their costs. The practical and conceptual obstacles to figuring out whether development pays its way, and thus whether exactions or other charges might be justified, are formidable. These calculations are hampered by the rational nexus standard, which, as described in chapter 4, normally requires local communities to demonstrate that exaction-financed facilities clearly are attributable to new development.

The rational nexus test has led many communities to adopt a three-step process for calculating impact fee formulas or schedules.[4] Local officials often understate their costs all along the way, as the calculation of the fee charged new single-family houses for county roads in Palm Beach, Florida, during the 1980s illustrates.[5]

The first step is to calculate the average daily use of the infrastructure service for the type of development. In the Palm Beach case, planners estimated that the average single-family household made twelve vehicle trips per day, each averaging six miles in length, for a total of seventy-two vehicle miles per day. The Palm Beach County commissioners decided to charge developers only for the first mile of each trip (for a total of twelve daily vehicle miles per household), assuming that no one could dispute that at least one mile of each trip was made on county roads.

The second step is to calculate the cost of providing the infrastructure service. Palm Beach computed the typical cost of building a lane-mile of road as $150,000 (in one direction) and estimated that each lane-mile had a daily capacity of 6,000 vehicles if a level of service of C (a traffic engineering measure of congestion) was maintained. A one-time capital cost of $25 per daily vehicle mile was determined ($150,000 divided by 6,000 vehicles). For twelve daily vehicle miles, the cost was $300 per household.[6]

The final step is to deduct funds available from other sources, such as state grants and contributions by current and future residents via, for example, gasoline taxes and local property taxes. When the Palm Beach fee was established in 1979, the methods for calculating these credits were not well developed. The county commissioners arbitrarily reduced the fee by five-sixths, to $50 per house, to make it safe from legal challenge. More elaborate methods have been developed since 1979, but the incentive to be conservative remains.[7] After devising a far more elaborate calculation, for example, the city of San Francisco determined that its costs of supplying transit service for downtown workers amounted to $10 per square foot of office space, then reduced the fee to $5 to ensure its legal defensibility.[8]

Local governments also may undercharge out of a desire to remain competitive in attracting new development. This motivation, while rarely explicit, probably is widespread. Manatee County, Florida, for example, deliberately reduced road impact fees charged for commercial, institutional, and industrial (but not housing) developments 40 to 75 percent below calculated costs to remain competitive with fees charged by neighboring counties.[9]

These several incentives to undercharge, taken together, easily can result in fees far smaller than total costs. A local jurisdiction will recover only 42 percent of its own costs if, to avoid legal challenge, it excludes 25 percent of its costs in each of the three steps in the typical fee calculation process. It will recover only 12.5 percent if it excludes 50 percent of its costs at each step. This is aside from the failure to charge for costs borne by other jurisdictions— federal, state, and local.

The tendency to undercharge may decline over time. Local officials may become less conservative in their calculations, for example, as they gain sophistication and practice in the art. Competition for low exactions also may abate as charging exactions becomes more widespread. The problem of jurisdictional spillovers also might be alleviated if the courts allowed local governments to collect on behalf of neighboring jurisdictions and higher levels of government. Nevertheless, the incentives to undercharge are so strong at present that many reforms would be necessary to approximate full cost recovery.

Exactions versus User Charges

Despite the incentives to undercharge, exactions may promote efficiency more effectively than the alternatives. Local property or sales taxes probably do not encourage efficient land or infrastructure use, so exactions may be the better choice. The more challenging competition comes from infrastructure user charges, which have a large potential to promote efficiency.[10] While exactions are assessed on the basis of the number of units of development (for example, per square foot per dwelling unit), user charges are assessed on the basis of actual consumption (for example, per thousand gallons of water, per bus ride, or per mile driven).

Exactions and user charges appear to promote efficiency in distinct ways. Well-structured exactions might provide incentives for developers to build in the right places, while user charges might encourage occupants of existing developments to economize in the use of infrastructure services. In fact, user charges can provide some incentives for efficient land development as well as infrastructure use, given that prospective buyers or tenants consider their expected user charges in calculating what they are willing to pay for newly developed property. Infrastructure user charges rarely are significant in real-world development decisions, however, in part because they seldom are structured to signal the different costs of serving different locations.

The Comparison in Theory

In theory, a combination of exactions and user charges would be best to simultaneously encourage efficient land and infrastructure use. Most economists would recommend user charges based on the marginal (or incremental) costs of supplying additional units of infrastructure service and exactions based on the marginal costs of connecting the development to the infrastructure systems. Both exactions and user charges would vary by location if their respective marginal costs also varied.

Such a strategy would entail a greater reliance on user charges than exactions, because infrastructure costs on the whole vary far more with use than with location-dependent connection costs.[11] Consider, for example, the cost of providing water service to a new housing unit. The water system costs most directly associated with connecting a new housing unit to the system (instead of with use) are those for installing a water pipe from the unit to the nearest trunk line in the existing distribution system. Most of the remaining water system costs depend on the amount of water residents consume. The capacity of the reservoir or the water treatment plant and the diameters of the water distribution mains will have to be larger, for example, if the new residents are expected to irrigate large lawns, operate swimming pools, and otherwise consume water on a grand scale than if they are expected to consume parsimoniously. Certain assumptions about average use of the water system have to be made up front, when the development of an area is being planned, so that adequate reservoir and distribution capacity will be available as development takes place. The expected usage will be lower, and thus facilities smaller, however, if marginal cost pricing is planned. And just because a forecast of average use is used in capital planning does not mean that capacity costs should not be allocated on the basis of actual use. Holding those households that consume more water (and raise the average over time) responsible for more of the capacity costs than those that consume less is only fair and efficient.

Excessive reliance on exactions instead of user charges will cause efficiency problems in at least two ways. First, exactions provide no incentives for existing residents to curb consumption. In the water example, costly future expansion of reservoir capacity might be avoided by curtailing consumption growth by existing, as well as new, residents. Second, exactions provide no incentive for new residents, once they have chosen where to live, to control consumption. Exactions geared to the capital costs of serving different locations may influence the siting of new development, but once it is occupied the new residents will face the same low user charges as existing residents. The lower the anticipated user charges, moreover, the larger the forecast of infrastructure consumption and capacity that the public sector must use in planning for new development.

The Comparison in Practice

Comparing exactions with an idealized system of user charges may be unfair. In practice, infrastructure user charges (like exactions) almost invariably are set well below the relevant marginal costs. In the first place, infrastructure authorities typically base their user charges on average cost, which usually, but not always, is much lower than marginal cost. California water districts most commonly receive water from two sources, for example: wells that tap local groundwater and massive federal and state water diversion projects that bring water from distant rivers, such as the Colorado, to California population centers. The water from the state and federal diversion projects costs the water district only $10 to $40 per acre foot, but the supply is limited and further diversions would be much more costly and provoke strong environmental opposition. Meanwhile, the cost of extracting local groundwater is $100 per acre foot or more. The California water districts price on the basis of average cost, say $60 acre foot, mixing in their cheap state and federal diversion water with their more expensive groundwater. In so doing, they encourage waste. If they charged $100 per acre foot (the marginal cost), not only would they be sure that every customer valued the water at least as much as the marginal cost of supplying it, but they also would reduce the pressures for new, even more costly, projects to expand supply.

Another way public authorities often underprice infrastructure use is by basing prices on historical instead of replacement costs. A reservoir built at the turn of the century, for example, may have depreciated very little, but the current cost of an additional or replacement reservoir would be several orders of magnitude larger than its original cost. If the bonds originally used to finance the reservoir have been paid off, moreover, public authorities often do not impose capital charges at all.

Finally, infrastructure services frequently are mispriced because charges are the same regardless of location, time of day, or season—while costs are variable. Highway construction and maintenance are financed mainly by motor fuel taxes, for example, which are a form of user charge. Motor fuel taxes are the same regardless of time of day or location, as fuel consumption rates change only modestly with speed and congestion. The marginal cost of providing for motorists varies enormously, however. Because highways are sized to meet peak, not off-peak, demand, for example, increases in off-peak motoring entail little cost. Highways also are much more expensive to construct in the center of a metropolitan area than on its periphery. While fuel tax receipts approximately cover highway construction and maintenance costs in urban areas, rush-hour and core area motorists are charged well below their marginal costs; those driving in off-peak periods and in outlying locations in general are overcharged.[12] The problem is not confined to highways. Water demand peaks in the summer, but water charges seldom vary with season, for example, and sewage and water rates are constant from location to location even though some sites clearly are more difficult to serve than others.

Modifying infrastructure user charges so that they more closely approximate marginal costs may be difficult, but the objections to doing so are not always convincing. One objection is that public infrastructure authorities often are constrained to collect only enough user revenues to cover their current costs, usually out of a concern to avoid burdening users unduly or a desire to impose fiscal discipline on authority managers. Marginal cost pricing would enable the authority to reap enormous profits if, as often appears the case, marginal costs significantly exceed average costs. Several ways exist of avoiding this problem, however, such as "lifeline" pricing in which a basic level of service, well below what most users will demand, is priced below marginal cost while extra (or marginal) units of service are priced at marginal cost.

A more difficult objection to answer is that collecting the appropriate user charges would impose enormous administrative costs on the authority or inconvenience to its customers, especially where marginal costs vary by location, season, or time of day. This objection most often is raised in the case of highways. Special rush-hour tolls on a few critical and congested facilities would do much to alleviate the problem of underpricing in some cities, however, and electronic methods of toll collection recently have been developed that greatly reduce collection costs and inconvenience.[13] For most other infrastructure services, such as water, sewage, and solid waste, moreover, the administrative difficulties of varying fees by location or season would seem relatively modest.

If, as a practical matter, charging infrastructure users their marginal costs in every circumstance is difficult, can exactions help compensate? The efficiency gains would depend in part on whether the exactions were designed to compensate for the specific shortcomings of the user charge system. From the perspective of promoting efficient land use, for example, exactions varying by location might be most important. The costs of providing infrastructure services differ considerably among locations in any metropolitan area because of diversification in topography, densities of existing developments, and distances from central infrastructure facilities or employment centers. By contrast, infrastructure user charges typically do not.

The efficiency gains also would depend on the extent to which the development types in the exaction or impact fee schedule accurately predict future infrastructure use. The number of commuting workers per square foot in an office building may vary enormously from average or typical levels, for example. A housing development may be occupied disproportionately by two-worker families or, at the other extreme, by retirees. Exactions will be a more reasonable second-best alternative to appropriate user charges in promoting efficient land use if the development types can be categorized to accurately reflect future consumption.

Given these conditions, the prospects for efficiency gain may be less where exactions are promulgated in an impact fee schedule or formula than where they are negotiated on a case-by-case basis. At present, the impact fee schedules or formulas typically employed appear too simplistic to spur greater land use efficiency. Fees on commercial development usually vary only by the square footage of the building, for example, and fees for housing may vary only by the square footage of the unit or the number of bedrooms and by the type (for example, single-family versus townhouse). A survey in the late 1980s revealed that only 5 percent of communities change their impact fees by location, although some notable exceptions exist.[14] San Francisco charges mass transit impact fees for offices in the downtown but not elsewhere, for example, and St. Luce County, Florida, charges fees nine times higher on its barrier island than on the mainland because of the high costs of building bridges to the island.[15] Some localities also will accept a lower fee if developers can demonstrate that their project has costs lower than the formula suggests, but the reverse appears to be rare.[16] By contrast, where exactions are negotiated on a case-by-case basis, local officials have more discretion to tailor the charge to the specific shortcomings of the user charge system, although whether this is a major consideration in many exaction negotiations is unclear.

Even if exactions do not differ much by location within a single community, they may promote efficiency by varying among communities. The relationship, however, between differences in exactions among communities and in local unit infrastructure costs is uncertain. Communities may impose higher than average exactions more out of concern about rapid growth or hot real estate markets, for example, than evidence of unusually high unit infrastructure costs. Communities also may impose charges similar to those of their neighbors, even though infrastructure costs vary, so as not to deter development unduly.

Exactions versus Growth Limits or Deteriorated Services

Exactions may be less efficient than idealized user charges, but they probably are more efficient than growth limitations. The marginal costs of growth could be so high in some communities that no development is the efficient solution. Where the costs of growth are not so high, however, exactions that cover or approximate those costs normally will be more efficient than a stringent limitation on growth. In the former case, developments with benefits that exceed their costs can proceed, while in the latter case they might not.

Comparisons between exactions and allowing local public services to deteriorate for lack of funding are more difficult. Allowing infrastructure services to deteriorate somewhat may be sensible if marginal costs are rising steeply. As an area becomes built-up and road expansion becomes more costly, for example, maintaining traffic congestion generally is not economical. Stated another way, the economically efficient level of congestion is higher in a high-density than a low-density city.[17]

Conclusions

Any conclusions about the relative efficiency of exactions have to be tentative, given that the evidence is limited and that any assessment is dependent on the particular circumstances involved. In theory, efficient land and infrastructure use would be best promoted by a system that relied more heavily on user charges than exactions to recoup most infrastructure costs. In practice, exactions might compensate for some of the deficiencies in existing user charges, but probably only when the exactions were carefully tailored to the deficiencies of the user charge system.

Exactions usually are more efficient than severely limiting growth, however. Whether exactions are better than allowing services to deteriorate is harder to say.

9

The Political Economy of Exactions

FOR ANALYTIC PURPOSES we have thus far treated aspects of the exaction phenomenon in relative isolation. We seek here to weave the themes that have emerged from these partial analyses into a coherent appraisal. These themes are, most notably, as follows: First, the recent surge in exaction usage is an epochal development in the history of American land use policy.[1] Second, even if one accepts the basic premise underlying exaction usage, that all new development should cover the full local cost of service expansion and mitigation attributable to it, wide room exists for dispute about the scope and scale of exactions that can be justified. Third, the most indisputable virtue of exactions is their utility as an instrument of growth conflict resolution, rather than as an instrument of fiscal or land use planning. Fourth, the growing popularity of exactions reflects a broader trend in American government toward regulation for revenue. The central premise of this trend—that responsibility for communal needs can be allocated objectively to private parties—is largely a myth. Finally, while the ascendancy of exactions owes less to their intrinsic virtues than to the growing unpopularity of leading alternatives, they merit recognition in many contemporary circumstances as the "least bad" option available.

Evolutionary or Epochal?

Exactions have become highly significant since the late 1970s in at least three major respects: as a source of revenue, particularly for public capital investments to accommodate growth; as an instrument for the resolution of local growth conflicts; and as a stimulus for the integration of land use regulation, public investment, and overall fiscal policy at the local level. These developments have represented adjustments to, and must be viewed in the context of, a sharp intensification of fiscal austerity and of conflict about the desirability of growth in most American localities. They are by no means, in short, isolated phenomena. They are critical elements, though, and salient markers of a set of land use policy changes that clearly, in our judgment, merit designation as epochal.

Sources of Impetus

Through the mid-1960s, business, labor, and media interests successfully nurtured a progrowth consensus in most localities. These groups shaped local opinion, financed campaigns, mobilized votes, and supplied a major share of candidates for local office (including lawyers, real estate agents, and insurance brokers as well as individuals directly engaged in development or land speculation). The progrowth consensus did not extend to all forms of development. Public housing projects, for example, were viewed negatively in most communities. But the zone of consensus was broad, and distinguishing between desirable and undesirable development generally seemed easy.

Since the late 1960s, the progrowth coalition has been increasingly countervailed at the local level by neighborhood, environmental, and taxpayer groups. What began as a pattern of neighborhood resistance to particularly unsettling projects has evolved into one of wide concern about the negative effects of development, both public and private, on the quality of life. These tendencies are most pronounced in affluent bedroom suburbs and in communities experiencing prolonged real estate booms, but they are evident to some degree almost everywhere.

We have analyzed the decline of the progrowth consensus and the concomitant rise of both antigrowth activism and exaction requirements from seven angles: neighborhood activism, environmentalism, the citizen tax revolt, cutbacks in federal aid, growing concern about infrastructure backlogs, proliferating federal and state mandates, and new perceptions emerging from the progress of fiscal impact analysis. These factors have, we maintain, at once intensified local controversy about growth, raised local consciousness about the need to accompany it with adequate public investment, and diminished access to the fiscal resources on which local governments previously relied to finance such investment.

Those anxious to avoid the negative impacts of growth may pursue a variety of strategies. On the one hand, they can oppose new development. If, on the other hand, they remain open to growth, they can strive to ensure the mitigation of its negative impacts. The sources from which mitigation funding might be obtained are local taxpayers, higher levels of government, and those who stand to profit if new development goes forward. (A final option frequently materializes after the fact—resigned acceptance of public service degradation as growing demand overwhelms existing capabilities. However, no one ever announces this strategy at the time development permits are under consideration.)

In practice, tax increases to facilitate development are generally out of the question; grants-in-aid are inadequate to meet existing local needs; and growth advocates continue to play a major role in the politics of most communities. It is in this context that local officials have turned increasingly to developers for public revenue to accommodate growth.

Trends

Only about 10 percent of American localities imposed exactions before 1960; by the mid-1980s, roughly 90 percent did so. Prior to 1960, nearly all exactions involved land donations or on-site, in-kind construction; by the mid-1980s, roughly three-fifths of all communities levied cash (impact fee) as well as in-kind exactions. Before 1960, almost all exactions were for core infrastructure (streets, water mains, and sewage lines); by the mid-1980s, exaction purposes commonly included open space, environmental facilities, and public buildings, and a few jurisdictions mandated developer commitments to social programs—either in the form of capital investment (for example, low-cost housing) or ongoing services (for example, day care).

Exaction dollar magnitudes have soared as well. The available data are fragmentary, but one survey of twenty-three localities in Southern California showed impact fees rising 511 percent from 1975 to 1983. A series of surveys by the Florida Advisory Commission on Intergovernmental Relations indicated that impact fees in that state tripled from 1985 to 1991. Exactions now comprise, as near as can be determined, 5 to 10 percent of new construction costs in most fast-growing communities and states. A 1991 survey of localities in several leading exaction states (mainly California, Florida, Oregon, and Washington) revealed average impact fees in the range of $5–7 per square foot for both residential and commercial developments. The average for a two thousand square foot house was about $12,000.

How Much Is Enough?

Exaction advocates maintain that considerable room for growth still exists, because the marginal cost of local infrastructure needed to serve a new residence was already in the range of twice this amount by the mid-1980s.[2] They may well be right. But systematic evidence as to "need" is lacking, and localities do not, it seems clear, routinely make investments of this magnitude to accompany new development.

The only hard evidence on public infrastructure investment, regrettably, is national in scale and refers to historic rather than marginal costs. Additionally, it aggregates investment for all purposes—renovation, replacement, and upgrading to meet new standards as well as capacity expansion; investment to serve rising per capita service demands as well as new demands attributable to growth; and investment to serve commercial and industrial as well as residential needs. The data are suggestive, however. They indicate that the entire net stock of state and local infrastructure as of 1990, on a historic cost depreciated basis, totaled $7,047 per capita in 1987 dollars. The locally owned share (financed in part by intergovernmental aid) was 62 percent, or about $4,400.

New gross investment by all levels of government combined—excluding that for defense, international relations, space, and postal service—totaled $138.4 billion in 1990, or roughly $551 per capita.[3] Localities expended 56 percent of this sum, or $308 per capita, but the revenue streams on which they drew included intergovernmental aid.[4] The U.S. government does not collect data on the revenue sources used to finance specific expenditures. It does, however, report the federal and state aid portion of overall local revenue, which was 37 percent in 1990.[5] Assuming that intergovernmental aid financed a comparable share of capital outlay expenditures, localities invested $194 per capita of their own-source revenue in 1990. The preponderance of this investment, almost certainly, was for purposes other than accommodating new growth. If one-third was to serve new growth (an estimate that we suspect is on the generous side), localities invested about $65 per capita for this purpose in 1990.

Let us assume further that one-half of this total was attributable to residential (as opposed to commercial, industrial, retail, governmental, and nonprofit) development. The result is an estimate of $33 per capita for the purpose of accommodating new residential development; or, since the average household consisted of 2.7 persons, $89 per household.[6] The annual rate of new housing construction during the 1980s averaged 1.8 percent of the existing stock.[1] This suggests that local investment of own-source revenue attributable to new housing was running as of 1990 in the range of $4,900 per new unit.

The disparity between these two sets of estimates is puzzling. Conceivably, they reflect actual differences between historic and marginal costs, but the evidence for such a conclusion is extremely weak. What is certain, though, is that the figures preferred by exaction advocates imply an extraordinarily high premium for access to new as opposed to existing infrastructure.

Catalysts for Compromise

The great political appeal of exactions is that they seem free to nearly everyone involved in local affairs. They do not show up on anyone's tax bill, and while they are likely to drive up developer prices they remain imperceptible even to purchasers as a distinct cost item. (Since purchaser identities are generally unknown at the time permit decisions are made, and even if known the individuals concerned are often outsiders to the community, their views do not count politically in any event.) So, faced with criticism for growing infrastructure inadequacies, local officials find in exactions a uniquely attractive instrument to finance at least the portion of community investment requirements that plausibly can be attributed to new development. Perhaps even more significantly, they find in exactions a marvelously flexible instrument for crafting compromises.

Developers are less sanguine about exactions, because they like to keep their costs down. But they typically view exactions as just one cost item among many, and they often perceive the alternatives to be prolonged local controversy or outright rejection of their plans. Their primary concern is to make money. If the total regulatory package—zoning restrictions, building codes, environmental rules, and exactions—leaves them room to do so, they almost always are disposed to go along. If not, they are inclined to look elsewhere for opportunities, or to wait for another day, rather than to engage in public protest or litigation. Delays are likely to cost them more than anything they can hope to gain, and they generally have a continued need for the favorable exercise of regulatory discretion.

In short, while increasingly significant as a source of revenue to finance new infrastructure, exactions are even more significant as a catalyst for the resolution of local conflicts that threaten to block development altogether.

Stimulus for Policy Integration

Local planning and land use regulation traditionally have been outside the mainstream of local decision making. Most frequently they have been entrusted to independent commissions and conceived as quasi-judicial (because their main component activity has been case adjudication). When actually planning, local land use agencies have tended to ignore fiscal and other immediate considerations, preferring to articulate long-term, "feel good" visions. As exactions have come into fashion, though, it has become increasingly apparent, first, that land use regulation is about community objectives, not just the resolution of private conflicts; and second, that to be effective as a communal instrument it must be thoroughly integrated with fiscal, environmental, and public works policy making. Where exaction financing is well advanced, these ideas are now taken for granted, and this integration is often far advanced.

Regulation for Revenue

The generic purposes for which regulation is deemed appropriate have gradually expanded over the past century. The initial purpose was to prohibit categories of behavior deemed antisocial in all circumstances; for example, conspiracy in restraint of trade, the marketing of adulterated products, or operating common carrier vehicles with reckless disregard for safety. Over time, regulation began to be employed as well for the control of behavior deemed appropriate in some circumstances but not others. Traditional zoning, for example, asserts a need to segregate socially valuable land uses in accord with local plans. The issue is not that any specific category, such as heavy industry, is antisocial, but rather that it should be located where its unpleasant side effects will least damage the interests of other land users. Next, policy makers concluded that many legitimate activities, even if carried out in appropriate circumstances, are prone to have unacceptable side-effects—for example, emissions of air pollutants in excess of public health standards—and that the responsible parties are properly required to avert such effects at their own expense. Finally, the idea has emerged, particularly since the 1960s, that regulation is a suitable method of revenue generation for public purposes even where considerable ambiguity exists about who is to blame for the communal needs to be addressed.

We reserve the term "regulation for revenue" for this final category. The bounds between categories are often less clear in practice than conceptually, but ambiguity is generally a sign that assignments of responsibility are discretionary.

Additional complications are introduced if we relax the premise that those to whom expenditures are attributable should pay. Most Americans agree, for example, that schools should be financed on the basis of egalitarian, not market, principles. Thus state aid, generated by broad-based income and sales taxes, has come in recent decades to exceed locally raised revenue as a nationwide source of school finance. Within local jurisdictions, moreover, no one argues that school resources should be allocated to neighborhoods in accord with their tax contributions, or that businesses should be exempt from contributing because they have no children.

Such cases, in which cost allocation is intrinsically more political than analytic, provide a wide-open door to regulation for revenue.

National, State, and Regional Perspectives

Any analysis of exactions would be severely skewed if supra-local patterns and trends were ignored.

The critical trend, reaching back to the 1960s, has been one of gradual withdrawal by the federal government from fiscal responsibility for infrastructure development. Whereas the federal share of core infrastructure investment (highways, transit, water, sewer, and aviation) was approximately one-half in the mid-1960s, it was one-sixth by the end of the 1980s. Federal aid for all purposes contracted severely in the 1980s, moreover, with devastating effects on state and particularly local finances. As a share of GNP, federal grants declined by one-third, from 3.6 percent to 2.4 percent. Simultaneously, the federal government moved sharply away from direct aid to localities. The local share of federal aid declined by nearly half, from 27 percent to 14 percent. The combined effect was a two-thirds reduction in federal aid by comparison with local own-source revenue, from 15 percent to 5 percent. Money is fungible, so scarcity in any policy domain unavoidably affects others.

The larger pattern, consistent throughout American history, is one of extreme, many would say excessive, reliance on local governments to regulate land use and finance public infrastructure. Local governments have a distinctive perspective on the nexus between real estate development and infrastructure demand—because of their small scale in relation to daily flows of goods and people and because of their traditional reliance on real property as a source of revenue. They can hope to capture the best features of new development (for example, tax revenue from a new office complex) while deflecting many of the worst (for example, expenditure requirements for schooling the office workers' children). They also fear that other localities will succeed better than they at this beggar-thy-neighbor game. Whatever the outcome, local governments are likely to associate infrastructure requirements with specific locational choices rather than with such aggregates as rising per capita incomes, changing patterns of production and distribution, rising environmental standards, and depreciation. The are likely to distinguish sharply, moreover, between current residents and employers, on the one hand, and those who will arrive if proposed developments go forward, on the other.

From a national standpoint, by contrast, new infrastructure requirements seem attributable mainly to aggregate trends rather than locational choices. The only real newcomers are immigrants, who tend to occupy old housing. States and regions have less comprehensive perspectives than the national government, but even they are large enough to contain the employment and shopping as well as housing locations of nearly all their residents, and to view the great majority of moves from existing to new structures as internal. They cannot hope to specialize in the most attractive fiscal categories of land use or to avoid many of the worst. By the same token, they rarely need fear as locational decisions are pending that they will be left with only the negative effects (for example, traffic jams generated by employment centers in neighboring communities). Finally, their principal sources of revenue are income and sales taxes, which rise automatically and unobtrusively with the level of economic activity, rather than property taxes, which rise only in the wake of highly visible reassessments or rate increases. For all these reasons, higher-level governments are generally committed to economic growth and view it as paying its own way.

Finally, localities in the fastest-growing regions, and particularly on their fringes, often grow far more rapidly than any state. The consequences are twofold. First, insofar as new development generates expenditure needs before it becomes a full contributor to public revenue streams, the burden on existing taxpayers is predominantly a function of the rate of growth. One percent annual growth may be scarcely noticeable, while a 10 percent growth rate may require large increases in revenue per capita. Second, insofar as new development has quality of life effects—for example, on traffic conditions, the disappearance of open space, and the appearance of neighbors with un-familiar behavior patterns—these are likely to be most noticeable when the rate of change is rapid. As statewide, and even regional, officials listen to constituents, therefore, they typically hear a broader range of messages about growth (many of them highly positive) than their counterparts in the fastest-growing localities.

Legal Constraints and Loopholes

State governments have participated in the exaction revolution almost entirely as regulators of local practice. Responding primarily to developer initiatives—legal suits in state courts, lobbying initiatives in state legisla-tures—they have coalesced in recent years around the rational nexus stan-dard, which provides that exactions can be used only to finance expenditures attributable to new development, that projects can be assessed no more than their proportionate shares of public investments attributable to multiple causes, that exaction requirements must be in accord with a local plan, and that expenditures of impact fee revenues must occur in timely fashion.

At face value, the rational nexus standard limits exactions to ensuring that existing residents suffer no harm, fiscal or otherwise, in consequence of new development. This is scarcely the end of the story, however. State laws and judicial precedents constrain localities insofar as they levy exactions by for-mula, but they have far less impact on discretionary, or negotiated, exactions. Even as state courts and legislatures have been articulating rational nexus constraints, moreover, they have become increasingly tolerant of discretion-ary land use regulation generally.

Discretionary regulation enables local officials to take account of the spe-cific circumstances of each case, including public opinion, but it also can extend review periods indefinitely and render investors highly vulnerable to informal demands. Where permitting is discretionary, developers often con-sider it prudent to volunteer exaction-type commitments. These are typically labeled "proffers" rather than exactions to signal their "voluntary" nature, but they scarcely seem voluntary to those who make them.

Equally important, though rarely discussed, the cost accounting estimates required by the rational nexus standard are inescapably rooted in policy de-cisions. No refinements in the techniques of fiscal impact analysis can alter this fact. The problem is that nearly all public expenditure requirements, including those for new infrastructure, arise from a wide variety of causes, and that decisions about who should pay involve value choices as well as technical findings.

Illustratively, in a community with both new housing and new commercial developments, what portion of the costs of serving commuting and shopping trips should be assigned to residences and what portion to the businesses? In theory, one might estimate the increase in vehicle mileage on local roads if the community allowed only new business development, compare this figure with the increase if only new residential development were allowed, and allocate costs accordingly. But such estimates require intrinsically uncertain judgments about where residents would work, and where workers would reside, in various scenarios. A likely conclusion, moreover, is that the two categories of development are truly "joint," in that there are dynamic feedback effects between residential and commercial development decisions.

Even more puzzlingly, to what extent should developers be held responsible for the "indirect" effects of activities in their buildings? The advocates of housing linkage, for example, maintain that new buildings attract new business activities, which in turn lure new employees from out of town, some of whom choose to live in the host community. Generating new jobs used to be considered unambiguously a good thing. According to linkage theory, however, it is a negative, because new housing market entrants tend to drive up housing prices, causing hardship for low-income households. It follows that office developers should be responsible for increasing the supply of affordable housing. Carrying the argument further, some believe that office developers should be responsible for any harm attributable to the employees of enterprises housed in older structures that do business with those in new developments. Such establishments may add workers, some of whom are from out of town, and so on.

Finally, no consensus exists on how the costs of functions deemed unsuitable for user financing should be allocated. Most local services are in this category, including education, police and fire protection, public health and social services, parks and libraries, judicial and incarceration services, and overhead administration. Many would add highway, transit, water, sewer, and other basic infrastructure services to this list, at least insofar as the "lifeline" requirements of low-income users are concerned. The costs of nearly all these services can be traced to specific residential neighborhoods, but to levy taxes or fees by location would violate the principle that the services should be available on the basis of need, regardless of ability to pay.

State courts rarely second-guess local findings on these matters, so long as local officials can demonstrate that they have used reputable cost allocation techniques, that they have made no egregious analytic errors, and that their exaction decisions are more or less rooted in their findings. The decisive requirement, in short, is to make a plausible, not a compelling, case.

Appraisal Criteria

While the courts and most participants in local land use policy making generally appraise exactions with reference to causality (that is, who can properly be held accountable for new expenditure requirements?), we find it more instructive to focus on outcomes (asking, most notably, what are the equity and efficiency consequences of reliance on exaction financing, by comparison with those of alternative policies?).

Equity

Virtually all contestants in land use debates can generally make persuasive arguments that their positions are most equitable, or fair. The explanation lies in their different answers to the following questions: What criterion of equity is most pertinent? Who ultimately bears the costs of exactions? And what are the most relevant alternatives with which exactions should be compared?

Local actors generally highlight the equity criterion of holding existing residents harmless; that is, of making sure that new development fully pays its own way. State governments, primarily at the urging of developers, emphasize the complement of this criterion, that new development should be required to pay no more than the costs directly attributable to it. Those concerned about equity in statewide and national policy debates, by contrast, stress the criterion of fiscal progressivity—assessment in accord with ability to pay. Companion themes are intergenerational equity and the promotion of socioeconomic integration.[8]

Who actually bears the costs of exactions? The popular view is that developers pay, since they are the ones who agree to the permit conditions and write the checks. Economists, however, paint a more complicated picture, noting that developers certainly try (though not always with success) to pass along all cost increases to their customers, with a markup for overhead, financing costs, and profit.

Developers are best able to recover their full exaction costs from consumers when the following three conditions are met: exaction requirements are stable (and thus have been reflected from the earliest stages of planning for current projects); all nearby communities that consumers view as similar impose comparable exactions (so evasion is difficult); and real estate markets are stable. Real estate development is a highly competitive business, so developers in stable markets generally have profit margins dictated by the returns to capital in alternative lines of business. If profit margins rise much above this level, production increases. If they decline much below it, production contracts. Also, similar communities in any given metropolitan area tend over time to levy comparable exactions, because they are exposed to similar market and political pressures. Exaction costs, as a result, cannot in the long run be borne by developers.

Landowners, too, are sensitive to the returns available from other options than sale to developers. Some of their alternative returns are denominated in terms of economic exchange (for example, earnings from farming or expectations of higher prices in the future), while others involve pleasure in use (for example, a farmer's reluctance to give up land that supports a way of life or an affluent homeowner's joy in possessing an estate-sized parcel).[9] But these returns are real, and they are responsive to movements in the price of land. So developers are rarely able to pass a significant share of their exaction costs back to landowners.

Consumers can avoid paying exaction costs in some circumstances, but these tend to be transitional. When exactions are rising, for example, developers are often caught with projects in the pipeline. The question before them at this point is not whether the project will yield adequate profit but whether the marginal benefits of proceeding outweigh those of cancellation. Even if they judge that they cannot raise prices, therefore, to offset their unanticipated exaction costs, they are likely to go forward. Likewise, in hot real estate markets where developers cannot keep up with demand and are earning above-normal profits, they frequently bear exaction costs. Because they are already charging what the market will bear, they cannot raise prices any further; but since their profits are so high they have no reason to curtail production. In this situation, local exaction requirements can function as a form of windfall profits tax.

Four points bear emphasis with respect to overheated real estate markets. First, they can result from ordinary market fluctuations or from government decisions to hold the supply of building permits below the level that the market will support. Second, pure market booms tend to burn out quickly, because developers increase production to the point of market glut. Third, tight markets sustained by permit restrictions typically are more long-lived, because developers are restrained from increasing production. They yield their largest windfalls, moreover, to those with great skill in pursuing permits rather than to those who simply own land or bring development skills to bear on it. Fourth, government-imposed supply restrictions are rarely significant at regionwide scale. Almost invariably, the central city and outer suburban jurisdictions are eager to grow, even if numerous inner suburbs are not.[10]

In considering who pays for exactions, finally, it is vital to consider ripple effects. While few empirical studies have been carried out, economic theory suggests that, to the extent exactions cause the prices of new buildings to rise, they pull up the prices of older structures as well. New and old properties compete in the same marketplace. So long as the premium that consumers are willing to pay for new space over old remains constant, both sets of prices move together. The consequences are vastly to magnify the cost of the original exaction from the standpoint of future buyers and renters. This increase does not generate any revenue for additional public improvements; it represents a pure windfall for current property owners. The transfer of wealth is in part intergenerational, because those who own property are on average considerably older than those who do not. More significantly, however, it is a transfer from less affluent to more affluent people.

Finally, how do exactions, particularly on residential development, compare with other serious policy options? We have focused on six, of which four are sources of public revenue (local property taxes, local sales taxes, local user fees, and intergovernmental aid) and two are alternatives to raising revenue (growth restrictions and neglect of public investment to accommodate growth). An underlying assumption in the following review of these alternatives is that residential exaction costs are generally borne by consumers.

The strongest case for exactions, by comparison with the realistic alternatives, is with reference to the criterion of holding current residents harmless. Only growth controls rank higher with reference to this criterion, and they do so by prohibiting rather than accommodating growth.

With reference to the criterion of avoiding discrimination against newcomers, on which state courts and legislatures have focused, the case for exactions is at best blurred. On the one hand, where exactions are based on painstaking rational nexus calculations, and where value choices are made explicit—for example, which costs should be allocated on the basis of usage and which on the basis of ability of pay, and how should levies on real property for common costs be allocated between the business and residential sectors—it seems reasonable to argue that the first order (direct cost) effects of exactions are roughly nondiscriminatory. On the other hand, the second-order (price ripple) effects tend to be highly discriminatory. In providing windfalls for existing property-owners, they severely penalize renters and future buyers. Negotiated exactions, moreover, often have little to do with rational nexus calculations and thus have considerable potential to discriminate even in their first-order effects.

The case for exactions—at least residential exactions—is particularly weak with reference to the criterion of progressivity. Residential exactions generally are levied on a flat-rate basis per room or per dwelling unit, without regard for price category. Consequently, they add a greater percentage to the cost of low- and moderate-income housing than to that of more luxurious housing. Although a few communities grant partial waivers for low- and moderate-income housing, it will be extremely difficult to alter the general pattern of regressivity so long as exactions are legally fees rather than taxes. If exactions are fees, they must be levied in accord with estimated usage instead of ability to pay. When states authorize waivers, they blur the distinction between exactions as fees and exactions as taxes.

Commercial exactions are another matter, because little can be said about who ultimately bears their cost. The eventual owners of newly developed commercial property are business enterprises, not end users. Like developers, they seek to recoup whatever they pay from their customers, who may themselves be other companies. Assuming that most enterprises charge what the traffic will bear regardless of their space costs, and that most have competitors in localities with lower exaction costs, exactions probably do not have significant effects on consumer prices. More likely, if the owners and renters of new space are unable to recoup their rent premiums, the demand for such space will diminish. Developers, in turn, facing weaker demand, will curtail production or shift their operations to communities with lower exaction costs. (And in the interim they may have to absorb some losses.)

Property taxes, while modestly regressive (the proportion of disposable income spent on housing tends to decline with income), are probably a good deal less regressive than exactions. Property taxes rise with property value, which tends roughly (though erratically from the standpoint of individual households) to correlate with household income.[11] Property tax increases, moreover, tend to deflate real estate prices—by raising the cost of carrying any given level of property value. If newcomers are lucky, the overall cost of ownership (capital and operating combined) may be unchanged in the wake of a property tax increase. What is a virtue from the standpoint of newcomers, though, is a vice from the standpoint of current owners; a property tax increase tends to reduce the value of their equity even as it increases their cost of operation. Not surprisingly, therefore, the property tax is the central focus of the contemporary tax revolt, and the last policy any local politician cares to advocate is a property tax increase to serve newcomers. Sales tax and user fee increases meet scarcely less resistance and tend to be even more regressive than property tax increases.

The option of permitting services to degrade, while never openly advocated, is often adopted, at least as one element of the community response to growth. Its effect is to spread the costs of growth, in the coin of service quality decline, throughout the community rather than concentrate them on newcomers. Distributional effects hinge on which services suffer. The poor, for example, have a greater stake in school than convention center improvements. In numerous circumstances, however, neglect at the margin is among the options most compatible with progressivity. The danger is that this strategy, if pushed too far, will generate a backlash in the form of demands for growth control.

Increases in intergovernmental aid have the greatest potential for progressivity, if financed by progressive federal and state taxes and distributed substantially on the basis of need. The allocation of aid for infrastructure has never been substantially need-based, however, and localities experienced severe cutbacks in overall federal aid during the 1980s. As of January 1993, the prospects appear favorable for a modest resurgence of federal infrastructure investment and, more generally, aid to localities. Numerous states that increased local aid during the 1980s, however, have struggled with their own fiscal crises during the early 1990s; and the greatest pressures they face for increased spending are in such domains as health, prisons, and education. Overall, it is difficult to imagine more than modest near-term relief for localities struggling to finance the public costs of growth.

The most realistic alternative to exactions in most communities under intense pressure to grow is particularly regressive. Growth controls, if stringent and widespread, are considerably more inflationary than exactions, because they force buyers to compete for an artificially restricted supply of new development. As with exactions, their inflationary effects ripple throughout the real estate markets to which they apply, and the windfall beneficiaries are existing property owners. Those frozen out of the community or placed in difficult financial straits are the least affluent participants in the local land use system.

Efficiency

Economists consider a levy "use efficient" if it requires consumers to internalize the marginal cost impacts of their decisions. The aim is to bring supply and demand into balance at a level that accurately reflects user willingness to pay. Household water usage tends to diminish sharply, for example, when localities shift from tax to metered charge financing. Residents start by fixing leaks and watering their lawns less frequently. If the prices become sufficiently high, they install such devices as low-flow toilets and shower heads.

While exactions might be structured to encourage use efficiency, they almost never are. They do tend to be higher in developing fringe communities than in localities near the core, so they act as a reminder to developers of the costs of sprawl. They do nothing to influence patterns of usage, however, once projects have been designed and constructed.

The serious question, then, is not whether exactions promote efficiency, but whether they are likely to substitute for policies that would. The most plausible contender is user charges. A sophisticated user charge system can differentiate rates by season, time of day, and even demand conditions monitored in real time, thereby holding down peak demand without imposing constraints during periods of slack capacity. The greatest value of such a revenue system is that it can enable service enterprises, whether public or private, to satisfy the greatest amount of demand with any fixed level of capacity. Thus, it may be feasible to defer, perhaps indefinitely, large-scale capacity expansion projects. If, for example, motorists with the least need to travel in peak hours could be induced by price differentials to travel off-peak, congestion and the pressure to build new highways would be sharply reduced.

While privately owned enterprises such as electric, phone, and airline companies have moved aggressively to exploit these principles in recent years, public agencies have not. Relevant market signals are almost entirely absent, most notably, in the highway sector, which accounts for roughly half of all infrastructure investment. Ironically, user levies (for example, gasoline taxes and vehicle registration fees) do cover most highway costs, but they are not designed to affect any motorist's decision about how much or when to drive.

One of the few things about which virtually all economists agree is that governments should rely more heavily on use efficient charges. Politicians are highly skittish about doing so, however, because they doubt their ability to persuade ordinary voters and media commentators that such charges are equitable. The problem is that most efficient price systems take no account of ability to pay. Economists respond that they can be structured to do so. Under pressure from state regulators, for example, numerous utilities now offer a basic minimum of service at a low (lifeline) price, making up for it with higher prices above that level. Governments adopting a road use charge system might, in similar fashion, issue vouchers to all vehicle owners for a basic level of use. This is extremely difficult to explain, however, and consumer groups are generally loathe to help because they view price systems as intrinsically less equitable than taxation.

More generally, the idea of calibrating prices to balance supply and demand is foreign to public debate. Politicians, and presumably most of their constituents, are much more at home with such concepts as equality of access, grandfathering of rights, and the need for revenue to finance historic costs (as represented by outstanding debt). When governments do impose charges, consequently, they rarely consider replacement prices or seek to influence demand with the aim of ameliorating pressure for expansion. Often, indeed, they set charges at even lower levels to solidify political support. California farmers who benefit from federal water projects, for example, pay as little as 10 percent of the current marginal cost of water, despite the existence of water crises in nearby urban areas. The source of this anomaly lies in policy decisions of the 1930s, which have been sustained by the political influence of their beneficiaries. There is a growing movement for tradeable water rights in arid parts of the United States and tradeable pollution permits; but there is little comparable support for reliance on charges to manage demand for urban infrastructure services. Even the airlines, for example, which are pioneers in the use of pricing to maximize yield from their own services, vigorously oppose such pricing by public airport authorities.

The other alternatives under consideration have no significant potential to promote efficiency. The option of growth restrictions, however, deserves a special word. Efficiency is about balancing supply and demand with a minimum of waste, not about walling off markets. Growth restrictions deny access to potential service beneficiaries without beginning to address the question of how the legitimate housing and public service claims of a growing population can be met with a minimum of waste.

Exactions Appraised

In principle, then, a variety of alternatives may be preferable to exactions. Intergovernmental aid and local broad-based taxes tend to be more progressive, user charges to be more efficient. The current reality in most growing jurisdictions, however, is that these options are politically unavailable for the purpose of accommodating new development, and that the public is ambivalent about how much growth to accept. The realistic alternatives, aside from exactions, are typically growth controls and passive neglect of infrastructure expansion. Growth controls are less equitable in most configurations than exactions. They offer no efficiency gains, and their most salient effects are either hardship for many low- and moderate-income households (if regional in scope) or accentuated urban sprawl (if growth is deflected from older communities to the metropolitan fringe). Neglect of infrastructure expansion is often preferable, but it is a policy with obvious limits. Few growing communities have sufficient infrastructure slack to rely on it for long without provoking a growth control backlash.

In this context, we believe, exactions merit recognition as an ingenious local adaptation to antitax and antigrowth pressures—highly imperfect, subject to abuse, and requiring state oversight, but often preferable to the likely alternatives.

Notes

Chapter 1

1. When monetary payments are viewed as substitutes for on-site, in-kind performance, they often are termed "in-lieu" fees. Legally, in-lieu fees can be used by local governments only to fund facilities for which they are authorized to mandate in-kind exactions. When monetary payments are viewed as user fees for connecting water and sewer systems, they frequently are known as "connection" fees. Where they are viewed as user fees to compensate public agencies for the cost of processing applications and inspections, they often are labeled "processing" fees.

See Brian W. Blaesser and Christine M. Kentopp, "Impact Fees: The 'Second Generation,'" *Journal of Urban and Contemporary Law*, vol. 38, no. 25 (1990), pp. 55–113, especially pp. 67–69, on the legal distinctions between in-lieu, connection, and impact fees. For a discussion that distinguishes several types of processing fees (for planning, engineering, and building department services) from other fee categories, see Bay Area Council, "Taxing the American Dream: Development Fees and Housing Affordability in the Bay Area" (San Francisco, 1988), especially p. 17.

These distinctions are fading in importance as more and more states provide broad authorization for monetary exactions. Until recently, however, the laws and judicial precedents of many states provided local governments with much clearer authority to levy fees in one or more of these specific categories than to levy impact fees more generally. While impact fees typically can be used for all of these purposes, they also can be drawn upon to fund a wide variety of off-site community investments—for example, road, waste treatment, and school improvements. The key legal test is whether the need for the improvements can be traced, at least in part, to the real estate projects on which the fees were levied. Where the facility need is traceable only in part to new development, the fee assessments are legally required to be proportionate.

2. See Donald G. Hagman and Julian Conrad Juergensmeyer, *Urban Planning and Land Development Control Law* (St. Paul: West Publishing, 1986), pp. 284–85; and Vicki Been,

" 'Exit' as a Constraint on Land Use Exactions: Rethinking the Unconstitutional Conditions Doctrine," *Columbia Law Review*, vol. 91 (1991), pp. 473–545, especially pp. 487–91.

3. The issue becomes far more complicated if the landowner is required to set aside land for a through-road and perhaps to defer nearby development until the community builds it. See Daniel R. Mandelker, "Interim Development Controls in Highway Programs: The Taking Issue," *Journal of Land Use and Environmental Law*, vol. 4 (Winter 1989), pp. 167–213, especially pp. 172–73, 179–81, 186–95, 210–13.

4. See the majority opinion of the U.S. Supreme Court in *Lucas v. South Carolina Coastal Council*, 1992 U.S. Lexis 4537 (1992), Section III:

> In 70-odd years of . . . regulatory takings jurisprudence we have generally eschewed any 'set formula' for determining how far is too far, preferring to 'engage in . . . essentially ad hoc, factual inquiries.' . . . We have, however, described at least two discrete categories of regulatory action as compensable without case-specific inquiry into the public interest advanced in support of the restraint. The first encompasses regulations that compel the property owner to suffer a physical 'invasion' of his property. In general (at least with regard to permanent invasions), no matter how minute the intrusion, and no matter how weighty the public purpose behind it, we have required compensation. . . . The second . . . is where regulation denies all economically beneficial or productive use of land.

This last point is elaborated upon, in footnote 7, as follows:

> Regrettably, the rhetorical force of our 'deprivation of all economically feasible use' rule is greater than its precision, since the rule does not make clear the 'property interest' against which the loss of value is to be measured. When, for example, a regulation requires a developer to leave 90% of a rural tract in its natural state, it is unclear whether we would analyze the situation as one in which the owner has been deprived of all economically beneficial use of the burdened portion of the tract, or as one in which the owner has suffered a mere diminution in the value of the tract as a whole. . . . The answer to this difficult question may lie in how the owner's reasonable expectations have been shaped by the State's law of property.

5. It may legitimately argue, furthermore, that an affordable housing requirement is no more expensive than a density restriction. It follows that the cost to developers of an affordable housing requirement can be offset, at least in part, by increases in allowable density. For a detailed description of one such program, including a density bonus provision, see Christie I. Baxter, *Moderately Priced Dwelling Units in Montgomery County, Maryland*, case C-16-91-1043.0 (John F. Kennedy School of Government, Harvard University, 1991). On inclusionary zoning more generally, see William A. Fischel, *The Economics of Zoning Laws: A Property Rights Approach to American Land Use Controls* (Johns Hopkins University Press, 1985), pp. 319–23, 327–29; Robert C. Ellickson, "The Irony of 'Inclusionary' Zoning," *Southern California Law Review*, vol. 54 (September 1981), pp. 1167–1216; and Donald Hagman, "Taking Care of One's Own through Inclusionary Zoning: Bootstrapping Low- and Moderate-Income Housing by Local Government," *Urban Law and Policy*, vol. 5 (June 1982), pp. 169–87.

6. In fiscal year 1990, property taxes accounted for 47 percent of local government own-source revenue nationwide and for 74 percent of local tax revenue. By comparison, property taxes accounted for only 1.5 percent of total state government own-source revenue and for 1.9 percent of state tax revenue. Bureau of the Census, *Government Finances: 1989–1990*, Series GF/90-5 (January 1992), table 29.

7. See John R. Logan and Harvey L. Molotch, *Urban Fortunes: The Political Economy of Place* (University of California Press, 1987), chapters 3–5; Paul E. Peterson, *City Limits* (University of Chicago Press, 1981), chapters 1–3, 7; John H. Mollenkopf, *The Contested City* (Princeton University Press, 1983), chapters 1–3, 7; Steven L. Elkin, *City and Regime in the American Republic* (University of Chicago Press, 1987), chapters 1–5; and Paul B. Kantor, *The Dependent City: The Changing Political Economy of Urban America* (Glenview, Ill.: Scott, Foresman, 1988), chapters 1, 2, 9–13. On the state perspective, see Peter K. Eisinger, *The Rise of the Entrepreneurial State: State and Local Economic Development Policy in the United States* (University of Wisconsin Press, 1988), chapters 1–4; and David Osborne, *Laboratories of Democracy* (Harvard Business School Press, 1988), chapter 8.

8. See Eisinger, *The Rise of the Entrepreneurial State*, chapters 1, 4, 10; Peterson, *City Limits*, chapters 2, 7; Shelly Metzenbaum, "Making the Most of Interstate Bidding Wars for Business" Ph.D. dissertation, John F. Kennedy School of Government, Harvard University, 1992; Ross J. Gittell, *Renewing Cities* (Princeton University Press, 1992); Robert Guskind, "The Giveaway Game Continues," *Planning*, vol. 56, no. 2 (February 1990), pp. 4–8; Alan A. Altshuler and Christopher Howard, "Local Government and Economic Development in the United States," in Project Liberty, John F. Kennedy School of Government, Harvard University, *Will Decentralization Succeed?: National, Regional, and Local Development in Multi-Party Democracies* (1991), pp. 39–49.

9. See Alan A. Altshuler, *The City Planning Process: A Political Analysis* (Cornell University Press, 1965), chapters 1, 2, 4; and Herbert J. Gans, *People and Plans: Essays on Urban Problems and Solutions* (Basic Books, 1968), pp. 57–65, 72–74.

10. See Robert H. Salisbury, "The Analysis of Public Policy: A Search for Theories and Roles," in Austin Ranney, ed., *Political Science and Public Policy* (Chicago: Markham Publishing, 1968), pp. 151–75, especially pp. 158, 167–74; Randall B. Ripley and Grace A. Franklin, *Bureaucracy and Policy Implementation* (Homewood, Ill.: Dorsey Press, 1982), pp. 72–73, 109–31; Douglas D. Anderson, "State Regulation of Electric Utilities," in James Q. Wilson, ed., *The Politics of Regulation* (Basic Books, 1980), pp. 3–41; Edward Mansfield, "Federal Maritime Commission," in Wilson, ed., *The Politics of Regulation*, pp. 42–74; Bradley Behrman, "Civil Aeronautics Board," in Wilson, ed., *The Politics of Regulation*, pp. 75–120; and James Q. Wilson, "The Politics of Regulation," in Wilson, ed., *The Politics of Regulation*, pp. 357–94, especially pp. 364–72.

11. See Alan Stone, *Regulation and Its Alternatives* (CQ Press, 1982), chapter 8; Martha Derthick and Paul J. Quirk, *The Politics of Deregulation* (Brookings, 1985); and Dorothy Robyn, *Braking the Special Interests: Trucking Deregulation and the Politics of Policy Reform* (University of Chicago Press, 1987).

12. See Michael N. Danielson, *The Politics of Exclusion* (Columbia University Press, 1976), especially chapters 3, 4, 7; Robert H. Nelson, *Zoning and Property Rights: An Analysis of the System of American Land Use Regulation* (MIT Press, 1977), chapters 1, 2, 4; Michael N. Danielson and Jameson W. Doig, *New York: The Politics of Urban Regional Development* (University of California Press, 1982), chapter 3; Sidney Plotkin, *Keep Out: The Struggle for Land Use Control* (University of California Press, 1987), chapter 1; and Yale Rabin, "Expulsive Zoning: The Inequitable Legacy of *Euclid*," in Charles M. Haar and Jerold S. Kayden, eds., *Zoning and the American Dream: Promises Still to Keep* (Chicago and New York: Planners Press, 1989), pp. 101–21.

13. See General Accounting Office, *Federal-State-Local Relations: Trends of the Past Decade and Emerging Issues*, Report HRO-90-34 (March 1990), chapter 3; U.S. Advisory Commission on Intergovernmental Relations, *Regulatory Federalism: Policy, Process, Impact, and Reform*, Report A-95 (February 1984); Donald F. Kettl, *The Regulation of American Federalism* (Johns Hopkins University Press, 1983), chapters 1–3, 8, and epilogue; David R. Beam and

Timothy J. Conlan, "The Growth of Intergovernmental Mandates in an Era of Deregulation and Decentralization," in Lawrence J. O'Toole, ed., *American Intergovernmental Relations*, 2d ed. (CQ Press, 1993), pp. 322–36; and Joseph F. Zimmerman, *Contemporary American Federalism: The Growth of National Power* (Praeger, 1992), chapters 4, 8, 9.

14. See Thomas W. Church and Robert T. Nakamura, *Cleaning Up the Mess: Implementation Strategies in Superfund* (Brookings, 1993), especially chapter 2.

15. Jan Paul Acton and Lloyd S. Dixon, *Superfund and Transaction Costs: The Experiences of Insurers and Very Large Industrial Firms* (Santa Monica: RAND, 1992), pp. 2–3.

16. The breakdown was 42 percent for external expenses (mainly legal) in connection with coverage disputes, 37 percent for external expenses to defend policyholders, 9 percent for internal administrative costs, and 12 percent for paying claims. Acton and Dixon, *Superfund and Transaction Costs*, tables 9, 14.

17. Acton and Dixon, *Superfund and Transaction Costs*, p. 30.

18. Four other states had systems based on the New Jersey model; that is, employing a formal, uniform surcharge on all hospital bills to finance a state uncompensated care fund. Many others had similar but more informal systems whereby, in regulating rates, they authorized hospitals to levy surcharges on paying patients to cover their own costs of uncompensated care.

The aspect of New Jersey's system ruled invalid was its application to union and company self-insurance plans. The court found that the federal government has preempted all regulatory responsibility for job-related benefits paid directly by companies and labor unions, even though it has not established any federal program to regulate such benefits. The provision in question is part of the Employee Retirement Income Security Act (ERISA), generally billed as protection for employee benefits. In practice, it also has become a major source of employee insecurity about health benefits, because federal courts have ruled that self-insurance plans can reduce benefits at any time, even after employees who thought they were covered become ill. Considerable debate has occurred about whether Congress intended such a broad exemption, but efforts to amend it have so far failed.

A major consequence of this regulatory exemption has been a major corporate shift from commercial health insurance to self-insurance in recent years. As of 1992, about 60 percent of paying hospital patients nationally were covered by self-insurance plans. Each new regulatory burden placed on the commercial health insurance system increases the cost disparity between commercial and self-insurance, thereby accelerating this trend.

See Joseph F. Sullivan, "Judge Voids Health Subsidy Covering New Jersey's Poor," *New York Times*, May 28, 1992, p. B7; Joseph F. Sullivan, "Judge Stays Rate Ruling for Hospitals," *New York Times*, June 5, 1992, p. B1; and Sarah Lyall, "Plan to Broaden Health Insurance: Cuomo and Legislators Agree on Coverage for the Sick," *New York Times*, June 8, 1992, p. A1. Also, editorial, "Free Care in a Free Fall," *Boston Globe*, June 6, 1992, p. 12.

19. Alan A. Altshuler and others, "The Cost of Clean: Why Washington Won't Pay," *Governing*, January 1992, pp. 45–51.

20. At the national level, a business countermobilization against environmental, safety, and other "social" regulatory initiatives generally is thought to have played a significant role in slowing the pace of social regulatory expansion during the late seventies and in reversing it during the Reagan years. See Samuel P. Hays in collaboration with Barbara P. Hays, *Beauty, Health, and Permanence: Environmental Politics in the United States, 1955–1985* (Cambridge University Press, 1987), pp. 311–28, 491–526; and Arthur Applbaum, *Michael Pertschuk and the Federal Trade Commission*, case C16-81-387. (John F. Kennedy School of Government, Harvard University, 1981).

21. Well-designed user charges are defined here as fees levied in such a fashion as to alert consumers to the marginal cost implications of their choices each time they consider whether to demand service (for example, to take an auto trip or water the lawn).

22. Exaction systems vary widely. Linkage exactions on office development to finance affordable housing, for example, are radically different in their distributive impact from residential exactions levied at a flat rate per unit to finance new roads and schools. For the sake of brevity, however, the focus here is on the latter, which are the most common form of exaction.

Chapter 2

1. See Ira Michael Heyman and Thomas K. Gilhool, "The Constitutionality of Imposing Increased Community Costs on New Suburban Residents through Subdivision Exactions," *Yale Law Journal*, vol. 73 (June 1964), pp. 1119–57, especially p. 1121; and Arthur C. Nelson, "Introduction," in Arthur C. Nelson, ed., *Development Impact Fees: Policy Rationale, Practice, Theory, and Issues* (Chicago and Washington: Planners Press, 1988), p. xxv.

2. Dean J. Misczynski, "Special Assessments," in Donald G. Hagman and Dean J. Misczynski, eds., *Windfalls for Wipeouts: Land Value Capture and Compensation* (Chicago and Washington: Planners Press, 1978), p. 311.

3. Robin L. Einhorn, *Property Rules: Political Economy in Chicago, 1833–1872* (University of Chicago Press, 1991), especially pp. 83–126. See also Misczynski, "Special Assessments," pp. 311–15.

4. Misczynski, "Special Assessments," pp. 311–15.

5. Bureau of the Census, *Government Finances: 1989–1990*, series GF 90-5 (December 1991), tables 18, 29. General own-source revenue excludes the revenues of government-owned utilities, liquor stores, and social insurance trust funds (for example, public employment retirement), which totaled $67.3 billion in fiscal year 1988.

6. Rachelle Garbarine, "Business Improvement Districts: A Special Tax Will Help Spruce Up around 34th Street," *New York Times*, September 11, 1991, p. B7.

7. See R. Marlin Smith, "From Subdivision Improvement Requirements to Community Benefit Assessments and Linkage Payments: A Brief History of Land Development Exactions," *Law and Contemporary Problems*, vol. 50 (Winter 1987), pp. 5–30; also, Heyman and Gilhool, "The Constitutionality of Imposing Increased Costs."

8. James E. Frank and Paul B. Downing, "Patterns of Impact Fee Use," in Nelson, ed., *Development Impact Fees*, pp. 3–21. The material cited is from p. 3. See also Thomas P. Snyder and Michael A. Stegman, *Paying for Growth: Using Development Fees to Finance Infrastructure* (Washington: Urban Land Institute, 1986), p. 22.

9. See Heymann and Gilhool, "The Constitutionality of Imposing Increased Costs," pp. 1121–22; Snyder and Stegman, *Paying for Growth*, pp. 10, 17–18.

10. John H. Mollenkopf, *The Contested City* (Princeton University Press, 1983), chapter 4; John R. Logan and Harvey L. Molotch, *Urban Fortunes: The Political Economy of Place* (University of California Press, 1987), chapters 3, 7; Paul Peterson, *City Limits* (University of Chicago Press, 1981), chapter 7; Bernard J. Frieden and Lynne B. Sagalyn, *Downtown, Inc.: How America Rebuilds Cities* (MIT Press, 1989), chapter 2. The term "pro-growth coalition" is Mollenkopf's. The term "growth machine" was coined by Molotch in a 1976 article, which, with revisions, constitutes chapter 3 of *Urban Fortunes*.

11. Alan A. Altshuler, *The City Planning Process: A Political Analysis* (Cornell University Press, 1965), chapters 1, 5; Michael N. Danielson and Jameson W. Doig, *New York: The Politics of Urban and Regional Development* (University of California Press, 1982), chapters 6, 9. See also Mollenkopf, *The Contested City*, chapter 4; Logan and Molotch, *Urban Fortunes*, chapters 3, 7; and Frieden and Sagalyn, *Downtown, Inc.*, chapter 2.

12. See Danielson and Doig, *New York*, chapter 9; Frieden and Sagalyn, *Downtown, Inc.*, chapter 4; Altshuler, *The City Planning Process*, chapters 1, 4; and Edward C. Banfield, *Political Influence* (New York: Free Press, 1961), chapters 5–7.

13. According to a survey of California developers by Ward Connerly and Associates, the time required to obtain all regulatory permissions increased from four-to-six months in 1970 to seventeen-to-thirty-two months in 1980. Each month of delay was estimated to add 1–2 percent to the cost per dwelling unit. Cited by Farhad Atash, "Local Land Use Regulations in the USA: A Study of Their Impacts on Housing Cost," *Land Use Policy* (July 1990), pp. 231–42. The material cited is from p. 235.

14. See Roger W. Caves, "Determining Land Use Policy via the Ballot Box: The Growth Initiative Blitz in California," *Land Use Policy* (January 1990), pp. 70–79.

15. On the civil rights movement, see Taylor Branch, *Parting the Waters: America in the King Years, 1954–63* (Simon and Schuster, 1988), especially chapters 10, 12, 21, 22; Benjamin Ginsberg and Martin Shefter, *Politics by Other Means: The Declining Importance of Elections in America* (Basic Books, 1990), pp. 40–47; and Madeleine Adamson and Seth Borgos, *This Mighty Dream: Social Protest Movements in the United States* (Routledge and Kegan Paul, 1984), pp. 71–137.

On neighborhood and consumer activism, see Harry C. Boyte, *The Backyard Revolution: Understanding the New Citizen Movement* (Temple University Press, 1980), chapters 1, 3, 6.

On the welfare rights movement, see Frances Fox Piven and Richard A. Cloward, *Poor People's Movements: Why They Succeed, How They Fail* (Pantheon Books, 1977), chapter 5.

On the movement for public service unionism, see Frederick C. Mosher, *Democracy and the Public Service*, 2d ed. (Oxford University Press, 1982), chapter 7; Theodore W. Kheel, "Introduction: Background and History," in A. Lawrence Chickering, ed., *Public Employee Unions* (San Francisco: Institute for Contemporary Studies, 1976), chapter 1; Jack D. Douglas, "Urban Politics and Public Employee Unions," in Chickering, ed., *Public Employee Unions*, chapter 6; David Lewin, "Collective Bargaining and the Right to Strike," in Chickering, ed., *Public Employee Unions*, chapter 9; Raymond D. Horton, "Economics, Politics, and Collective Bargaining: The Case for New York City," in Chickering, ed., *Public Employee Unions*, chapter 11; A. H. Raskin, "Conclusion: The Current Political Contest," in Chickering, ed., *Public Employee Unions*; and Jack Stieber, *Public Employee Unionism: Structure, Growth, Policy* (Brookings, 1973), chapters 6, 8.

On the environmental movement, see Charles O. Jones, *Clean Air: The Policies and Politics of Pollution Control* (University of Pittsburgh Press, 1975), chapters 4–7; Samuel P. Hays, *Beauty, Health, and Permanence: Environmental Politics in the United States, 1955–1985* (Cambridge University Press, 1987), chapters 1–3, 8–15; and Robert Cameron Mitchell, "From Conservation to Environmental Movement: The Development of the Modern Environmental Lobbies," in Michael J. Lacey, ed., *Government and Environmental Politics: Essays on Historical Developments since World War Two* (Woodrow Wilson Center Press, 1989), pp. 81–113.

16. See Frieden and Sagalyn, *Downtown, Inc.*, chapter 3.

17. See, for example, Martin Anderson, *The Federal Bulldozer: A Critical Analysis of Urban Renewal, 1949–1962* (MIT Press, 1964).

18. See Herbert J. Gans, *The Urban Villagers* (Free Press, 1962), chapters 13, 14; Jane Jacobs, *The Death and Life of Great American Cities* (Random House, 1961), chapters 15, 16; and Marc Fried, "Grieving for a Lost Home: Psychological Costs of Relocation," in James Q. Wilson, ed., *Urban Renewal: The Record and the Controversy* (MIT Press, 1975), pp. 359–79. For a retrospective synthesis, see Frieden and Sagalyn, *Downtown, Inc.*, chapters 2, 3.

19. See Frieden and Sagalyn, *Downtown, Inc.*, pp. 49–54.

20. See Alan A. Altshuler and Robert W. Curry, "The Changing Environment of Urban Development Policy: Shared Power or Shared Impotence?" *Urban Law Annual*, vol. 10 (1975), pp. 3–41.

21. See Frieden and Sagalyn, *Downtown, Inc.*, pp. 49–54; Bernard J. Frieden and Marshall Kaplan, *The Politics of Neglect: Urban Aid from Model Cities to Revenue Sharing* (MIT Press,

1975), chapters 2, 9, 10; and William J. Stull, "From Urban Renewal to CDBG: Community Development in Nine Cities," in C. F. Sirmans, ed., *Research in Real Estate*, vol. 2 (JAI Press, 1982), pp. 185–230.

22. Federal highway expenditures in constant dollars more than doubled from 1956, when the Interstate Highway Program was enacted, to 1965 and continued rising slightly through 1971. Over the following four years, however, they declined by 37 percent, to a level only one-third higher than in 1956. A more specific indicator of the decline in new federally aided highway construction is the rate at which residents were relocated from their homes to make way for it. That rate declined by four-fifths from 1968–69 (when the rate was 64,000 residents per year) to 1975–76 (13,300 per year). Alan A. Altshuler with James P. Womack and John R. Pucher, *The Urban Transportation System: Politics and Policy Innovation* (MIT Press, 1979), pp. 37–42, 340–42.

23. See Joseph DiMento and LeRoy Graymer, eds., *Confronting Regional Challenges: Approaches to LULUs, Growth, and Other Vexing Governance Problems* (Cambridge, Mass.: Lincoln Institute of Land Policy, 1991), especially Frank Popper, "LULUs and Their Blockage: The Nature of the Problem, The Outline of the Solutions," pp. 13–30.

24. For an account of the environmental movement, see Jones, *Clear Air*, chapters 4–7; Hayes, *Beauty, Health, and Permanence*, chapters 1–3, 8–15; and Mitchell, "From Conservation to Environmental Movement," in Lacey, ed., *Government and Environmental Politics*, pp. 81–113.

25. See Bernard J. Frieden, *The Environmental Protection Hustle* (MIT Press, 1979), chapters 1, 5, 9, 10, 11. Frieden was unable to find cases of environmentalists supporting proposed developments.

26. Frank Levy and Richard C. Michel, *The Economic Future of American Families* (Washington: Urban Institute Press, 1991), table 2.1.

27. Levy and Michel, *The Economic Future*, chapter 3, especially table 3.1.

28. Levy and Michel, *The Economic Future*, p. 11.

29. Congressional Budget Office (CBO), "Measuring the Distribution of Income Gains," memorandum (March 1992), table 1 and p. 2. Adjusting for declining household size, the figures look only slightly different. Average household income rose 15 percent from 1977 to 1989. Of the total growth in after-tax income, more than two-fifths accrued to the richest 1 percent of households, three-fifths to the top 5 percent, and four-fifths to the top 20 percent. The income share of the richest 1 percent rose from 8 to 13 percent in this tabulation, while that of the bottom 40 percent declined from 17 to 14 percent. Only the bottom 20 percent of households experienced absolute income decline. CBO, "Measuring the Distribution of Income Gains," table 2. Critics of the adjustment for household size emphasize that, to maintain constant living standards, smaller households have to spend more per capita than larger households.

The accentuation of after-tax income inequality since the mid-1970s has been due to a combination of private market and public policy changes. Of the latter, the most important have been changes in the federal tax structure: particularly, sharp cuts in high-end tax rates on personal incomes (with the top rate falling from 70 to 31 percent), and massive increases in social insurance payroll taxes. While the overall effective federal tax rate for all groups combined remained virtually unchanged from 1977 to 1988 (declining from 22.8 to 22.7 percent), households with the highest incomes enjoyed a dramatic reduction in their effective tax rate. For those in the top 1 percent, the cut was from 39.2 percent of pre-tax income to 29.3 percent. For those in the top 5 percent, the cut was from 32.5 percent to 27.4 percent. Meanwhile, nearly all groups below the top 10 percent experienced an increase in their effective tax rate. CBO, *The Changing Distribution of Federal Taxes: 1975–1990* (October 1987), pp. 11–17, 41–48.

30. The year 1989 marked the end of a major economic boom, and opportunities for addi-

tional labor force participation by women were nearly exhausted. Expectations were for house-hold incomes to rise more slowly, if at all, during the 1990s than during the prior two decades.

31. U.S. Advisory Commission on Intergovernmental Relations (ACIR), *Significant Features of Fiscal Federalism: 1991*, vol. 2, report M-176-II (October 1991), tables 18, 22.

Government expenditures rose even more rapidly than receipts in the period 1955–75, as the federal government discovered the political joys of Keynesian economics. The federal budget deficit equaled 1 percent of GNP in 1955, whereas it equaled 4.3 percent in 1975, a figure only slightly exceeded during the worst deficit years of the mid-1980s.

The sense of public austerity was accentuated after 1975 by the inability of governments, having gone about as far as they could in the area of deficit spending, to increase spending without adopting commensurate increases in taxes or charges. By the measure of expenditures, the public sector share of GNP rose by fully half from 1955 to 1975: 25.0 percent to 37.5 percent. The following fifteen years witnessed no growth in share at all; government expenditures totaled 37.3 percent of GNP in 1990. ACIR, *Significant Features of Fiscal Federalism*, vol. 2, tables 18, 22.

32. While public sector revenue growth was nearly all on the state-local side in 1955–75, expenditure growth was divided more equally between the national and state-local levels. Each gained roughly six percentage points of GNP share. Federal expenditures rose from 16.9 to 22.8 percent of GNP, while state and local expenditures rose from 8.1 to 14.7 percent. The conse-quence at the federal level was a massive shift from surplus (roughly 1 percent of GNP in 1955) to deficit (more than 4 percent of GNP in 1975). ACIR, *Significant Features of Fiscal Federalism*, vol. 2, tables 18, 22.

33. ACIR, *Significant Features of Fiscal Federalism*, vol. 2, tables 18, 22.

34. *Nordlinger* v. *Hahn*, 60 U.S.L.W. 4563 (1992).

35. ACIR, *Significant Features of Fiscal Federalism*, table 22. State-local revenues and ex-penditures tend to be more stable than GNP, so their share tends to rise in periods of economic downturn.

36. ACIR, *Significant Features of Fiscal Federalism*, vol. 2, table 18.

37. ACIR, *Significant Features of Fiscal Federalism*, vol. 2, table 24.

38. Grants-in-aid made a comeback in the early Bush budgets, rising by roughly 18 percent in real terms from 1989 to 1991, and from 2.4 to 2.8 percent of GNP. ACIR, *Significant Features of Fiscal Federalism*, vol. 2, table 24.

39. The federal aid changes are from ACIR, *Significant Features of Fiscal Federalism*, vol. 2, tables 24, 38. Table 38 does not include adjustments for inflation; we did the calculations, taking the annual adjustment factors from table 24. The U.S. economy grew by 27 percent in real terms from 1979 to 1989. See *Economic Report of the President, February 1992*, table B-2.

40. ACIR, *Significant Features of Fiscal Federalism*, vol. 2, tables 24, 38.

41. See Pat Choate and Susan Walter, *America in Ruins: Beyond the Public Works Pork Barrel* (Washington: Council of State Planning Agencies, 1981); Associated General Contractors of America, *America's Infrastructure: A Plan to Rebuild* (Washington: May 1983); Congressional Budget Office, *Public Works Infrastructure: Policy Considerations for the 1980s* (April 1983); *National Infrastructure Advisory Committee Report to the Joint Economic Committee of Congress* (February 1984); David Alan Aschauer, "Why Is Infrastructure Important?" in Alicia H. Mun-nell, ed., *Is There a Shortfall in Public Capital Investment?* Conference Series no. 34 (Federal Reserve Bank of Boston, June 1990), pp. 21–50; Alicia H. Munnell, "How Does Public Infra-structure Affect Regional Economic Performance?" In Munnell, ed., *Is There a Shortfall in Public Capital Investment?*, pp. 69–103; National Council on Public Works Improvement (NCPWI), *Fragile Foundations: A Report on America's Public Works* (February 1988); and Office of Technology Assessment, *Rebuilding the Foundations: State and Local Public Works Financing and Management*, OTA-SET-447 (March 1990).

42. Spending for operation and maintenance grew slightly over this period, from 1.3 to 1.5 percent of GNP. NCPWI, *Fragile Foundations*, p. 8.

43. These figures include facilities developed with federal aid. The states and localities owned 85 percent of total U.S. public nonmilitary capital stock in 1990. Federally owned nonmilitary capital stock rose more slowly than the state-local stock in this period, declining from 25 percent to the combined federal-state-local total in 1950 to 17 percent in 1970 and 15 percent in 1990. The 1990 totals (in 1987 dollars) were state-local fixed capital stock, $1,771.7 billion; and federal nonmilitary capital stock, $317.2 billion. All figures were estimated by the Bureau of Economic Analysis, Department of Commerce, reported in John C. Musgrave, "Fixed Reproducible Tangible Wealth in the United States, Revised Estimates," *Survey of Current Business* (January 1992), table 16.

44. Douglas Holtz-Eakin has developed state-specific estimates of the state and local capital stock through 1988. He estimates that total state and local capital averaged $5,811 per capita in 1982 dollars as of 1988 and that the core physical infrastructure component (streets and highways, sewer facilities, and local utilities) averaged $3,209 per capita. He also estimates that localities owned 62 percent of total state and local capital in 1988. Douglas Holtz-Eakin, "State-Specific Estimates of State and Local Government Capital," Department of Economics and Metropolitan Studies Program, Syracuse University, and National Bureau of Economic Research, January 1992, tables 1, 3, 4.

45. *Budget of the United States Government, Fiscal Year 1993*, part 3, table 29-3. The absolute figures in 1987 dollars were $14.0 billion in 1965, $15.2 billion in 1980, and $5.3 billion in 1990.

46. The figures in this paragraph are from Enhance Reinsurance Company, *Infrastructure Investment: A Historical Overview* (New York: 1991), p. 4, 6, graphs 9, 14; and unpublished tables provided by Sheila Brody of Enhance Reinsurance Company.

NCPWI, in *Fragile Foundations*, considered four categories in addition to those analyzed (in considerably greater detail) in the Enhance study. The five categories on which the Enhance study focused, however, were the largest in dollar volume and accounted for 85 percent of total estimated capital assets. Highways alone accounted for 51 percent. See NCPWI, *Fragile Foundations*, especially pp. 42–43.

47. Overall capital outlay figures are from *Bureau of the Census, Government Finances: 1989–1990*, table 11. These data break down expenditures by level of government, but they do not distinguish intergovernmental from other revenues. The federal aid data are from *Budget of the United States Government, Fiscal Year 1992*, pt. 6, table XVIII-4.

48. See Aschauer, "Why Is Infrastructure Important?"; Munnell, "How Does Public Infrastructure Affect Regional Economic Performance?"; and NCPWI, *Fragile Foundations*, p. 1.

49. See John Landis and Cynthia Kroll, "The Southern California Growth War," in John J. Kirlin and Donald R. Winkler, eds., *California Policy Choices*, vol. 5 (University of Southern California, School of Public Administration, 1989), pp. 129–63; also, Anthony Downs, *Stuck in Traffic: Coping with Peak-Hour Traffic Congestion* (Brookings and Lincoln Institute of Land Policy, 1992), chapter 1.

50. Traffic volume data are for all motor vehicles (cars, trucks, buses, and motorcycles). See Federal Highway Administration, Department of Transportation, *Highway Statistics Summary to 1985* (1985), pp. 225–32; and Federal Highway Administration, *Highway Statistics 1989* for the years 1986–89, p. 181. Population data exclude military personnel overseas. See ACIR, *Significant Features of Fiscal Federalism*, table 7. For estimates of average annual rates of traffic increase by decade, see table 5-1.

51. These are nationwide figures. See Altshuler, *The Urban Transportation System*, pp. 340–41.

52. Reported in Downs, *Stuck in Traffic*, p. 11.

53. Landis and Kroll, "The Southern California Growth War," p. 158. Douglas Holtz-Eakin estimates that whereas the per capita stock of state and local capital in California rose 2.1 percent annually from 1961 to 1974, it declined at a rate of 1.4 percent annually from 1975 through 1978. California ranked fifty-first among the fifty states and the District of Columbia in the latter period. By 1988, moreover, it ranked forty-seventh on the measure of accumulated net stock of core infrastructure capital (streets and highways, sewers, and government-owned utilities). Holtz-Eakin, "State-Specific Estimates of State and Local Government Capital," tables 4, 8, 9.

54. Landis and Kroll, "The Southern California Growth War," pp. 130–33, 141, 146, 158. Early data from the 1990 census long form survey indicate that, among states with average commute times above the national average, California experienced the greatest increase during the 1980s, roughly 10 percent (2.2 minutes per trip). By comparison, the national increase was 3 percent (0.7 minutes). Within California, the greatest increases were in outer suburban counties around the largest metropolitan areas. Average commute times jumped from roughly 22 to 28 minutes in Riverside and San Bernadino counties (outside of Los Angeles) and Solano County (outside of San Francisco). Federal Highway Administration, Department of Transportation, New Perspectives in Commuting, prepared by Alan E. Pisarski (July 1992), pp. 19, 22, 26–27. This report does not include data from the San Diego area.

While the census indicates that average travel times nationally rose from 1980 to 1990 (21.7 to 22.4 minutes), the Nationwide Personal Transportation Survey, which is conducted every six to eight years, indicates that they declined from 1983 to 1990 (20.4 to 19.7 minutes). Federal Highway Administration, Department of Transportation, New Perspectives in Commuting, p. 19. It seems clear that no great stock should be placed on small changes reported by these surveys.

55. U.S. Advisory Commission on Intergovernmental Relations, Federal Preemption of State and Local Authority, draft report (May 1989), appendix A, cited in General Accounting Office, Federal-State-Local Relations: Trends of the Past Decade and Emerging Issues, report HRD-90-34 (March 1990), p. 31. Throughout the nation's entire history prior to 1960 125 preemption statutes were enacted, 39 in the 1960s, 95 in the 1970s, and 91 from 1980 through 1988. For a more detailed review of developments through the early 1980s, see U.S. Advisory Commission on Intergovernmental Relations, Regulatory Federalism: Policy, Process, Impact, and Reform, report A-95 (February 1984), chapters 1, 3.

For a list of some more expensive new mandates enacted during the 1980s, see Joseph F. Zimmerman, Contemporary American Federalism: The Growth of National Power (Praeger, 1992), pp. 74–76. Zimmerman notes, for example, that in a single 1986 act Congress directed local governments to control eighty-three additional drinking water contaminants. See p. 75.

56. This account of the Lovell study is drawn from ACIR, Regulatory Federalism, pp. 156–62.

57. Zimmerman, "Federalism in the United States: The Preemption Revolution," paper presented at the Maxwell Graduate School, Syracuse University, October 1990, p. 15. One of the most expensive cases of mandate compliance became an issue in the 1988 presidential campaign, when Vice President George Bush made an issue of the slow pace of the federally mandated, $4 billion Boston Harbor cleanup. Governor Michael S. Dukakis, the Democratic presidential nominee, responded that the federal government, while requiring the massive project, had agreed to make only a miniscule contribution ($100 million) toward its cost. For a good summary, see Fox Butterfield, "Fight on Harbor Cleanup Goes On," New York Times, February 3, 1990, p. 11. Subsequently, the federal budget for fiscal 1992 included another $100 million, and President Bush requested a third federal contribution of $100 million as part of his budget for fiscal 1993. Community Relations Office, Boston Harbor Project, Massachusetts Water Resources Authority, July 1992.

58. See Allan D. Wallis, "Growth Management in Florida," Working Paper (A. Alfred Taubman Center for State and Local Government, John F. Kennedy School, Harvard University,

August 1991), especially pp. 2–3, 34–38, 48–73, 92–95; and Thomas G. Pelham, "Adequate Public Facilities Requirements: Reflections on Florida's Concurrency System for Managing Growth," *Florida State University Law Review,* vol. 19 (1992), pp. 973–1052.

59. Joseph F. Zimmerman, *Contemporary American Federalism: The Growth of National Power* (Praeger, 1992), pp. 182–83; and Walker, "The Evolution of Intergovernmental Regulation," p. 9.

60. See Michael N. Danielson, *The Politics of Exclusion* (Columbia University Press, 1976), especially pp. 50–74; Danielson and Doig, *New York,* pp. 78–105; William A. Fischel, *The Economics of Zoning Laws: A Property Rights Approach to American Land Use Controls* (Johns Hopkins University Press, 1985), chapter 15; and Yale Rabin, "Expulsive Zoning: The Inequitable Legacy of *Euclid,*" in Charles M. Haar and Jerold S. Kayden, eds., *Zoning and the American Dream: Promises Still to Keep* (Chicago and Washington: Planners Press, 1989), pp. 101–21.

Chapter 3

1. Given that many exactions still are in-kind, no tabulation based on local government records would be comprehensive in any event.

2. The formal Census Bureau definition is "charges for current services and [the] sale of products in connection with general government activities." The other main nontax revenue categories are interest, special assessment, utility, liquor store, and social insurance trust fund receipts. See Bureau of the Census, *Government Finances: 1989–90,* series GF/90-4 (January 1992), p. vii and table 1.

3. Paul B. Downing and James E. Frank, "The Growing Role of User Charges in Financing City Governments," Working Paper (Florida State University, October 1989), pp. 2, 4 and table 6. As of 1987, five states had ratios of current charge to property tax revenue of more than 3.0 (Alabama, Arkansas, Oklahoma, West Virginia, and Wyoming), while ten had ratios of 0.3 or less (Connecticut, Hawaii, Maine, Maryland, Massachusetts, Nevada, New Hampshire, New Jersey, North Carolina, and Rhode Island).

4. Paul B. Downing, "The Revenue Potential of User Charges in Municipal Finance," paper prepared for the Taxes, Resources and Economic Development (TRED) Conference on Financing Local Government in the 90s, Lincoln Institute of Land Policy, October 4–5, 1991, table 1. Current charges accounted for 30–37 percent of local own-source general revenue in five of the ten federal regions, all of them rapidly growing (West North Central, Mountain, Pacific, West South Central, and East South Central). By contrast, they accounted for only about one-sixth of local own-source general revenue in the New England and Middle Atlantic regions.

5. Elizabeth D. Purdum and James E. Frank, "Community Use of Exactions: Results of a National Survey," in James E. Frank and Robert M. Rhodes, eds., *Development Exactions* (Chicago and Washington: Planners Press, 1987), pp. 123–52, especially p. 124 and table 6-2. The response rate for jurisdictions with populations above 100,000 was 57 percent; that for smaller jurisdictions was 32 percent. Regrettably, no regional or state-by-state breakdowns were available from this survey.

6. *Ibid.,* table 9. The leading categories were as follows: land dedication for drainage (9.5 percent), sewage treatment (9.2 percent), and new roads (8.7 percent); build/install requirements for drainage (8.6 percent); and new roads (7.0 percent).

7. *Ibid.,* pp. 126–37.

8. *Ibid.,* recalculated from table 6-5, eliminating nonresponses and "not applicable" responses.

9. Surprisingly, 4.1 percent of the respondents claimed that they required land set-asides for

low- or moderate-income housing prior to 1950 and 3.4 percent claimed to have required actual construction. No adoptions of this type took place from 1950 through 1959, however; the pre-1950 exactions cited may have been special wartime initiatives. Purdum and Frank, "Community Use of Exactions," table 6-9.

10. We have chosen not to report Purdum and Frank's findings with respect to the diffusion of exactions for low- and moderate-income housing, because these seem to be in conflict with their findings about current practice—not to mention with a vast array of other scholarship highlighting the exclusionary orientation of most American localities. Purdum and Frank report in table 6-9 that, at one time or another, fully three-quarters of all localities have adopted requirements that developers build or make cash contributions for affordable housing. In table 6-3, by contrast, they find the following percentages of communities reporting that they "frequently or always" imposed affordable housing exactions at the time of the survey: land dedication, 2.5 percent; build or improve, 3.8 percent; cash, 0.1 percent. Adding communities that "sometimes" imposed such requirements, the figures were 6.8 percent, 8.3 percent, and 3.2 percent, respectively.

Another Purdum and Frank finding that we doubt, and have chosen not to cite, is that as of the mid-1980s exactions were still used only rarely for off-site purposes. The problem here is that their questionnaire was poorly designed to elicit this information. Consequently, the responses, along with a high nonresponse rate, are open to various interpretations. Two questions just prior to the one about the location of facilities for which cash payments were utilized, for example, focused on in-lieu fees (substitutes for in-kind requirements) instead of impact fees (almost always intended for off-site usage). The key question, finally, did not ask whether cash payments were ever used for off-site purposes. Instead, it asked how they were used "in general." (Respondents were offered four choices: on-site, within one-half mile of the site, off-site, and no location requirement. The following question offered still another option: that location might vary by facility type. The questionnaire appears in Purdum and Frank, "Community Use of Exactions," pp. 148–52.)

How, then, should the answers be interpreted? Only 23 percent of the respondents said that in general they applied cash payments "on-site." Even fewer, just 8 percent, answered "adjacent to the site" or "off-site." Twelve percent answered "no location requirement," which suggests that they were free to use cash payments off-site; six percent answered that location might vary. Altogether, then, 26 percent chose answers compatible with frequent off-site usage of cash payments. These constituted 55 percent of all those responding. Finally, given the way the questionnaire was worded, some who replied that "in general" they utilized cash payments on-site sometimes may have applied them off-site.

11. Purdum and Frank, "Community Use of Exactions," table 6-9. The data were reported for five-year blocks of time and in three categories (land dedication, build/install, and cash). Information was not available on the degree of overlap among localities in the three categories. Construction of table 3-1 was based on the assumption that in each time period the number of separate adopting localities was two-thirds of the combined percentage for all three exaction forms or the percentage for the most favored form, whichever was greater. For example, the totals for school exaction adoptions in the decade 1960–69 were as follows: land dedication, 25 percent of respondent localities; build/install, 14 percent; and cash, 4 percent. Two-thirds of the combined total is twenty-eight percent. The lower bound possibility is 25 percent.

12. Gus Bauman and William H. Ethier, "Development Exactions and Impact Fees: A Survey of American Practices," Law and Contemporary Problems, vol. 50 (Winter 1987), pp. 51–68.

13. Bauman and Ethier, "Development Exactions and Impact Fees," p. 59. This study split the country into six "regions": California, the remainder of the West, the Midwest, the South, the Middle Atlantic states, and New England.

14. Calculated on the basis of Bauman and Ethier, "Development Exactions and Impact Fees," tables 2 and 5. The simple measure of 1984 housing starts is a very weak indicator of community growth, because it ignores overall community size, nonresidential growth, and cumulative effects of years of community growth or stagnation.

15. Edward J. Kaiser, Raymond J. Burby, and David H. Moreau, "Local Governments' Use of Water and Sewer Impact Fees and Related Policies: Current Practice in the Southeast," in Arthur C. Nelson, ed., *Development Impact Fees: Policy Rationale, Practice, Theory, and Issues* (Chicago and Washington: Planners Press, 1988), pp. 22–36.

16. James E. Frank and Paul B. Downing, "Patterns of Impact Fee Use," in Nelson, ed., *Development Impact Fees*, pp. 3–21. The material cited is from pp. 19–20.

17. Florida Advisory Council on Intergovernmental Relations (FACIR), *1991 Florida Impact Fee Report*, 91-2 (September 1991), pp. 5–7, 20; FACIR, *Impact Fee Use in Florida: An Update*, 89-8 (July 1989), pp. 10, 13, 34; and FACIR, *Impact Fees in Florida*, (November 1986), p. 69. The survey methodology evolved over time, so these results are not entirely comparable. The 1986 survey, for example, included 98 municipalities: all those with populations in excess of twenty thousand plus 34 smaller municipalities thought by other respondents to levy impact fees. The 1989 survey included 131 municipalities: all those with more than fifteen thousand residents plus 50 smaller jurisdictions thought by regional planning council staff to be using impact fees. The 1991 survey included all 390 Florida municipalities regardless of population. As the numbers of municipalities included in the survey grew, the response rate declined. The 1986 survey was conducted first by phone, with a follow-up mail survey of those who reported using impact fees, and at least partial responses were obtained from every jurisdiction. Phone follow-ups were used in 1991 to ensure 100 percent county representation, but the municipalities were surveyed exclusively by mail, and only 44 percent responded.

18. See Purdum and Frank, "Community Use of Exactions," table 6-5.

19. Thomas P. Snyder and Michael A. Stegman, *Paying for Growth: Using Development Fees to Finance Infrastructure* (Washington: Urban Land Institute, 1986), pp. 75–76.

20. Bay Area Council, *Taxing the American Dream: Development Fees and Housing Affordability in the Bay Area* (San Francisco: 1988), pp. 2–6, 18–19. All figures in the report are in current dollars; we determined the inflation adjustments. The consumer price index rose 21 percent in this period. In virtually all cases, the council noted, fees were levied on a per-unit basis, without regard to value. Thus, the proportionate burden was far greater on lower than higher priced homes, often approaching 10 percent.

21. Bay Area council, *Taxing the American Dream*, pp. 5, 7.

22. The increase percentages noted were in current dollars. Combined impact fee revenues for the reporting jurisdictions totaled $279 million in fiscal year 1991. FACIR, *Florida Impact Fee Report 1991*, table 3. A more detailed examination of the 1988 survey data by council staff revealed that impact fees averaged about 3.5 percent of new home prices, with high-end fees in the range of 5–6 percent. FACIR, *Impact Fee Use Update*, pp. 31–32. These figures did not take into account developer markups. Thomas P. Snyder and Michael A. Stegman estimated in a 1986 study of Colorado Springs, Colorado, that a normal markup for overhead, financing, and profit would add 28 percent. Cited in James C. Nicholas, Arthur C. Nelson, and Julian Conrad Juergensmeyer, *A Practitioner's Guide to Development Impact Fees* (Chicago and Washington: Planners Press, 1991), p. 63.

23. James C. Nicholas and Geoff Pappas, "Impact Fees on the Rise, Again" *Growth Management Studies Newsletter*, vol. 6 (Holland Law Center, University of Florida, July 1991), pp. 1–4. For additional detail on survey results through 1990, see Nicholas and others, *A Practitioner's Guide to Development Fees*, pp. 2–9. The inflation-adjustments are our own, based on the consumer price index. See *Economic Report of the President, 1992*, table B-56.

24. Comparison by the authors of data reported in Nicholas and Pappas, "Impact Fees on

the Rise, Again," with that reported in James C. Nicholas with Kellie Ruscher, "Impact Fees on the Rise," *Growth Management Studies Newsletter*, vol. 5, no. 2 (Holland Law Center, University of Florida, June 1990), pp. 1–4. We are unable to adjust for one jurisdiction that dropped out of the survey from 1990 to 1991, reducing the sample from thirty-three to thirty-two jurisdictions. As of 1991, the average impact fee totals in the thirty-two jurisdictions surveyed, exclusive of water and sewer fees, were: $4,606 per single-family home, $4,013 per thousand square feet of general retail space, $3,247 per thousand square feet of general office space, and $1,772 per thousand square feet of general industrial space. The residential total, including water and sewer fees, was $7,691. Estimating water and sewer fees for the nonresidential categories was impossible because they varied even within jurisdictions. Nicholas and Pappas, "Impact Fees on the Rise, Again," p. 3.

25. Association of Bay Area Governments (ABAG), *Development Fees in the San Francisco Bay Area: An Update* (Berkeley, January 1982), p. 39.

26. The most prevalent type of social exaction, if one chooses to label it as such, is inclusionary zoning, which does pertain to residential development. As discussed in chapter 1, however, we have omitted inclusionary zoning from detailed consideration in this volume because, both in form and legal rationale, it resembles traditional zoning more than it resembles other types of exactions.

The form of inclusionary zoning is simple regulation of what land uses can be developed on given plots of land. Regulators who engage in inclusionary zoning add some items that developers would prefer to have omitted, but communitywide zoning has always sought to shape the mix of uses rather than simply to give developers their head. (The aspect of inclusionary zoning that does arguably make it a form of exaction is that it requires developers to include money-losing activities in their mix.)

The legal rationale for inclusionary zoning likewise is rooted squarely in zoning, not exaction, theory. The traditional justification for zoning includes a claimed community right, in pursuit of valid public objectives, to regulate the land use mix within its boundaries. The core justification for exactions, however, is that developers may be required to internalize certain public costs directly attributable to their activities. Additions to the supply of market rate housing do not in any obvious sense contribute to the need for affordable housing. Indeed, by adding to the overall supply of housing, they should (via trickle down) alleviate that need. Inclusionary zoning, therefore, must rest legally on the community's right (and in a few states its obligation) to pursue socioeconomic balance in its residential mix.

27. Teresa R. Herrero, "Housing Linkage: Will It Play a Role in the 1990s?" *Journal of Urban Affairs*, vol. 13, no. 1 (1991), pp. 1–19. The material cited is from p. 1.

28. Those with mandatory programs were San Francisco, Sacramento, Santa Monica, Berkeley, Palo Alto, and Menlo Park, California; Boston and Cambridge, Massachusetts; and Princeton and Cherry Hill, New Jersey. Those with voluntary programs were Miami, Orlando, and Tampa, Florida; Hartford, Connecticut; Jersey City, New Jersey; and Seattle, Washington. See Herrero, "Housing Linkage," table 1; and Neil S. Mayer and Bill Lambert, "Flexible Linkage in Berkeley: Development Mitigation Fees," in Nelson, ed., *Development Impact Fees*, pp. 242–56, especially pp. 244–52.

Several of these localities—Boston, San Francisco, Seattle, Miami, and Hartford—also have inclusionary zoning programs. Other major cities with such programs include New York, Denver, and Washington, D.C. See W. Dennis Keating, "Responding to the Impact of Downtown Development: Linkage Programs and Comprehensive Planning," in Nelson, ed., *Development Impact Fees*, pp. 219–26; and Nina J. Gruen, "A Case History of the San Francisco Office/Housing Linkage Program," in Douglas Porter, ed., *Downtown Linkages* (Washington: Urban Land Institute, 1985), pp. 42–51. The nation's best-known program of mandatory inclusionary zoning is that of Montgomery County, Maryland. It has been in operation since the mid-1970s, applies to all new developments of more than fifty residential units, and includes a density bonus provision. See Christie I. Baxter, *Moderately Priced Dwelling Units in Montgomery County, Maryland*, case C16-91-1043.0 (John F. Kennedy School of Government, Harvard University, 1991).

Other useful sources on commercial-residential linkage include Robert Collin and Michael Lytton, "Linkage: An Evaluation and Exploration," *The Urban Lawyer*, vol. 21, (Summer 1989), pp. 413–46; and John A. Henning, Jr., "Mitigating Price Effects with a Housing Linkage Fee," *California Law Review*, vol. 78 (1990), pp. 721–53.

29. Peter Dreier and Bruce Ehrlich, "Downtown Development and Urban Reform: The Politics of Boston's Linkage Policy," *Urban Affairs Quarterly*, vol. 26 (March 1991), pp. 354–75, especially pp. 359–665.

30. Quoted in Donald L. Connors and Michael E. High, "The Expanding Circle of Exactions: From Dedication to Linkage," *Law and Contemporary Problems*, vol. 50 (Winter 1987), pp. 69–83. The material cited is from p. 81. See also Lawrence Susskind and Gerard McMahon, "Reframing the Rationale for Downtown Linkage Programs," in Rachelle Alterman, ed., *Private Supply of Public Services* (New York University Press, 1988), p. 203–18.

31. Dreier and Ehrlich, "Downtown Development," pp. 366–67.

32. Gruen, "A Case History of the San Francisco Office/Housing Linkage Program," in Porter, ed., *Downtown Linkages*, pp. 42–43. A California state council on competitiveness recently made the same point more generally. Reporting that it had found development fees per standard single-family home (1,650 square feet) as high as $34,000 in one jurisdiction and more than $20,000 in a number of others, the council stated, "Having depressed the supply of affordable housing by exactions, and with a shrinking supply of federal dollars to finance affordable housing, cities and counties have reacted by adopting still more exactions on other projects, *i.e.*, mandatory inclusionary housing programs and housing trust funds. These programs require that residential and commercial projects provide solutions to the community's lower-income housing problems as a *quid pro quo* for project approval. Masked as a density bonus incentive, these techniques are little more than a private subsidy for what should be public obligations borne by society as a whole." Council on California Competitiveness, *California's Jobs and Future* (April 23, 1992), p. 42. For more general criticisms in the same vein, see Bernard J. Frieden, *The Environmental Protection Hustle* (MIT Press, 1979), chapters 4–6, 10; and Robert C. Ellickson, "The Irony of Inclusionary Zoning," *Southern California Law Review*, vol. 54 (September 1981), pp. 1167–1216.

33. Linda L. Hausrath, "Economic Basis for Linking Jobs and Housing in San Francisco," in Nelson, ed., *Development Impact Fees*, pp. 257–66, especially pp. 260–65. Sacramento's linkage program, based on a similar technical analysis, currently is on appeal to the U.S. Supreme Court. The plaintiffs charge that Sacramento, despite its studies, has not adequately demonstrated that commercial development is a cause of low-income housing need. The city prevailed at the district and circuit court levels. See *Commercial Builders of Northern California v. City of Sacramento*, 941 *Federal Reporter*, pp. 872–78, for the opinion of the Ninth Circuit Court of Appeals.

34. Mayor's Office of Economic Planning and Development, City and County of San Francisco, "Annual Revision of Office/Affordable Housing Production Program (OAHPP) In Lieu Fee" (March 23, 1992). For historical detail on the linkage fee program see Mayor's Office of Economic Planning and Development, City and County of San Francisco, *Annual Revision of the Office/Affordable Housing Production Program (OAHPP) Planning Code Section 313* (December 1990).

35. Gruen, "A Case History of the San Francisco Office/Housing Linkage Program," in Porter, ed., *Downtown Linkages*, pp. 44–47.

36. Chester Hartman, *The Transformation of San Francisco* (Rowman and Allanheld, 1984),

pp. 261–62. See also Brad Paul, "San Francisco Growth Management," case C16-90-948.0 (John F. Kennedy School of Government and Graduate School of Design, Harvard University, 1988), p. 9.

37. Meyer and Lambert, "Flexible Linkage in Berkeley," in Nelson, ed., *Development Impact Fees*, pp. 244–55.

38. Forrest E. Huffman, Jr., and Marc T. Smith, "Market Effects of Office Development Linkage Fees," in Nelson, ed., *Development Impact Fees*, pp. 267–77. The material cited is from p. 272.

Chapter 4

1. This and the following two paragraphs draw substantially on Elizabeth A. Deakin, "The Politics of Exactions," in Rachelle Alterman, ed., *Private Supply of Public Services: Evaluation of Real Estate Exactions, Linkage, and Alternative Land Policies* (New York University Press, 1988), pp. 96–110.

2. The extent to which developers can pass costs on to consumers or back to landowners depends on a wide variety of market circumstances. See chapter 7.

3. See Charles Siemon, "Who Bears the Cost?" *Law and Contemporary Problems*, vol. 50 (Winter 1987), pp. 115–26, especially p. 122.

4. See Brian W. Blaesser and Christine M. Kentopp, "Impact Fees: The 'Second Generation,'" *Journal of Urban and Contemporary Law*, vol. 38, no. 25 (1990), pp. 63–69; Ira Michael Heyman and Thomas K. Gilhool, "The Constitutionality of Imposing Increased Community Costs on New Suburban Residents through Subdivision Exactions, *Yale Law Journal*, vol. 73 (June 1964), pp. 1119–57, especially pp. 1122–25; Steven B. Schwanke, "Local Governments and Impact Fees: Public Need, Property Rights, and Judicial Standards," *Journal of Land Use and Environmental Law*, vol. 4 (Winter 1989), pp. 215–47, especially pp. 221–24; Julian Conrad Juergensmeyer, "The Legal Issues of Capital Facilities Funding," in Alterman, ed., *Private Supply of Public Services*, pp. 51–65; Fred P. Bosselman and Nancy Stroud, "Legal Aspects of Development Exactions," in James E. Frank and Robert M. Rhodes, eds., *Development Exactions* (Chicago and Washington: Planners Press, 1987), pp. 70–103, especially pp. 70–75.

5. See Theodore C. Taub, "Exactions, Linkages, and Regulatory Takings: The Developer's Perspective," *Urban Lawyer*, vol. 20 (Summer 1988), pp. 515–96, especially p. 518.

6. Taub, "Exactions, Linkages, and Regulatory Takings," p. 519, cites two California cases of the mid-1980s. More generally, see Heyman and Gilhool, "The Constitutionality of Imposing Increased Community Costs on New Suburban Residents through Subdivision Exactions," pp. 1122–23; and Schwanke, "Local Governments and Impact Fees," p. 221.

7. On local home rule authority as a basis for levying exactions, see Blaesser and Kentopp, "Impact Fees," pp. 86–93.

8. Donald G. Hagman and Julian Conrad Juergensmeyer, *Urban Planning and Land Development Control Law* (St. Paul: West Publishing, 1986), pp. 203–06; Taub "Exactions, Linkages, and Regulatory Takings," pp. 519–20; Schwanke, "Local Governments and Impact Fees," pp. 221–30.

9. See Schwanke, "Local Governments and Impact Fees," pp. 224–30; Blaesser and Kentopp, "Impact Fees," pp. 64–66; Hagman and Juergensmeyer, *Urban Planning and Land Development Control Law*, pp. 207–08; and Richard J. Roddewig, "Recent Developments in Land Use, Planning and Zoning Law," *Urban Lawyer*, vol. 22 (Fall 1990), pp. 719–831, especially pp. 780–83.

10. See Hagman and Juergensmeyer, *Urban Planning and Land Development Control Law*, pp. 284–85; and Vicki Been, "'Exit' as a Constraint on Land Use Exactions: Rethinking the

Unconstitutional Conditions Doctrine," *Columbia Law Review*, vol. 91 (1991), pp. 473–545, especially pp. 487–91.

11. Until the 1960s, the predominant view was that exactions generally were appropriate only if public investments were "specifically and uniquely attributable" to the developments involved. The idea of combining exaction revenues from groups of projects—or of combining exaction and tax revenues—to finance projects attributable to multiple causes and of utilizing cost accounting methods to allocate responsibilities fairly was first fully developed by Heyman and Gilhool in their landmark 1964 article, "The Constitutionality of Imposing Increased Community Costs on New Suburban Residents through Subdivision Exactions," pp. 1119–57.

12. Schwanke, "Local Governments and Impact Fees," pp. 234–39; Taub, "Exactions, Linkages, and Regulatory Takings," pp. 528–33; and Blaesser and Kentopp, "Impact Fees," pp. 62–63.

13. The underlying premise of exaction financing is that old residents should not subsidize new. From a legal standpoint, however, the reverse is equally true; that is, new residents must be protected from subsidizing old. Consequently, communities must grant credits to any development against exaction liabilities for tax payments that its owners and occupants have made, or are expected to make, toward the financing of facilities to serve existing development. See James C. Nicholas, Arthur C. Nelson, and Julian Conrad Juergensmeyer, *A Practitioner's Guide to Development Impact Fees* (Chicago and Washington: Planners Press, 1991), chapter 10.

14. For discussions of the rational nexus standard and its evolution, see R. Marlin Smith, "From Subdivision Improvement Requirements to Community Benefit Assessments and Linkage Payments: A Brief History of Land Development Exactions," *Law and Contemporary Problems*, vol. 50 (Winter 1987), pp. 5–30; "Note: Municipal Development Exactions, the Rational Nexus Test, and the Federal Constitution," *Harvard Law Review* (March 1989), pp. 992–1012; Schwanke, "Local Governments and Impact Fees," pp. 234–44; and Taub, "Exactions, Linkages, and Regulatory Takings," pp. 528–33.

15. Blaesser and Kentopp, "Impact Fees," pp. 73–81, 102–106; David L. Callies, "Review Essay: Impact Fees, Exactions, and *Paying for Growth in Hawaii*," *University of Hawaii Law Review*, vol. 11 (Fall 1989), pp. 295–333, especially pp. 306–10; Schwanke, "Local Governments and Impact Fees," p. 233; and Taub, "Exactions, Linkages, and Regulatory Takings," pp. 529–30.

16. Schwanke, "Local Governments and Impact Fees," pp. 233–34; Blaesser and Kentopp, "Impact Fees," especially pp. 60–61; Taub, "Exactions, Linkages, and Regulatory Takings," pp. 528–29.

17. 107 S. Ct. 3141 (1987). See, on evolving California practice, Jane H. Lillydahl and others, "The Need for a Standard State Impact Fee Enabling Act," in Arthur C. Nelson, ed., *Development Impact Fees: Policy Rationale, Practice, Theory, and Issues*, pp. 121–34, especially pp. 123–25, and Daniel J. Curtin and Richard L. Crabtree, "Development Fees: What Nexus Is Sufficient?" *Los Angeles Daily Journal*, April 14, 1992, p. 7.

18. Stewart E. Sterk, "*Nollan*, Henry George, and Exactions," *Columbia Law Review*, vol. 88 (1988), pp. 1731–51, especially p. 1750. See also Jerold S. Kayden, "Land Use Regulations, Rationality, and Judicial Review: The RSVP in the *Nollan* Invitation," pt. 1, *Urban Lawyer*, vol. 22 (Summer 1991), pp. 301–31; Schwanke, "Local Governments and Impact Fees," pp. 240–45; and Taub, "Exactions, Linkages, and Regulatory Takings," pp. 580–84.

19. 107 S. Ct. 3141 (1987), pp. 3146–51.

20. Kayden, "Land Use Regulations, Rationality, and Judicial Review," pt. 1, p. 331. Part 2 of this article, focusing entirely on lower court disagreement about the meaning of the *Nollan* decision, is forthcoming.

21. The nine are Arizona, California, Florida, Georgia, Illinois, Maine, Texas, Vermont, and Virginia. Blaesser and Kentopp, "Impact Fees," p. 71. James Nicholas, during a telephone

conversation in July 1992, identified nine other states with specific impact fee enabling statutes as of 1992: Hawaii, Indiana, Maryland, Nevada, New Hampshire, North Carolina, Oregon, Washington, and West Virginia.

22. Caryl Brinson Sumner and Ed Sumner, "Impact Fees under Georgia's New Statute," *Georgia Municipal Association Information Series*, vol. 11 (June 1990). The quotation is from the statute, as quoted by the authors on p. 8. A condensed version of this article, with the same title, appeared in the *Growth Management Studies Newsletter* (Holland Law Center, University of Florida, November 1990), pp. 1–4 and (June 1991), pp. 2–4.

23. Lillydahl and others, "The Need for a Standard State Impact Fee Enabling Act," p. 123.

24. Ibid., pp. 123–25.

25. Arnold M. Howitt, *Implementing Growth Management in Maine*, case study (Taubman Center for State and Local Government, John F. Kennedy School of Government, Harvard University, 1992).

26. See Douglas R. Porter, Patrick L. Phillips, and Terry J. Lassar, *Flexible Zoning: How It Works* (Washington: Urban Land Institute, 1988); Terry Jill Lassar, *Carrots and Sticks: New Zoning Downtown* (Washington: Urban Land Institute, 1989); and Richard H. Cowart, "Negotiating Exactions through Development Agreements," in Alterman, ed., *Private Supply of Public Services*, pp. 219–33.

27. See Porter and others, *Flexible Zoning*, pp. 85–92; and Robert H. Nelson, *Zoning and Property Rights: An Analysis of the System of American Land Use Regulation* (MIT Press, 1977), pp. 138–40, 154–66.

28. See Colleen Grogan Moore, *PUDs in Practice* (Washington: Urban Land Institute, 1985).

29. Lawrence Susskind and Gerard McMahon, "Reframing the Rationale for Downtown Linkage Programs," in Alterman, ed., *Private Supply of Public Services*, pp. 203–18.

30. *Nollan v. California Coastal Commission*, 107 S. Ct. 3141 (1987). The material cited is from p. 3149 n. 5. See also Been, "'Exit' as a Constraint," pp. 491–92: "If the government is allowed to spend the exaction in any way it chooses, the government will have an incentive to impose land use regulations not because it is truly concerned about the damage that development will cause to the public, but because it sees the 'sale' of exemptions from the regulation as a source of funds, or because it sees the exemptions as a form of capital that it can use to grant favors to its supporters. . . . If exactions may be spent only for germane projects, on the other hand, . . . the pressure to overregulate will decrease accordingly."

31. Susskind and McMahon, "Reframing the Rationale for Downtown Linkage Programs," in Alterman, ed., *Private Supply of Public Services*, p. 203.

32. Douglas R. Porter, "Will Developers Pay to Play?" in Nelson, ed., *Development Impact Fees*, pp. 73–80. The material cited is from p. 78.

33. Nancy Stroud, "Legal Considerations of Development Impact Fees," in Nelson, ed., *Development Impact Fees*, pp. 83–95. The material cited is from p. 87.

34. Cowart, "Negotiating Exactions," in Alterman, ed., *Private Supply of Public Services*, p. 224.

35. Cowart, "Negotiating Exactions," in Alterman, ed., *Private Supply of Public Services*, p. 223. The California statute, like the impact fee enabling statutes, was the product of a developer initiative and an alliance with some local officials (plus, in this case, environmentalists). State judicial doctrine held that every permit required for a development project was conditional until all were secured. That is, if new rules were promulgated during the review period, permissions already granted could be withdrawn. California developers were eager for permits to vest as they were received. Local officials, supported by environmental groups, wanted clear authority to negotiate permissions and exactions. The development agreement statute was the result.

36. See Lassar, *Carrots and Sticks*, chapter 4; Susan R. Diamond, "Upping the Ante in the Approval Process," *Urban Land*, September 1992, pp. 31–33; and Richard C. DeLeon, *Left Coast City: Progressive Politics in San Francisco 1975–1991* (University Press of Kansas, 1992), chapter 8.

37. Lassar, *Carrots and Sticks*, pp. 20–26.

38. Peggy L. Cuciti, "Exactions through Annexation Agreements: A Case Study," in Alterman, ed., *Private Supply of Public Services*, pp. 234–49.

39. Thomas P. Snyder and Michael A. Stegman, *Paying for Growth: Using Development Fees to Finance Infrastructure* (Washington: Urban Land Institute, 1986), pp. 78–79; and Barry Light, "A Public Official's Experience with Public/Private Development: Battery Park City, New York," in Rachelle L. Levitt and John J. Kirlin, eds., *Managing Development through Public/Private Negotiations* (Washington: Urban Land Institute and American Bar Association, 1985), pp. 41–47.

40. Snyder and Stegman, *Paying for Growth*, p. 78.

41. Bernard J. Frieden and Lynne B. Sagalyn, *Downtown, Inc.: How America Rebuilds Cities* (MIT Press, 1989), pp. 222–27.

42. Malcolm D. Rivkin, "Negotiating with Neighborhoods," in Levitt and Kirlin, eds., *Managing Development through Public/Private Negotiations*, pp. 65–76; and Susskind and McMahon, "Reframing the Rationale for Downtown Linkage Programs," in Alterman, ed., *Private Supply of Public Services*, pp. 203–18.

43. Frieden and Sagalyn, *Downtown, Inc.*, pp. 152–53.

44. In fiscal 1990, "charges and miscellaneous general revenue" accounted for 23 percent of state and 37 percent of local own-source general revenue. Bureau of the Census, *Government Finances: 1989–90* series GF/90-5 (December 1991), table 2.

45. Hawaii is an exception, at least insofar as inclusionary zoning is concerned. The state regulates conversions of private agricultural land for urban uses and has adopted a policy of requiring residential developers of such land to set aside 60 percent of their units for households with incomes below 120 percent of the statewide median. Local governments in Hawaii did not impose exactions as of 1989. See Callies, "Review Essay," pp. 296–98.

Of the other (very few) cases that have come to our attention in which state agencies have imposed exactions, none have involved fund raising to finance public facilities or services. The beach easement exaction at issue in the *Nollan* case is a good example. (The California Coastal Zone Commission is a state agency.) While it might have reduced the market value of the Nollans' property, it did not require them to make a financial outlay.

46. Eighty-eight percent of Americans over the age of five lived in the same state in 1990 as five years earlier. Of those who moved to a different house beteen 1985 and 1990, 79 percent remained within the same state; 57 percent remained within the same county. Bureau of the Census, "The Nation's Economic, Social, and Housing 'Portrait' Drawn from 1990 Census Long Form," press release, May 29, 1992, table 1.

47. The Supreme Court's 1992 decision upholding California's Proposition 13 may presage a shift in doctrine with respect to the right to the travel. Explicitly, however, the Court ruled only that the plaintiff in this case had no standing to raise the issue, because she herself had not moved to California from out-of-state. *Nordlinger* v. *Hahn*, 60 U.S.L.W. 4563 (1992), especially p. 4566. The California Court of Appeal found that Proposition 13 does not violate the right to travel because it "bases each property owner's assessment value on acquisition value, irrespective of the owner's status as a California resident or the owner's length of residence in the state," and thus any benefit to longtime California residents on average is merely "incidental" (p. 4565).

48. Bureau of the Census, *Government Finances: 1989–1990*, table 1.

Chapter 5

1. See, for example, Dick Netzer, "Do We Really Need a National Infrastructure Policy?" *Journal of the American Planning Association*, vol. 58 (Spring 1992), pp. 139–43; Alicia H. Munnell, ed., *Is There a Shortfall in Public Capital Investment?* Conference Series no. 34 (Federal Reserve Bank of Boston, 1990); and National Council on Public Works Improvement, *Fragile Foundations: A Report on America's Public Works* (February 1988).

2. See Office of Technology Assessment, *Rebuilding the Foundations: State and Local Public Works Financing and Management*, OTA-SET-447 (March 1990).

3. See Charles A. Lave, "Future Growth of Auto Travel in the U.S.: A Non-Problem," in Jefferson W. Tester, David O. Wood, and Nancy A. Ferrari, eds., *Energy and the Environment in the Twenty-First Century* (MIT Press, 1991), pp. 227–29.

4. Lave, "Future Growth of Auto Travel in the U.S."; and Alan A. Altshuler and others, *The Future of the Automobile: The Report of MIT's International Automobile Program* (MIT Press, 1984), pp. 110–11. For a conflicting view, see Arlee T. Reno, "Personal Mobility in the United States," in *A Look Ahead: Year 2020*, Special Report 220 (Transportation Research Board, 1988), pp. 369–93, especially pp. 382–83.

5. Lave, "Future Growth of Auto Travel in the U.S."

6. Hypothetical calculations of this type might be possible, but many of the parameters needed are not available. Economists' estimates of the income elasticities of household infrastructure would be of limited use, for example, because few estimates separate the effects of income from the effects of larger and higher quality residences that typically accompany higher incomes.

7. This is not an unreasonable guess when comparing the trends in driving and household growth in table 5-1.

8. South Coast Air Quality Management District and Southern California Association of Governments, *Air Quality Management Plan: South Coast Air Basin* (Los Angeles, 1989); and Genevieve Giuliano, "Is Jobs-Housing Balance a Transportation Issue?" in *Transportation Research Record 1305* (National Research Council, TRB, 1992), pp. 305–12, especially p. 306.

9. See, for example, Robert Cervero, "Jobs-Housing Imbalance and Regional Mobility," *Journal of the American Planning Association*, vol. 55 (1989), pp. 136–50, especially p. 139.

10. The discussion here summarizes planning and engineering cost estimates for different types of urban form. Another approach is statistical comparison of actual costs in a cross section of communities. This literature is not reviewed here because it has dealt with aggregate measures of density or form (such as gross population density at the city or county level) and not the more detailed design concerns of infrastructure and land use planners. Cross-section statistical studies, however, generally find little or no cost savings from higher density. For an example of one of the best recent studies, see Helen F. Ladd, "Population Growth, Density and the Costs of Providing Services," *Urban Studies*, vol. 29, no. 2 (1992), pp. 273–95.

11. For the most comprehensive review of this literature, which reaches different conclusions than those presented here, see James E. Frank, *The Costs of Alternative Development Patterns: A Review of the Literature* (Washington: Urban Land Institute, 1989). For an excellent review of some older studies, see John F. Kain, "Urban Form and the Costs of Urban Services," Discussion Paper No. 6, revised (Program on Regional and Urban Economics, Harvard University, May 1967).

12. See Frank's review of the Wheaton and Schussheim, Isard and Coughlin, and Urban Land Institute studies in *The Costs of Alternative Development Patterns*, pp. 11–23.

13. Real Estate Research Corporation (RERC), *The Costs of Sprawl: Environmental and Economic Costs of Alternative Residential Development Patterns at the Urban Fringe*, 3 vols.

(1974). More recent studies reach similar conclusions and appear to include similar flaws; see, for example, Robert B. Smythe and Charles D. Laidlaw, *Residential Growth in Loudon County: Density-Related Public Costs* (Washington: American Farmland Trust, 1984) as summarized in Robert A. Blewett and Arthur C. Nelson, "A Public Choice and Efficiency Argument for Development Impact Fees," pp. 282–83 in Arthur C. Nelson, ed., *Development Impact Fees: Policy Rationale, Practice, Theory, and Issues* (Chicago: Planners Press, 1988).

14. RERC estimated that school costs would vary considerably, assuming townhouses and apartments would be occupied by smaller households with fewer school children. Altshuler and others have pointed out that this assumption confuses a cost comparison of building densities with a cost comparison of different family types. See Alan A. Altshuler, "Review of *The Costs of Sprawl*," *Journal of the American Institute of Planners*, vol. 43 (April 1977), pp. 207–09; and Duane Windsor, "A Critique of *The Costs of Sprawl*," *Journal of the American Planning Association*, vol. 45 (July 1979), pp. 279–92.

15. See, for example, Altshuler, "Review of *The Costs of Sprawl*"; Windsor, " A Critique of *The Costs of Sprawl*"; and Alan A. Altshuler, *The Urban Transportation System: Politics and Policy Innovation* (MIT Press, 1979), pp. 379–93.

16. RERC also assumed that the walk-up and high-rise apartments would have only 1,000 and 900 square feet of living space, respectively, while single-family homes would average 1,600 square feet per dwelling unit. These differences in the interior space affect the estimates of housing structure costs (which are not reported here) but not the estimates of infrastructure costs. RERC, *The Costs of Sprawl: Detailed Cost Analysis* (1974), table 12.

17. In the two low-density communities, the costs of sprawl are confused with the costs of neighborhood types. The low-density planned community contains 75 percent cluster homes, while the low-density sprawl community contains only 25 percent cluster homes. RERC, *The Costs of Sprawl: Detailed Cost Analysis*, p. 90.

18. Richard B. Peiser, "Does It Pay to Plan Suburban Growth?" *Journal of the American Planning Association* 50 (Autumn 1984), pp. 419–33. See also Richard B. Peiser, "Density and Urban Sprawl," *Land Economics*, vol. 65 (August 1989), pp. 193–204.

19. Peiser, "Does It Pay to Plan Surbuban Growth?" pp. 426–27.

20. Ibid., p. 425.

21. Downing reported his costs as $39.93 per household on an annualized basis. We determined the estimated $500 figure based on Downing's assumption of an 8 percent discount rate. See Paul B. Downing and Richard D. Gusteley, "The Public Service Costs of Alternative Development Patterns: A Review of the Evidence," in Paul B. Downing, ed., *Local Service Pricing and Their Effect on Urban Spatial Structure* (University of British Columbia Press, 1977), pp. 63–86, especially p. 84. Some of the results also are summarized in Paul B. Downing and Thomas S. McCaleb, "The Economics of Development Exactions," in James E. Frank and Robert M. Rhodes, eds., *Development Exactions* (Chicago and Washington: Planners Press, 1987), pp. 42–69, especially pp. 46–49.

22. See Kain, "Urban Form and the Costs of Urban Services," pp. 20–22.

23. Cervero, "Jobs-Housing Imbalance and Regional Mobility," pp. 140–41.

24. See, for example, P. A. Stone, *The Structure, Size and Costs of Urban Settlements* (Cambridge University Press, 1973), p. 92.

25. The planners estimate 1.2 fewer daily peak period trips into the central area per additional housing unit in the central area; David M. Nowlan and Greg Stewart, "Downtown Population Growth and Commuting Trips: Recent Experience in Toronto," *Journal of the American Planning Association*, vol. 57 (Spring 1991), pp. 165–82.

26. Giuliano, "Is Jobs-Housing Balance a Transportation Issue?" pp. 307–11.

27. Commuting trip lengths of all types have been growing, but suburb-to-suburb work trips are shorter on average than suburb-to-central business district or central-city work trips. As a

result, the migration of jobs from the central city to the suburb should reduce work trips. See Peter Gordon, Ajay Kumar, and Harry W. Richardson, "Congestion, Changing Metropolitan Structure, and City Size in the United States," *International Regional Science Review*, vol. 12, no. 1 (1989), pp. 45–56.

28. Cervero, "Jobs-Housing Imbalance and Regional Mobility," p. 139.

29. Unfortunately, no recent comparisons have been made of planned and unplanned communities; see R. Zehner, *Access, Travel and Transportation in New Communities* (Cambridge, Mass.: Ballinger, 1977) as summarized by Giuliano, "Is Jobs-Housing Balance a Transportation Issue?" p. 310.

Chapter 6

1. For a review of cost/revenue analysis in the 1940s and 1950s, see William L. C. Wheaton, "Applications of Cost-Revenue Studies to Fringe Areas," *Journal of the American Institute of Planners*, vol. 25 (November 1959), pp. 170–74.

2. A number of fiscal impact manuals were produced during this period, most notably Robert W. Burchell and David Listokin, *The Fiscal Impact Guidebook: Estimating Local Costs and Revenues of Land Development* (Department of Housing and Urban Development, Office of Policy Development and Research, 1979); and Robert W. Burchell and David Listokin, *Practitioner's Guide to Fiscal Impact Analysis* (Center for Urban Policy Research, Rutgers University, 1980).

3. See, for example, Thomas P. Snyder and Michael A. Stegman, *Paying for Growth: Using Development Fees to Finance Infrastructure* (Washington: Urban Land Institute, 1986); James C. Nicholas, *The Calculation of Proportionate-Share Impact Fees* (Chicago: American Planning Association, 1988); James C. Nicholas and Arthur C. Nelson, "Determining the Appropriate Development Impact Fee Using the Rational Nexus Test," *Journal of the American Planning Association*, vol. 54 (Winter 1988), pp. 56–66; and David Listoken, "Impact Fees: A Fair Share Framework," in Susan G. Robinson, ed., *Financing Growth: Who Benefits? Who Pays? And How Much?* (Washington: Government Finance Research Center, Government Finance Officers Association, 1990), pp. 109–33.

4. Snyder and Stegman, *Paying for Growth*, p. 42.

5. See, for example, Wheaton, "Applications of Cost-Revenue Studies to Fringe Areas," p. 171.

6. Robert Dahl, "The City in the Future of Democracy," address to the 1967 annual meeting of the American Political Science Association.

7. Practical problems include the limitations on bond lives and local bonding capacities noted by Stegman and Snyder. An additional and most confusing conceptual problem is the argument that none of the capital costs should be allocated to future users once the investment is made because the investment is then a "sunk" cost and no additional capital outlays are required for its continued use. In practice, few investments are completely "sunk," however, as the land or, in some cases, the facilities could be converted to other productive uses if the facility no longer was needed. Moreover, the use of an already built facility imposes other short-run social costs for which users should, in theory, be charged. Increasing use of a road adds to the congestion fellow motorists suffer, for example, while increasing water consumption adds to the risks of drought or reduced water quality, especially as the local reservoir approaches capacity. These costs of congestion, drought, or water quality do not appear on government budgets. They might equal or come close to the amortized capital costs that are included in government budgets, however, especially if valuable alternative uses are available for the land or facilities or if the economies of scale or the lumpiness of the investments are modest.

8. Boise-Cascade Center for Community Development, *The Relative Importance to Mont-*

gomery County of Selected Economic Activities: A Benefit/Cost Study, report prepared for the Economic Development Commission, Montgomery County, Maryland, 1970.

9. Bain's study was not officially adopted by the Montgomery County Council. Henry Bain, "Highway Costs and Revenues of an Additional Worker in Montgomery County, Maryland," report prepared for the Transportation and Environment Committee, Montgomery County, Maryland, 1989.

10. If some office workers lived inside the county, Bain would have had to allocate some of the commuting costs to the residential developments in the county that housed those workers.

11. John R. Meyer and José A. Gómez-Ibáñez, *Autos, Transit, and Cities* (Harvard University Press, 1981), pp. 198–205.

12. Many of these methodological problems have been noted by others. Especially useful is J. Richard Recht, "Rose Bushes Have Thorns," in Arthur C. Nelson, ed., *Development Impact Fees: Policy Rationale, Practice, Theory, and Issues* (Chicago: Planners Press, 1988), pp. 380–87.

The methodological problems of fiscal impact analysis depend in part on the specific purposes for which it is used. The focus here is on the simplest and most limited use: to determine whether new development will generate more government revenues than costs, assuming that the existing structure of government taxes and fees is fixed. Fiscal impact analyses also often are used to revise government taxes or fees so that new development or different types of development will pay their fair share of government costs. Seemingly a straightforward extension of the simpler form of analysis, it raises additional complex questions discussed in chapter 7.

13. The difficulty of allocating costs is less troubling if some of the public services whose costs comfortably can be allocated to particular types of development exhibit diseconomies of scale; that is, increasing cost per residence or business served. The marginal costs for such public services will be greater than the average costs, so allocating responsibility based on marginal costs will generate a "profit," which might cover some or all of the costs of social services.

14. For example, Burchell and Listokin, *Practitioner's Guide to Fiscal Impact Analysis.* Most recent analyses follow the convention recommended in the manuals; see, for example, Tishler and Associates, Inc., "Fiscal Evaluation of Seven Land Use Prototypes," December 1989, and American Farmland Trust, "The Costs of Community Services in Deerfield, Massachusetts," July 1, 1991, both reprinted in Lincoln Institute of Land Policy, *Does Land Conservation Pay? Determining the Fiscal Implications of Preserving Open Land* (Cambridge, Mass., 1992).

15. For example, Nicholas, *The Calculation of Proportionate-Share Impact Fees;* Snyder and Stegman, *Paying for Growth;* or Listokin, "Impact Fees: A Fair Share Framework."

16. Arthur Andersen, Inc., *Downtown Highrise District Cost-Revenue Study Update,* report prepared for the San Francisco Chamber of Commerce, April 1981, as cited in Brad Paul, "San Francisco Growth Management," case C16-90-948.0 (John F. Kennedy School of Government and Graduate School of Design, Harvard University, 1988), exhibits 3 and 4.

17. David Jones, *Downtown Highrise District Cost/Revenue Study,* report distributed by San Franciscans for Reasonable Growth, February 1981, as cited in Paul, "San Francisco Growth Management," exhibits 5 and 6.

18. Note that even Jones omitted education, presumably because the city did not run the schools.

19. The results reported here are from a preliminary version of Helen Ladd's study; see Helen F. Ladd, "Effects of Population Growth on Local Spending and Taxes" (Cambridge, Mass.: Lincoln Institute of Land Policy, April 1990). A later paper that concentrated on spending only and gave less detailed results is Helen F. Ladd, "Population Growth and Local Public Spending," typescript, Duke University, April 1992.

20. Ladd, "Effects of Population Growth," tables 4, 6, and 7 interpreted on pp. 18–19. Ladd reported that growth had less effect when she controlled for changes in state and local responsibilities as well as changes in income and demography (p. 32). She measured changes in state and

local responsibilities by changes in the local share of total state and local spending in the state where each county was located. Fast-growing counties tended to be located in states where the state share of local spending was declining, so she got a U-shaped relationship between real spending and growth. According to her estimates, higher growth rates were associated with modest declines in spending up to a 26 percent population growth rate (over seven years) and with modest increases in spending when population growth exceeded 26 percent. These results may be misleading, however, because her measure of changing state and local responsibilities effectively included local spending as an independent as well as a dependent variable.

21. Ladd's transportation category included capital outlays for transportation, while the capital outlays and interest categories included expenses for all government functions. Ladd, "Effects of Population Growth," pp. 17–18.

22. Ladd's early versions of the analysis also considered the impact of residential growth only and ignored the effects of commercial or industrial development. Fast-growing counties typically experienced nonresidential as well as residential development, and, thus, some of the spending increases Ladd attributed to population growth may have been caused by nonresidential development. When Ladd controlled for the effects of changes in jobs per capita in later versions, however, the results were affected only slightly (mainly by increasing the rate of population growth at which spending rose at above average rates). Compare Ladd, "Effects of Population Growth on Local Spending and Taxes" and Ladd, "Population Growth and Local Public Spending."

Chapter 7

1. For the most comprehensive exposition, see Andrejs Skaburskis, "The Burden of Development Impact Fees," *Land Development Studies* vol. 7 (1990), pp. 173–85. See also F. E. Huffman and others, "Who Bears the Burden of Development Impact Fees," *Journal of the American Planning Association*, vol. 54 (1988), pp. 49–55; Charles E. Connerly, "The Social Implications of Impact Fees," *Journal of the American Planning Association*, vol. 54 (1988), pp. 75–78; Charles J. Delaney and Marc T. Smith, "Development Exactions: Winners and Losers," *Real Estate Law Journal*, vol. 17 (1989), pp. 195–220; and Larry D. Singell and Jane H. Lillydahl, "An Empirical Examination of the Effect of Impact Fees on the Housing Market," *Land Economics*, vol. 66 (February 1990), pp. 82–92.

2. Housing exaction formulas often vary the exaction by the number of bedrooms or the structure type (for example, single-family detached or townhouse) but not by square footage or value. Office, retail, or industrial building exactions often are proportional to the square footage, so that the buyers or tenants may have more options to evade by contracting for less space and using that space more intensively.

3. Additional opportunities exist for property buyers and renters to evade exactions. For example, buyers and renters of housing may be able to win higher wages from their employer to compensate for higher local housing prices. This is likely, however, only if the demand for local labor is strong and workers are willing to move from one metropolitan area to another in search of higher wages and lower housing prices. Nonresidential property buyers and tenants also may be able to pass on a portion of the cost to consumers of their products or services or their workers.

4. The increase takes place because the site is bypassed in favor of development at the periphery, so the premium it can command as a more convenient commuting location rises. See Richard J. Arnott and Frank D. Lewis, "The Transition of Land to Urban Use," *Journal of Political Economy*, vol. 87, no. 1 (1979), pp 161–69. The material cited is from p. 163.

5. Skaburskis, "The Burden of Development Impact Fees," p. 178.

6. The slowdown in the rate of growth of the community also will reduce the rate at which

the commuting premium for a developed property at any given location will be expected to appreciate, however, which will hurt the landowner.

7. Skaburskis, "The Burden of Development Impact Fees," p. 179.

8. Singell and Lillydahl, "An Empirical Examination of the Effect of Impact Fees on the Housing Market."

9. Developers might respond by building higher quality housing for two reasons. First, the percentage price increase will be smaller on a high-quality than a low-quality house, if, as is most frequently the case, the cost of the exaction does not rise proportionately with quality and price. Second, buyers of high-quality houses may be less price sensitive.

10. The data consisted of 429 sales of new or existing houses. To control for a hot market, the researchers included thirty-six dummy variables, one for each month in which houses were sold. To control for quality, the researchers estimated a hedonic price equation including variables for interior square footage, lot size, number of bedrooms, number of baths, and the age of the structure.

11. Another explanation advanced by the authors is that developers used the new fees as an excuse to recover other development charges and requirements Loveland imposed in the past (which were estimated to cost $5,000 to $7,000 per unit). This seems highly unlikely, however, because the developers should have been able to pass on the charges when they were imposed if the exactions were passed on. See Singell and Lillydahl, "An Empirical Evaluation of the Effect of Impact Fees," p. 89.

12. Charles J. Delaney and Marc T. Smith, "Impact Fees and the Price of New Housing: An Empirical Study," AREUEA Journal, vol. 17, no. 1 (1989), pp. 41–54.

13. Dunedin prices increased relative to all three neighbors, but in only two of the three cases was the increase statistically significant. Delaney and Smith, "Impact Fees and the Price of New Housing," p. 51.

14. The researchers neither reported the statistical significance of the price differential after six years nor compared the later differential with the impact fee.

15. Andrejs Skaburskis and Mohammad Qadeer, "An Empirical Estimation of the Price Effects of Development Impact Fees," Queen's University, Kingston, Ontario, 1992; and Arthur C. Nelson and others, "Price Effects of Roads and Other Impact Fees on Urban Land," in Transportation Research Record 1305 (Washington: National Research Council, TRB, 1992), pp. 36–41.

16. This study estimated that the amount of the price increase was dependent on the rate of growth of the housing stock. Each $1 in fee was associated with a $1.88 increase in lot prices at a growth rate of zero and a $1.23 increase at a growth rate of 2.33 percent per year. The researchers did not explicitly state that fees were paid before the land sale, but some of their adjustments to the data appear sensible only if this was the case. See Skaburskis and Qadeer, "An Empirical Estimate of the Price Effects of Development Impact Fees," pp. 6 and 16.

17. Land price increases would be expected even when the fee is paid later because landowners and developers who expected to pass the fee forward to property buyers would delay the development of vacant sites on the urban periphery. Nelson and others, "Price Effects of Roads and Other Impact Fees on Urban Land," pp. 38 and 40.

18. Buyers and tenants of residential property have some options for passing exactions on to employers, but these seem less likely. See note 3 in this chapter.

19. See Charles E. McClure, "The 'New View' of the Property Tax: A Caveat," National Tax Journal, vol. 30, no. 1: 69–75; or Harvey S. Rosen, Public Finance (Homewood, Ill.: Irwin, 1985), pp. 482–87.

20. Notice that the property tax burden is almost the opposite of the exaction burden for landowners. Capital owners (including landowners) bear the common or minimum property tax because it is applied to all forms of capital in all jurisdictions and therefore is not easily avoided

by investors. Exactions, by contrast, are applied to newly developed houses or buildings only and thus usually can be evaded by holding land in agricultural uses or by shifting to other lines of business. Only in communities where exactions are higher than usual will landowners bear part of the exaction cost (if development proceeds in the high-exaction community at all).

21. While prices for new homes increased by $3,800, prices for existing homes rose by $7,000. The researchers got this result even though they included house age as one of the measures of house quality in their statistical analysis of housing prices. The result is surprising because the price increase for new and old homes should be about the same if buyers regard them as close substitutes. See Singell and Lillydahl, "An Empirical Examination of the Effects of Impact Fees on the Housing Market," pp. 89–90.

22. The children of existing residents may eventually inherit their parents' property and thus gain a large portion of the windfall initially captured by their parents. State and federal inheritance taxes will reduce the portion of the windfall they receive, however.

23. Some observers contend that exactions also are an unfair burden on newcomers because the existing residents benefit from new development in the form of higher property and land values. See Timothy Beatley, "Ethical Issues in the Use of Impact Fees to Finance Community Growth," in Arthur C. Nelson, ed., *Development Impact Fees: Policy Rationale, Practice, Theory, and Issues* (Chicago: Planners Press, 1988), pp. 339–61, especially pp. 342–44. This argument ignores the possibility that growth (in the absence of exactions) might lead to higher taxes to finance infrastructure or deteriorated infrastructure services.

24. This presumes that the pressures for growth would not simply be funneled to a neighboring community that had imposed no limits and was regarded as a close substitute by most home buyers or renters. In that case, a growth moratorium in the first community would have no effect on housing prices, but neither would the imposition of exactions in the first community because exactions also would divert growth to the neighbor.

25. See McClure, "The 'New View' of the Property Tax"; or Rosen, *Public Finance*, pp. 482–87.

26. For a review of the incidence of the sales tax, see Rosen, *Public Finance*, pp. 456–58.

27. User charges might appeal to other notions of equity, however, as many regard charging users for the costs of the services they consume as fair.

28. It may be less progressive than one might think, however, given that pension funds and insurance companies with many moderate-income clients own a substantial share of American companies.

29. Many of these arguments have been cited by others; see particularly Charles E. Connerly, "Impact Fees as Social Policy: What Should Be Done?" in Nelson, ed., *Development Impact Fees*, pp. 362–72.

30. Economists disagree as to whether property tax obligations are capitalized into housing prices or not. If they are capitalized, however, a property tax increase would reduce housing prices, while a tax reduction would increase prices.

31. This calculation assumes that either the property tax increase or the exaction would be borne by the tenants or owner-occupants of developed property. The former is likely in jurisdictions whose property taxes are high already, so that they are borne fully by consumers of capital.

Chapter 8

1. See, for example, Robert A. Blewett and Arthur C. Nelson, "A Public Choice and Efficiency Argument for Development Impact Fees," in Arthur C. Nelson, ed., *Development Impact Fees: Policy Rationale, Practice, Theory, and Issues* (Chicago: Planners Press, 1988), pp. 281–89, especially p. 285; and Franklin J. James, "Evaluation of Local Impact Fees as a Source of Infra-

structure Finance," *Municipal Finance Journal*, vol. 11 (Winter 1990), pp. 407–20, especially pp. 411–12. For a skeptical view more consistent with this chapter, see Douglass B. Lee, "Evaluation of Impact Fees against Public Finance Criteria," in Nelson, ed., *Development Impact Fees*, pp. 290–312.

2. Another category, less important here, is services that prevent individuals from harming others. Often such behavior is simply prohibited or protective services are required at private, not public, expense. Businesses and individuals are obligated by law to limit the pollution they generate, for example, and parents are required to inoculate their school-age children against communicable diseases. Sometimes such services are provided at public expense, however, when private parties are unable or unwilling to pay. The government may pay for the cleanup of a polluted site when the responsible private parties cannot be identified or are insolvent, for example, or provide free inoculations to children from poor households.

3. This discussion assumes that the exactions are charged on the residences of the households using those social services. The equity problems may be less if the exactions are charged on the businesses that employ workers from those households given that the burden of nonresidential exactions may be more widely distributed among the business owners and customers as well as employees.

4. James C. Nicholas and Arthur C. Nelson, "Determining the Appropriate Development Impact Fee Using the Rational Nexus Test," *Journal of the American Planning Association* 54 (1988), pp. 56–66.

5. James C. Nicholas, "Florida's Experience with Impact Fees," in James C. Nicholas, ed., *The Changing Structure of Infrastructure Finance* (Cambridge, Mass.: Lincoln Institute of Land Policy, 1985), pp. 45–58.

6. Palm Beach officials, like those in many other communities, considered only capital costs in setting the fee, perhaps to avoid the (often incorrect) challenge that operating costs should not be included in fees because they already are recouped by user charges.

7. Nancy Stroud, "Legal Considerations of Development Impact Fees," *Journal of the American Planning Association*, vol. 54 (Winter 1988), pp. 29–37, especially p. 32; Nicholas and Nelson, "Determining the Appropriate Development Impact Fee Using the Rational Nexus Test," p. 58; and James C. Nicholas, *The Calculation of Proportionate-Share Impact Fees* (Chicago: American Planning Association, 1988).

8. Brad Paul, "San Francisco Growth Management," case C16-90-948.0 (John F. Kennedy School of Government and Graduate School of Design, Harvard University, 1988).

9. Mark P. Barnebey and others, "Paying for Growth: Community Approaches to Development Impact Fees," *Journal of the American Planning Association*, vol. 54, no. 1 (1988), pp. 18–28, especially p. 26.

10. The argument that user charges might promote efficiency better than exactions has been made by Lee, "Evaluation of Impact Fees against Public Finance Criteria."

11. Our view on this issue conflicts with those of many fiscal planners, who argue that exactions ought to be used to recover the capital costs of infrastructure; and user charges, to recover the operating costs. Such a practice would result in heavier reliance on exactions than user charges, because many forms of infrastructure are capital extensive. However, the appropriate distinction is not between capital and operating costs but between costs that vary with connection and costs that vary with consumption.

12. For example, see John R. Meyer and José A. Gómez-Ibáñez, *Autos, Transit, and Cities* (Harvard University Press, 1981), p. 205.

13. Ibid., pp. 218–27. Another problem is that highway users are not accustomed to paying tolls for local streets, and thus the imposition of tolling would be highly unpopular. See José A. Gómez-Ibáñez, "The Political Economy of Highway Tolls and Congestion Pricing," *Transportation Quarterly*, vol. 46, (July 1992), pp. 343–60.

14. James E. Frank and Paul B. Downing, "Patterns of Impact Fee Use," in Nelson, ed., *Development Impact Fees*, pp. 3–21. The material cited is from p. 19.

15. Nicholas and Nelson, "Determining the Appropriate Development Impact Fee Using the Rational Nexus Test," p. 59.

16. For example, Manatee County, Florida; see Barnebey and others, "Paying for Growth," p. 27.

17. Meyer and Gómez-Ibáñez, *Autos, Transit, and Cities*, p. 187.

Chapter 9

1. The factual material in this chapter for the most part has been documented previously. Noted here, consequently, are only those statements of which this is not the case.

2. Nicholas and colleagues, for example, estimate that the cost of new or expanded local facilities to serve a single new dwelling unit "exceeds $20,000." They cite as evidence a 1982 estimate by the California Office of Planning and a 1986 estimate by the Florida Advisory Committee on Intergovernmental Relations. The Florida study itself merely cites a 1983 oral statement by James Frank (more than $22,000) and a 1973 estimate by Paul B. Downing and Richard D. Gustely ($24,359 when adjusted for inflation to 1985). We have been unable to obtain the California study. See James C. Nicholas, Arthur C. Nelson, and Julian Juergensmeyer, A *Practitioner's Guide to Development Impact Fees* (Chicago and Washington: Planners Press, 1991), p. 1; and Florida Advisory Council on Intergovernmental Relations, *Impact Fees in Florida* (November 1986), pp. 89–90.

The average price of a new single-family home in Florida as of 1985 was $68,062. Nicholas and others, A *Practitioner's Guide to Development Impact Fees*, p. 90. Conceivably, then, a locality might have justified exactions that—if passed through by the developer with no markup for overhead, financing, or profit—would have increased the average cost of new housing by one-third.

3. The capital outlay figures are from Bureau of the Census, *Government Finances: 1989–1990*, series GF 90/5 (December 1991), table 11. The population estimates, also by the Bureau of the Census, are reported in U.S. Advisory Commission on Intergovernmental Relations, *Significant Features of Fiscal Federalism: 1991*, 2, report M-176-II (October 1991), table 6.

4. Bureau of the Census, *Government Finances*, table 11.

5. Ibid., table 29. Localities obtained 62.8 percent of general revenue from their own sources in fiscal year 1990, 33.6 percent from state aid (which included federal aid pass-throughs), and 3.6 percent from direct federal aid.

6. Bureau of the Census, "The Nation's Economic, Social, and Housing 'Portrait' Drawn from the 1990 Census Long Form," press release, May 29, 1992, tables 1 and 3.

7. The new construction figures, which include mobile homes and on-site replacements for demolished housing, are from William C. Apgar, Jr., George S. Masnick, and Nancy McArdle, *Housing in America: 1970–2000* (Joint Center for Housing Studies, Graduate School of Design, and John F. Kennedy School of Government, Harvard University, 1991), exhibit 6.4. Net housing stock growth has been considerably smaller than these figures suggest because of subtractions from the housing inventory, which average 0.5 percent annually. We are indebted to William C. Apgar, Jr., for the estimates of housing inventory in noncensus years, which are based on unpublished research by the Joint Center for Housing Studies, Harvard University.

8. Formally defined, progressive revenue sources take a rising percentage of income as income itself rises. Their polar opposites, regressive revenue sources, take a declining percentage of income as income rises. Revenue sources that take a constant proportion of income at all income levels are labeled proportional. We define a set of arrangements as equitable from an

intergenerational standpoint to the extent that younger households, which do not own much property in aggregate, face government-imposed barriers to obtaining property no greater than those that most current property owners encountered at comparable stages in their own life cycles. We define a set of arrangements as equitable from a socioeconomic standpoint to the extent that it facilitates community integration by income class and race.

9. John R. Logan and Harvey L. Molotch maintain that the great majority of contemporary land use disputes are best understood as contests between groups in pursuit of exchange values and opponents (most notably, residents and environmentalists) who are preoccupied with safeguarding use values. *Urban Fortunes: The Political Economy of Place* (University of California Press, 1987), chapters 2, 4, 6.

10. John D. Landis judges that the main urban regions of California were exceptions during the 1980s—although he finds that housing shortfalls and price increases were no greater in communities with than without formal growth caps. The explanation, he believes, is that localities without formal caps routinely achieved comparable effects by ad hoc regulation. John D. Landis, "Do Growth Controls Work? A New Assessment," *Journal of the American Planning Association* (Autumn 1992), pp. 489–508, especially pp. 499–501.

11. This correlation is particularly rough in California, which has explicitly chosen to stress preference for existing property owners over ability to pay as indicated by current values. Proposition 13 of 1978, it will be recalled, precludes localities from reassessing property except at the time of sale. A subsequent amendment enables state residents to move without losing their historic assessments, so long as they pay no more for their new home than the sale price of their old.

Index

171